The Life-Changing Power of Group Psychometry

Kim McCauley, Ph.D.

BALBOA.PRESS
A DIVISION OF HAY HOUSE

Balboa Press books may be ordered through booksellers or by contacting:

Balboa Press
A Division of Hay House
1663 Liberty Drive
Bloomington, IN 47403
www.balboapress.com
844-682-1282

Because of the dynamic nature of the Internet, any web addresses or links contained in this book may have changed since publication and may no longer be valid. The views expressed in this work are solely those of the author and do not necessarily reflect the views of the publisher, and the publisher hereby disclaims any responsibility for them.

The author of this book does not dispense medical advice or prescribe the use of any technique as a form of treatment for physical, emotional, or medical problems without the advice of a physician, either directly or indirectly. The intent of the author is only to offer information of a general nature to help you in your quest for emotional and spiritual well-being. In the event you use any of the information in this book for yourself, which is your constitutional right, the author and the publisher assume no responsibility for your actions.

Photographer for the front and back cover images: Melissa Leer
Instagram: LeersEYEview

Print information available on the last page.

ISBN: 979-8-7652-5753-1 (sc)
ISBN: 979-8-7652-5755-5 (hc)
ISBN: 979-8-7652-5754-8 (e)

Library of Congress Control Number: 2024924872

Balboa Press rev. date: 01/15/2025

Contents

Part 3: Advice for Giving Psychometry Readings

Part 4: The Benefits of Being in a Psychometry Group

Dedication

This book is dedicated to all past, present, and future psychometry/ meditation groups. May your commitment to soul growth continue to heal and expand spiritual communities across the globe.

Acknowledgments

This book would not have been possible without the love and support of our psychometry/meditation group family. My heart overflows with gratitude for them and especially for my wife and daughter.

I'd also like to thank my friend and editor, Neola Mace. Her honesty, skill, and support helped me focus, organize, and finish this book with a sense of joy.

Introduction

Looking up the word "psychometry" on the internet prompts images of a psychic with special powers tuning in to the history of an object as well as a description of its owner.

Although at one time this view of psychometry may have been the case, in this book, I offer a different approach—one that, when used in a group setting along with meditation and a healing circle, offers even more enrichment.

Everyone brings a small object and in turn gives and receives a message, something even a newcomer can do. If this sounds intimidating or too mystical, I hope to provide information in this book that will not only ease your fears but show you how powerfully supportive, empowering, and loving a group like this can be.

Specifically, this new approach consists of being open to receive a message that will be helpful to another person—the one who brought the object. For our purposes, specifics about the history of the object is much less important than the message it fosters for the participant. In psychometry, the object is just a conduit for the sharing of helpful information, and it doesn't require any special practice or psychic gifts.

Ted Andrews, who wrote a book on the subject of psychometry, says, "Everyone is psychic,"[1] and Laura Day has said in many of her workshops, "Everyone is intuitive." Also, according to Day, the less familiar a reader is with a subject or topic, the more his or her intuition "comes into play!"[2]

---

[1] Ted Andrews, *How to Develop and Use Psychometry* (St. Paul, MN: Llewellyn Publications, Vanguard Series, 1994), 11.

[2] Laura Day, *Practical Intuition: How to Harness the Power of Your Instinct and Make It Work for You* (New York: Villard-Random House, 1996), 11.

The meditation/psychometry group that I started in my own home is just one version among a myriad of other kinds of spiritual circles, but it's very special—so special that most of the women in the group call it "life-changing."

I'm writing this book to share some of these wonderful experiences and guide others who might want to create a similar group of their own. My hope is that you remember three key takeaways from this book.

1) First, everyone has the ability to give a helpful message. We can label it as the product of intuition, Spirit, God, our higher self, inner guidance, or sensory information that works like a radio signal from our body's electromagnetic field. There is nothing to fear with that. Nothing.

2) Second, no one needs to have any experience in being a "psychic reader" to participate.

3) Third, and most importantly, meeting with others for the purpose of sharing helpful intuitive information deepens each person's sense of belonging, self-confidence, spiritual insight, and personal growth.

I hope that as you read this book, you'll be picturing yourself seated among us and growing with us. I also hope that eventually you will become part of a group that meets regularly or consider starting one of your own.

PART 1

Explaining Psychometry

"The third-eye person has always been the saint, the seer, the poet, the metaphysician, or the authentic mystic who grasps the whole picture. We need true mystics who see with all three sets of eyes. Some call this movement conversion, some call it enlightenment, some transformation, and some holiness."[3]
— Richard Rohr

---

[3] Richard Rohr, "Third Eye Seeing," Center for Action and Contemplation, published June 3, 2022, https://cac.org/daily-meditations/third-eye-seeing-2022-06-03.

CHAPTER 1

A Psy-chomo-what Group?

"I host a psychometry and meditation group that meets in my home."

"A psy . . . com-o . . . ? What?"

People react with a variety of facial contortions—tilting their heads, squinting their eyes, or raising their eyebrows in a way that suggests I may have initiated a subject that sounds either too academic or too "woo-woo."

"Psychometry is the use of an object as a conduit for giving a reading, generally a message for the person who brought it. In our psychometry group, we have a guided meditation first, then I pass around a bowl with everyone's object in it. Each person in the group pulls out an object that's not their own and writes down the message they receive."

Before I finish that first sentence, my listeners are already glaring incredulously—unless, of course, they have heard about the group from a mutual friend.

Since the initial days of starting the group, I learned, rather quickly, that "the group"—in terms of what it's called, how it works, and why it's made such a difference for the attendees—could not be explained adequately in a brief conversation. The value of what we do within the group would require an ongoing dialogue with each person who regularly attends, and although I've included some of their stories in the following chapters, I cannot adequately capture the nuances of their spoken words, wonderful personalities, and life-changing wisdom.

Similarly, psychometry/meditation group participants can also have difficulty putting their experiences from the meeting into words. For example, on her third visit, a new attendee, Lynda, happened to see me in the Unity church a couple of days afterward. Her whole face glowed as she expressed her appreciation for what had occurred the previous Friday night. She thanked me over and over, but what touched me most was that not only during the group meeting but also in our after-church conversation, Lynda's excitement was magnetic. I mentioned this book to her and asked her if she would be willing to write about her experience. Her immediate response was "I don't think I could even have the words to express how amazing it was!"

As she shared a bit more, Lynda admitted that, yes (like most people), her first time doing a psychometry reading felt a bit intimidating and that even though she benefitted from it, she still had a few doubts. The second time she participated, she received her girlfriend's object from the bowl (which always has a scarf on top of it so that no one can see which item they are picking). Because she knew her girlfriend (and future wife), Amy, so well, it took a leap of faith for Lynda to resist doubts in her ability to distinguish between what came from her previous knowledge or imagination and her intuition. She said that she hoped whatever she received would be valuable for Amy and decided to trust her inner voice. The reading she gave turned out to be very good, but her next visit validated everything.

In her third meeting, she told all of us that the moment she pulled the object—a ring—from the bowl, she immediately felt joy and love flooding around her. The intensity was palpable, real, and deep. Like the rest of the group, Lynda wrote down what she received and waited till it was her turn to share. As she spoke and held the ring in the air to see who the reading was for, her close friend Claudia spoke up and said, "That's mine." After Lynda read what she had written, both of them looked as if they would burst into happy tears and hugged. Claudia then explained that it was her wedding ring and that she and her husband were very much in love and planned to celebrate their first wedding anniversary that week.

The evening touched Lynda so much that, two days later, she reiterated to me once again that what she felt that night was so special that she wanted to continue to join us as often as she could.

Our group consists of a range of people: from newbies who have very little awareness of their intuition to some who have far-above-average natural gifts. A few others have honed their special abilities for several years. Most of the regular attendees, however, would place themselves between the beginning and midrange stages.

As a former professor of writing and university administrator, I am analytical and detail oriented. I feel the need to double-check information. But as soon as I started experiencing what energy feels like and how it works for me—in healing sessions and giving readings—I was hooked. This work (if we can really call it that) surprises me, humbles me, and excites me.

However, despite the goal of giving and receiving readings, perfecting these amazing intuitive abilities is not the main focus. This may sound surprising given the fact that what we do requires using our intuition. The overarching focus, the genuine benefit, and true power of this psychometry/meditation group stems from focusing our energy on helping one another. The famous intuitive, author, and teacher Laura Day emphasizes this over and over in her own work. In *Practical Intuition*, she writes, "If I had one message to share with you in this book, it would not be, 'You are intuitive.' It would be, 'We are all more capable of giving help than we realize.'"[4] The value of our intuition is not just a personal tool; it grows from the connection we have with others and in our efforts to support and build an even greater sense of community in each other's lives.

After reading the next two chapters that provide an introduction to psychometry, you're welcome to pull up a chair and join us as I describe a typical evening with the group. I will do my best to lead you on this journey without heavy terminology or paranormal tales from woo-woo-ville. It's my hope that these pages will be an inspiring collection of the life-changing experiences we've shared as well as a guide for those who seek to create a psychometry/meditation group of their own.

---

[4] Day, *Practical Intuition*, 176.

CHAPTER 2

What Is Psychometry?

Have you ever held an object and felt as if you could feel its history or sense something unique about the person who owned it? If so, even without knowing it, you may already have practiced a form of psychometry (also sometimes referred to as psychoscopy or clairtangency).

The term *psychometry* originated in 1842 from American physician Joseph Rodes Buchanan, who combined the Greek words *psyche*, as a designation for soul, and *metron*, to indicate measurement. Ted Andrews, modern-day author of *How to Develop and Use Psychometry*, reiterates this definition, mentioning that the word *psychometry* translates as "soul measuring."[5] Andrews further explains that psychometry is the act of reading an "energy imprint," or more specifically, "the ability to detect something about a person or event through the sense of touch."[6] But the act of touching the object is only part of the process. The energy imprint, Andrews explains, "becomes a bridge between ordinary sensory perception to the more intuitive."[7] The main focus for the reader is sensing the energy emanating from the object, which could carry an imprint of a person's character or a past event. William Denton, a nineteenth-century geologist who continued Buchanan's research onward from the mid-1800s, refers to psychometry as discovering "the soul of things," a fitting title for his own book on the subject.

---

[5] Andrews, *Psychometry*, 25.
[6] Andrews, *Psychometry*, 14-15.
[7] Andrews, *Psychometry*, 13.

Even today, as part of their sessions, psychics who work as mediums can ask a client to bring an item belonging to a particular person—living or dead—so that they can enhance their connection to that individual's energetic imprint. The item then becomes a conduit for receiving details that might be helpful. Sometimes a psychic who touches an item of clothing or jewelry from a missing person or artifact from a crime scene can provide clues to the police for follow-up. This is a form of psychometry, but it's only a small example of the many ways it can be applied.

According to Andrews, psychometry does not usually provide information about the future, but he notes that it's possible: "Someone who is capable of seeing the pattern of the past in the life of the individual through the object can usually make very viable predictions based on that data."[8]

There are three different kinds of psychometry, Andrews says, which can frequently "overlap."[9] The types vary by subject, according to whether they involve

- objects,
- locations, or
- persons.

The most common type concerns objects—their history and previous ownership. The object's energy imprint will hold any significantly emotional or stressful event, which can be read by anyone who tunes into it. The ancients revered relics and amulets because they felt those objects were imbued with healing power. It's not uncommon for people today to revere sacred objects and use them for healing as well.

Location psychometry may be something many of us have felt from time to time when we enter a place that feels like we've visited before, or we walk into a room that feels energetically peaceful and calming, or the opposite—creepy and uncomfortable. When a Realtor shows a house that is still furnished but has been empty for a while, it can often feel lifeless or soulless. Or when a family moves into a new home, it takes a while for their own energy to settle into it, even long after the furniture is in place.

---

[8] Andrews, *Psychometry*, 25.
[9] Andrews, *Psychometry*, 25-26.

Pat, who has been attending the group since its first year, told me about her experience with location psychometry when she went on vacation out west:

> While several of us were on our way to Mount Shasta, we were in a restaurant. I couldn't even eat. I believe we were in a restaurant where there had been a massacre many years ago because we were right by water, and I think it was probably an Indian settlement. It was overwhelming, and I don't know if I've had a feeling like that in a long time. But I just got up and left. I couldn't stay there.

Location and object psychometry can blend, just as Andrews explains. For example, in his book, *The Soul of Things*, Denton mentions that a stone from Jerusalem and one from Dover Beach might have the same chemical elements in them, but "they are as different psychometrically as the history of the United States is from that of Greece."[10] In one of Denton's psychometry experiments, his test subject and sister, Mrs. Cridge, held a rock in her hands, presumably with her eyes closed because he says specifically that the object was "unseen by her."[11] When she held the rock, she described images of what she saw, as if she was a witness to its origin:

> I see the ocean, and ships sailing on it. This must be an island, for the water is all around. Now I am turned from where I saw the vessels, and am looking at something most terrific. It seems as if an ocean of fire was pouring over a precipice, and boiling as it pours.[12]

Denton then explains that the rock was a piece of lava from Kilauea, Hawaii, and was part of the "ocean of fire" from a volcano that erupted there in 1840.

---

[10] William Denton and Elizabeth M. Foote Denton, *The Soul of Things* (Boston: Walker, Wise and Company, 1863), 298, https://archive.org/details/soulthingsorpsy00dentgoog.
[11] Denton and Denton, *The Soul of Things*, 38.
[12] Denton and Denton, *The Soul of Things*, 38.

The third type, person psychometry, is also something we experience, perhaps on a daily basis without knowing it. We can read someone's mood even from a distance or have a sense about the character of someone from a first impression. As observers, we rely on the minute details of other people's body language and facial expressions to give us signals. But reading someone's energy goes beyond that. Our bodies naturally produce an electromagnetic field which extends several feet beyond the surface of our skin. Everyone has a specific energetic fingerprint which can vary on the surface depending on how grounded, stressed, or healthy a person is, but on a deeper level, the energy of who we are at our core stays pretty much the same. People who work in energy healing can pick up on these levels—what is on the surface, what might be buried deeper, and the core being of who a person is. Sensing all of this is their starting point, and what they do is a unique form of "person psychometry" that can also transform to become a reading and a healing at the same time.

No matter how much I try to explain how a reading comes to be, it's still much of a mystery to me. I once heard Laura Day explain in one of her workshops that the same stream of energy can either be read for information or manipulated for healing. Specifically, a psychic can pinpoint and read an energy thread to sense information about the future; a "healer"[13] can sense energy flow, too, but more specifically in terms of identifying and remedying imbalances in the electro-magnetic field of the physical body. During a session, a practitioner attuned to a patient's energy flow will work with the person to release blockages and create a template that re-patterns the flow toward wholeness. Talk therapy carries "energy" as well; a therapist dialogues with a client to create a template for re-patterning and wholeness, which could occur through alternative therapy, dream work, or in a traditional session.

---

[13] Despite my use of the term "healer," I believe that the client is the manager of his or her own healing, with the "Universe" and the practitioner assisting in the process. The word "healing" implies that there was a problem and that a client is "all fixed now," but it's almost never as black and white as that. Therapy in any form, whether it's counseling, physical therapy, or energy work, can be complex. As Laura Day explains, people are "systems"; their genetic structure as well as how they eat, handle stress, relationships, etc. all contribute to a person's wellness.

In my own energy sessions with clients, I've seen a variety of results ranging from barely noticeable shifts to sudden, extraordinary transformations. For example, a few years ago, I worked with a 70-something year-old woman who asked for help with her hearing (let's call her Anne). While Anne was lying face-up on the table, I scanned her energetic field by hovering my hands about six inches above her body. As I did, I sensed some strong, prickly waves coming from the right side of her torso; the strongest sensations originated specifically from the auric field above her breast. As I hovered over this part of her field to support her healing process, I heard a song pop into my head: "The Love of Money" by the O'Jays. It was certainly not my favorite song or something I had just heard on the radio, so I thought it might be a message for Anne. I admit that I struggled with whether to tell her what I heard. I had to trust that she and I could work together to make sense of this seemingly random piece of information.

So, when it was time for Anne to sit up, regain her balance and reflect, I asked if we could talk about what I sensed. I explained that the energy I felt near her breast might be a sign that she is over-nurturing someone else and under-nurturing herself. Since it appeared on the right side of her body, I asked whether she might be sacrificing quite a bit of her energy to a male in her life. Anne raised her eyebrows. It was a challenge to explain to a 70-something year old woman that I not only felt a strange sensation over her breast but also heard the refrain, "Money, Money, Money."

Despite the awkwardness of the moment, I sang a few lines of the song to her. As I did, her eyes widened even more and her mouth dropped. She told me that her grandson had asked her for money, and she felt a bit uncomfortable because she gave him nearly $10,000 the previous year, and now he was asking for more. I had no idea this was going on in Anne's life. Through the session, we learned that she wasn't truly "listening" to her own needs. She came in asking for help with her hearing, but the body is holistic. As she thought of granting this second request for financial help from her grandson, her energy field "spoke up" on her behalf; too much life force was leaking from the symbol of nurturance—her breast. Overall, the session helped this client regain balance in her life. She became more aware of her needs and could then make a decision based on the signals her body had been sending.

Regarding any sort of intuitive reading, it's important to remember that no one can be correct 100 percent of the time because any reading must necessarily be interpreted into words. Errors can occur even in the reiteration of an image or a feeling because both are difficult to communicate accurately. We are all susceptible to making assumptions or overanalyzing something rather than merely stating something heard, seen, or felt.

The same could be true regarding the reception of an intuitive or psychic message because not all messages resonate with the recipient—at least not necessarily at the time they are received. The nuances of a message can be influenced by the personality of both the reader and recipient. For example, in his treatise on psychometry, published in 1893, J. R. Buchanan describes an individual session in which he places an envelope with his signature "on the head" of a "psychometer," his term for "reader." The psychometer then goes on to describe what he sees intuitively:

> [T]he scene of a leader or adventurer, marching on toward
> a distant height . . . . He appeared to be covered, as to his
> head, by a species of Roman helmet, which rendered him
> insensible to the missiles and weapons which he expected
> to encounter.[14]

Buchanan was pleased, calling this a "happy sketch."[15] The helmet covering his head, Buchanan said, related to his current neurological studies and the description of himself as an adventurer. Marching upward depicts his efforts toward scientific advancements. As protection, the helmet "was a good illustration," he says, of how he has needed to become "indifferent to the applause or disapprobation of mankind."[16] Also interesting in the reading is that Buchanan's psychometer told him that his work was located in Cincinnati and that the person he described had a connection with Lower Market Street. At the time of the reading, Buchanan worked as a professor of physiology at the Eclectic Medical Institute in Cincinnati. And, as the reader mentioned, Buchanan explains that he grew up on

---

[14] Joseph Rodes Buchanan, M.D. *Manual of Psychometry* (Boston: Frank H. Hodges, 1893), 69.

[15] Buchanan, *Manual*, 69.

[16] Buchanan, *Manual*, 70.

Lower Market Street. All this information came from the psychrometer's use of a sealed envelope containing only Buchanan's signature.

In his interpretation of the reading, particularly of the image of the helmet and of a leader marching "toward a distant height," Buchanan knew it was not literal and understood its symbolism. Readings often have this quality.

Sometimes, however, a reading can be quite literal, referring, for instance, to an actual car that might need repair or an upcoming trip someone is planning. Once I received a psychometry reading that told me to "ignore the loud" and reminded me that I did not have all the information regarding the situation. The previous week, someone had yelled at me quite strongly, and it was true that all the pieces of the situation had not yet fallen into place. When I was able to truly "ignore the loud," I had a better glimpse of the truth, which not only eased my fears but helped me see the entire situation in a less judgmental way. Even though I was still feeling the sting of someone yelling at me, I became more open than usual to reflecting on this message. That reflection helped me soften my attitude and is one of the many rewards from practicing psychometry with others. We can learn and grow in a helpful, positive way that feels empowering.

PART 2

Group Psychometry

"[W]ho is your community? . . . If you're called to the prophetic task, and I think in some aspects all of us are—where is your prophetic community that will feed you and support you and guide you and help you?" [17]

— *Barbara Holmes*

[17] Barbara Holmes, "Prophets Belong in Community," Center for Action and Contemplation, Richard Rohr's Daily Meditations, January 4, 2023, https://cac.org/daily-meditations/prophets-belong-in-community-2023-01-04.

CHAPTER 3

What Is Group Psychometry?

Group Psychometry is Unique

When I began researching the topic of psychometry for this book, I read publications, looked online, and listened to various podcasts on the subject. What I discovered is that psychometry is not a common practice, and most websites in America associate it with psychological testing—something completely different than what we are discussing here.

Also, the kind of psychometry that involves reading the energy emanating from an object is not traditionally associated with groups and is generally practiced in isolation or in one-to-one settings. The usual scenario goes like this: a reader, usually a person who considers themselves to be psychically-inclined, holds an object and provides information regarding its history, the current or previous owner, and any other relevant details. On one podcast, the hosts described going to a used clothing store and, on the show, discussed what they had picked up intuitively from the energy of the items. Later in the podcast, they held objects that each other brought to the show and reported what they felt emanating from each. The female hosts seemed to prefer the term "clairtangency" over psychometry, although they referred to both.[18]

---

[18] Laura Wong and Kaitlyn Graña, "Psychometry," May 2023, in *Third Eye Bind*, Spotify podcast audio, Episode 33, 1:17, https://open.spotify.com/episode/1WbGnNkXMdpJfI2Plt9ri0?si=46eb22bab4f54edf.

In most cases, whether we're watching a TV show, listening to a podcast, or reading something on the topic of intuition, a featured clairvoyant tends to be the only person providing psychic information; others are merely the recipients.

What I'm referring to in this book is something much different. The group does not require a professional psychic to provide readings for each person. Instead, we take for granted that everyone is intuitive and can provide a helpful reading for someone else, so every person who attends is responsible for giving a reading. But even though everyone is intuitive, giving a reading requires interpersonal sensitivity and a degree of courage. Overall, it takes perception to a whole new level.

The group we've set up has a particular format. After a healing circle and group meditation sets the tone, each person picks an object (hidden in a bowl under a scarf) and writes down a reading for the person who brought it. When placing our object in the bowl, all of us try to hide what we bring so that no one sees. Then, when we choose someone else's object from the bowl, not knowing whose object we have allows our impressions to be free of mental assumptions and interferences.

This general description, though, cannot possibly capture the essence of what it's like to experience the group. In my interviews with participants, I discovered how much each person treasured the meetings and what they received from them. Dee, a ministerial student in the group, characterizes her appreciation in terms of "belonging" and "transformation":

> The embodied feeling of acceptance and belonging is delightful. Kim's honoring of each of us—by being an intuitive gatekeeper for the group—and the camaraderie that has been preserved over the years speaks richly to me. Peter Block, author of *Community: The Structure of Belonging* says, "The future is created one room at a time, one gathering at a time. Each gathering needs to become an example of the future we want to create. This means that the small group is where transformation takes place . . . The small group gains power with certain kinds of conversations. To build community, we seek conversations where people show up by invitation rather than mandate

and experience an intimate and authentic relatedness." The constant reminder that psychometry contributes to our individual wholeness as well as wholeness that the world desperately needs allows me to believe that we are touching many more than just the lives in the room.

I truly believe that we do, indeed, touch "many more than just the lives in the room." Hopefully these positive transformations in whatever form are occurring in small groups across the world. But for now, let's pause and go back to the "lives in the room" to observe a typical meeting with the group. Other than experiencing it yourself, live and in person, the best route to understanding what we do in the group is to sit in vicariously as you read the next chapter and follow along.

CHAPTER 4

Example of a "Typical" Group Meeting

Although "A Typical Group Meeting," is part of this chapter's title, nothing about a psychometry meeting could ever be classified as typical except for the format. Part 5 of this book provides some direction on how to create and organize a group of your own like this. It includes a suggested timeline, pros and cons to consider when hosting, choosing a location, and managing the group, so there's no need to pause this narrative to decipher all of the "how tos" just yet.

In the following account, the readings are all real, having occurred at one point or another in the last seven or eight years of my note-taking. I've included a few images of the actual readings I've received during that time and a couple that people in the group have given me permission to copy. The dates on them may be varied, but all are examples of what an amazing experience this "group reading" process can be.

Preparing the Space

We create a sacred space first, minimizing interruptions. Our intention is for each person to feel welcome and safe, free from the fear that what they say or write will be judged.

As Participants Arrive

We place our own objects in the bowl underneath the scarf, and as others arrive, we remind them to place theirs in the bowl before we officially start.

Sometimes I have soft music playing but not always. We chat, arrange whatever snacks guests have brought in the eating area, and catch up. Most of the people who attend are friends, so catching up is easy.

I make sure that everyone in the group who wants a reading has placed their object in the bowl, and that the bowl is still covered with a scarf so that no one sees each other's objects. All are aware that in order to receive a reading, they must provide one. If they put an object in the bowl, it's their commitment to choosing a different one when we pass the bowl around and then writing a reading in exchange. During the time I've hosted my own group, I've only had one person decide to just observe and not give or receive a reading.

After some light snacks while standing around the kitchen counter, we circle up and all sit down after about fifteen to twenty minutes.

At this point, all of us make sure that we have pen and paper as well as a sturdy magazine underneath to serve as a "writing desk."

Special Instructions for New Participants

Although every group is different, since I've hosted psychometry in my home for over a decade now, it's rare for us to include a new person because we only have so many seats and limited time.

New participants tend to need extra encouragement and more detailed information on providing as well as receiving a reading. (I share more information on all of this at various points in the book.)

Sharing Positive Affirmations

After getting comfortable in their seats, everyone begins the process of focusing their attention toward the group as a whole. Just looking to my left and right around the group seems to start this, and when I begin by saying something like, "Welcome! I'm so glad you are all here tonight ..." etc., conversations wind down and everyone's attention seems to fall naturally into place. This part does not come from years of teaching or lapsing into my "teacher voice." It's the energy of the group itself, a commitment all of us have established through months of loving the magical moments we will be enjoying with each other over the next couple of hours.

I explain our process of beginning with affirmations and give an example: "I am Kim, and I am balanced." Others follow around the circle, in order, counterclockwise.

"I am Lynda, and I am thankful."

"I am Amy, and I am excited to be here."

"I am Esther, and I am at peace."

"I am Allie, and I am blessed."

And so on. Sometimes, to ground us even more, or when there are new guests attending, we go around a second time. In addition to this being a beneficial way to start, it's another way for newcomers to learn everyone's name.

Creating the Healing Energy of the Circle

The next step is starting the healing circle.

I ask everyone to stand in a circle and close their eyes. I lead them in an exercise to center, cleanse, and ground the individual and group energies. I ask participants to try to sense the warmth of their hearts through focused breathing, then visualize taking this energy into the Earth and back up— from their feet to their heads and back down again.

After this, I ask them to hold out their hands, left palm up and right palm down. As they hover over each other's hands without touching, palms up to palms down, we sense the energy connections and allow them to flow to the right, counterclockwise, from person to person, to open the energy of the circle. Consciously, we send love to the person standing on our right; some members can see the patterns of energy moving in a circle while others say that it's so palpable that they can feel it in their hands.

Even when we are not part of a group, each of us is surrounded in a bubble of our own electromagnetic energy, whether we can feel it or not. Connecting these auric bubbles while we stand together centers us to the group energy, solidifies our goal of helping each other, and protects us from distractions.

I ask everyone to say the names of those who need healing, including themselves, either silently or aloud. We can hear whispers of names and sometimes a sigh in place of a name. We are still hovering over each other's hands at this point. And as the voices become quiet, I ask them to move their right hand in a flat, counterclockwise circle above the other person's left hand. We all do this in unison, all of our left hands remain still while our right hands move in circles above. This builds even more energy, and as it grows stronger, I ask them to see rainbows of healing light reaching each person and situation in need of support, wherever and however they need it most.

The vibrations grow stronger, and from this powerful feeling of intention, we hold hands and repeat our healing affirmation: "Healing rays . . . from the Divine Source of all power…are penetrating my body . . . making me perfectly whole."

Even though we are using the words "my" and "me" in the affirmation, we know that what we are sending is a blessing to others as well as ourselves. We set the intention for healing in our own individual lives and in the lives of others we know. As a group, we also send light, peace, and healing to various parts of the world—to those we don't know who are suffering or need support.

The action of standing, sensing energy, moving it with our hands, and vocalizing it is like a symbolic ritual. It moves our prayer from an emotional or mental space into the physical realm for outward manifestation.

Group Meditation

After the healing circle, people in the group tend to look dreamy-eyed, so sitting and readying ourselves for the guided meditation feels natural and welcome. I usually lead the meditation and don't tend to plan what I'm going to say ahead of time. Since you are joining us as I narrate this particular evening, I'll ask you to join us in the group meditation as you read.

> Take a deep breath and hold it for a few seconds. When you exhale, open yourself wide enough to release anything from your day that feels stuck. You can exhale with a big breath through your mouth or through your nose. No judgment here. Just let it out. Feel free to do another big exhale or two, whatever you need to do until your breath flows normally, in perfect rhythm for you.

Focus now on your heart. Imagine your heart energy opening . . . growing warmer and warmer . . . as if the image of a candle flame is hovering over your chest, gently flickering with each breath. Allow this warmth to spread until it extends beyond the perimeter of your torso, down to your arms and hands, down your legs and into your feet. It reaches down into the Earth and then back up again. After a few moments, it travels farther upward, reaching above your head . . . and then traveling back down again in a beautiful, rhythmic cycle. The energy surrounding you pulses softly, and your mind becomes quiet as you go deeper into this warmth, vibration, and breath.

As you feel the gentle vibrations on your skin, become aware of the energy field surrounding you, ready for you to send healing to the multidimensional parts of your self—whether the areas are physical, emotional, mental, or spiritual. Send the vibration of your inner light to these areas now and also to various parts of your life. Take a few moments to refresh your commitment to self-development and love. Know for certain that as you heal, others are healing, too—those within our circle as well as our families, extended families, friends, and acquaintances.

Extend this light to your home, your workplace, to schools and governments. Picture positive outcomes, compassion, and wisdom transforming areas of the world that are suffering conflict or hunger. See this, feel this. . . . Take a minute or so in the silence to picture this clearly.

After these moments of silence, you will become aware that you are letting go. When you release these intentions, know that the vibrant template we are creating here makes a difference.

It's time now to allow that powerful, world-encircling light to be absorbed back into each of us, re-centering and re-energizing every cell. As it does, breathe it in. Bathe yourself in its life-enriching energy.

Dwell within this light for a few moments. As it lifts, you land gently back into this moment . . . into this room . . . to where you are sitting. When you're ready, open your eyes.

Starting Off the Readings

As each person takes a moment to fully arrive back into the group, I reach for the bowl with the objects and pass it to my right.

We've learned to respect the sacredness of the meditation time which then transfers to the receptive space for writing our messages. If my intuition prompts me to select an object as I start passing the bowl, I will; otherwise, I wait till the end and choose the last item. On the rare chance that I receive my own object, I will ask someone to switch with me.

The group remains silent while each person writes down notes or draws sketches about what they are receiving. Heads raise and lower as people write in the silence. Some stare into space while others close their eyes. Some look at their objects, and others just hold them, loosely or tightly, using one or both hands. Words ebb and flow, filling blank pages. After about 15 minutes, a couple people may still be writing, adding whatever extra words or phrases they feel prompted to add.

"Do you still need a few more minutes?" I ask.

"No, it's ok to get started while I finish up," I hear.

I take a minute before I look at the group, "Who would like to start?"

Elizabeth's Reading for Helen

Elizabeth smiles broadly, "I will." Then she holds up the object she happened to pick. "Who brought this?" she asks, holding a keychain with a crystal on it. Helen raises her hand.

Elizabeth looks at Helen, holds up the paper, and shares her reading aloud with all of us. "I sense a need for self-care and protection. Travel and protection are featured, but so is having fun. I heard, 'Don't eat too many strawberries,' and 'You are YES.'"

Helen jumps from her chair as Elizabeth hands her the reading and the keychain. "I just came back from a Disney cruise, which of course included travel and fun. My daughter was eating strawberries every day at that time, lots of strawberries, so 'Don't eat too many strawberries' was a joke between us. Also, recently, I made a commitment to saying 'yes' as much as possible, rather than saying 'no' automatically in some situations. You're right about my being 'yes,' so that's a wonderful validation. Thank you."

As people comment on a reading they've just given or received, some share a little bit about any life challenges they might be having, but only as they surface through the words. Rarely do those develop into a group discussion for any length of time. Our group provides support, but it does not function like a support group.

Thankfully, no one has ever tried to control the group, dominate the discussion, or tell us that we're "doing it all wrong." I believe that, somehow, the group has been divinely protected from that.

Continuing With All the Readings

Helen's Reading for Lynda

Since Helen has just received a reading, it's her turn to go next, so she holds up the object she retrieved from the bowl, a sea-band bracelet.

Lynda raises her hand.

All of us are still grinning from Helen and Elizabeth's exchange about the idea of saying "yes" as much as she can yet saying "'no' to strawberries."

Helen holds the paper and reads aloud, "Lynda, try to create more space inside your mind. Take deeper breaths." She pauses and then transitions to the next part of the message, "I saw sheep playing leapfrog."

All of us giggle as we picture the image.

"I see intense passion." She pauses for a moment. "Breathe deeply. It's time to speak up or anger may ensue. If you feel tranquil after speaking up, you will have the confirmation you need. A warrior woman came through. You are experiencing a huge energy output and may need a psychic re-charge. Are your sinuses bothering you? I see a need for letting go of possible resentment underneath."

Lynda hugs and thanks Helen. "That was such confirmation, Helen. Oh my." As she sits down, Lynda explains that she, too, just came back from a Disney trip which inspires a few oohs and ahhs.

"During the trip," Lynda says, "I recognized what a difficult time my son has been having with anxiety, so we have been working with him in hope of helping him ease that through breathing exercises. You're right on target with that." Also, she said, "I have to tell you that I've just started doing some inner child work, and some emotions are definitely rising to the surface through that. I guess I'm on the right track. Thanks again, Helen."

Lynda's Reading for Amy

Lynda looks at her wife, Amy, sitting next to her. "I think this is yours, but I tried not to focus on that because I wanted the reading to be helpful for you. I hope it will be, that is."

Amy takes the pendant Lynda handed to her and smiles, "I understand. I would feel the same way if I knew an object was yours, too. So let's hear it!"

Lynda picks up the page and reads, "A sheet snaps, flung into the air. Maybe it's a duvet cover? I see a new start, ripples in the water. Connection. A breeze blows dust and dirt away. It brings fulfillment and understanding. Don't leave the sheet hanging, though. Don't squander the opportunity. I see three guides swaddling a baby."

As she looks at Amy and hands her the paper and the pendant, both of them twinkle, as if their eyes expresss a secret code they've kept for each other.

Amy reviews the scope of the reading and explains, "I love the snapped sheet! There's lots to clean in my world. I do feel guided and comforted in the process, so I must be the baby. No, I AM the baby!"

While several of us smile at this, Cathleen pipes up and adds, "Well either you're the baby or you're three sheets to the wind!"

Amy's Reading for Allie

Laughing and composing ourselves after the joke, all of us take a deep breath as Amy holds up a ring. "Whose is this?"

Everyone looks at each other, and Allie clears her throat and speaks up, "I brought that tonight."

Amy hands the ring to Allie, sits back down, and starts reading. "The theme here for you now is 'deep transformation.'"

"I saw the image of a black and yellow butterfly. I sensed that you must know absolutely who you are in order to progress to your next evolution—which is signaled by a deep acceptance of yourself. I also had the sense that this ring has the energy of a maternal grandmother or mother, a close bond. I heard a bell ringing, a triangular bell and saw children in uniform. The color blue was prominent. At the end of the reading, I heard that you are learning to truly let go. You are already in a butterfly state." Amy places the reading in her lap for a moment as the words sink in.

"There's more," Amy says, continuing. "I also saw a candle and heard, 'The Light of God is in you always.' I sense that you are guarded. This is perhaps a guardian angel who is always with you. I see leaves blowing and hear rustling as a means of catching your attention and reminding you that you have help whenever you want. There is no need to be careful in asking. Doors swing open. Go for it. Water bubbles up. Notice. Learn and listen sooner rather than later. Love surrounds you: Two people, open to magnitude of love. Get out of your head and into the experience of love."

As Allie pulls a tissue from her pocket, she wipes a tear and gives Amy a hug. Even though all of us were still sitting down, it felt to me as if it was a group hug. Over a year ago, Allie had lost her partner to cancer, and the energy of support for her grieving process filled the room.

Allie tells us that she is getting to know her guardian angel and that the candlelight represents a memorial. "Yes," Allie said, "I have been going through a lot of personal changes, both internal and external. Transformation is a good word for that. This ring is my mother's, so thank you for picking up on that."

She sniffed as she spoke to us and bolstered herself to tell us the rest. "Before I arrived here tonight, a dear friend said, 'I love you' to me . . . and honest to goodness it felt as if those words had directly come from my mother's spirit."

Laura, who is sitting next to Allie, pats her arm, and the woman on Allie's other side reaches around her shoulder for a sideways hug. We all sit for a few moments in the quiet as Allie soaks it all in.

After the meeting was over, Allie expressed to me that she felt as if the message about love surrounding her was from her mother, which she said, "gives me a lot of joy."

Allie's Reading for Esther

When Allie is ready to share what she received for someone else, she holds the object up and looks around the circle, asking who brought it.

Esther smiles, and says, "Oh, that's mine." People around the circle lean in to get a glimpse at the tiny little object, a ceramic squirrel.

And as everyone relaxes back, ready to listen, Allie explains that as she listened within for what to write, one phrase really stood out as very important, as if it were written in bold letters: "See God as your soulmate."

As I listened, I was amazed to hear such a powerful message imparted through the energy of such a small, unassuming creature.

The one who brought the tiny squirrel, Esther, closes her eyes for a moment and takes a breath. Instead of being tense, the sacredness of her pause looks like a prayer. As her eyes open, Esther expresses her gratitude for such a confirming reading in terms of how well it describes her close connection with God. "Yes, I have that closeness with God—or, that is, I strive to."

Sitting on the floor, rocking back and forth as she speaks, Esther tells us about her inner life. "God is absolutely the most important thing to me, and I talk with God, or Spirit—or however you want to name it—throughout the day, as often as I can. That is what makes me happy."

Esther's Reading for Elizabeth

Esther, still sitting on a floor pillow, holds up a piece of jewelry, which Elizabeth claims.

Esther closes her eyes again, spontaneously giving her reading from memory. She holds the necklace in her hands. At first it seems as if she is in a trance, but throughout her reading, she opens her eyes occasionally as she laughs and checks her notes.

"You are amazing! You are supported with all of your efforts by the Universe for you are recognized as a messenger of love. I see love at your center. You are a messenger, chosen, to bring context—a certain feeling or thinking about others—into some kind of a business encounter. The situation needs love to be brought into it. The encounter looks perfect to everyone else in theory, but in actuality, it is cold and dry. Yes, put love there. It's needed. Also, this is about something else. I'm hearing that you have to cry. Yes, you have to cry. Go to a movie and let your tears roll . . . Let go of unhealed feelings. Your forgiveness is flowing. Your purification process is done."

Esther's Reading for Elizabeth

At this point, Elizabeth starts digging for a tissue. She struggles through the tears to explain that her daughter, her only child, has just moved from Florida to Seattle.

Most of us in the group know that Elizabeth and her daughter have a very close relationship, one that stimulates each other's growth in loving, supportive ways.

"It's been so hard. I just can't tell you. I haven't let myself feel it completely, and I've held back the tears so often. Thank you, Esther, thank you for this."

Elizabeth's partner, Eileen, puts her arm around her.

The rest of us wait, holding the space for her to let it out.

One woman says, "We're here for you, Elizabeth. Anytime you need to talk, we're here."

Another says, "Remember, we love you."

After a minute or so, Elizabeth says, "Thanks, my friends. I know. I can feel your support." She lifts her head. "Now, ok, so I've already given a reading. We'll need a volunteer to go next."

Maritza's Reading for Suman

Maritza volunteers and holds up a bracelet with three beads.

Suman looks at it, and says, "Oh, that's mine," and smiles.

As Maritza reads, she occasionally turns over her paper to show a drawing that supplements or emphasizes her reading. "This is what I must tell you. Sing from your psyche …"

At this, Suman starts laughing, "Oh! Oh my goodness."

Maritza keeps going, "Movement to the right side. I sense the need for more power in your adrenals. Sound is very important, singing, vibrations coming from the throat."

Suman laughs and says, "Well, I can't sing. There's just no way any harmonic sound is coming out of my throat." Her reaction, shaking her head and declaring herself totally incapable of singing, prompts us all to grin and laugh, too.

It lightens the mood, for sure.

"But I can identify with this, regardless," Suman said, "because the three beads are associated with Shiva and the throat chakra. I'm certainly learning more about how to nurture the power of speaking my truth and, of course, my own inner willpower. Thank you, Maritza."

As Maritza rises from her seat, she shows her drawing with its flowing patterns of energy and hands it to Suman.

Suman kisses the air near Maritza's cheek, "Mmuwa! Thank you, my friend."

Suman's Reading for Kim

As Suman sits down, she holds up a ring and a piece of paper. "I don't know whose this is, but the reading really surprised me."

I looked toward the sofa at Suman and told her that the ring was mine.

She tilts her head, and says incredulously, "Are you guys building a house?"

Everyone's eyes widen as they look toward Rita and me.

I say, "Yes, we are, but we haven't told anyone about it yet."

All around the circle, we could hear a few "Wows" and expressions of amazement. "You are?" "Will you still be local?"

"Yes, yes, we will. It's nearby, just ten minutes from here."

"Well then," exclaims Suman, as she shows us the picture she drew of a concrete square with rebar poles sticking up along the corners. "Does it look anything like this?"

"That's just what it looks like now. I'm amazed, Suman."

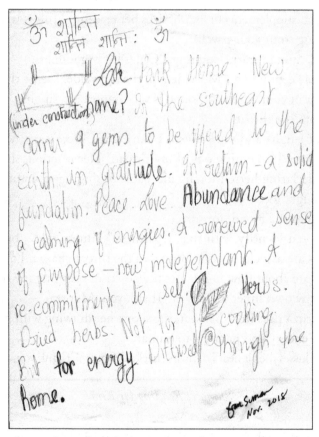

Suman's reading for me, November 2018. Note the importance of having pens that work well. This one ran low on ink, so she retraced some words.

She then starts reading what she wrote. "Lake. Park. Home. New home under construction?"

"Yes, it's a new house by a lake," I say.

Everyone's eyes grow even wider.

Suman continues, "In the Southeast corner, nine gems are to be offered to the Earth in gratitude. In return, a solid foundation. Peace. Love. Abundance and a calming of energies. A renewed sense of purpose, now independent. A re-commitment to self. Herbs. Dried Herbs. Not for cooking but for energy, diffused through the home."

As she passes the reading to me, Rita and I look more closely at the picture. It is a moment we'll never forget—confirmation of our new adventure and that everything is working out according to our intentions. Building a house is expensive and stressful, so hearing that there will be "abundance" as well as "a calming of energies," comforted us.

"Thank you so much, Suman! Wow, we are just so grateful for this."

"My turn next," I say, looking at Suman, "but I need to take a deep breath first. You're a hard act to follow!"

Everyone chuckles. Suman's reading is, indeed, amazing.

"Now, it's not me doing this. I just write down whatever nonsense pops into my head," Suman reminds us.

Kim's Reading for Cathleen

I look down at the page in my hand, not knowing who had brought the small gold ring and hold it up. "Whose is this?"

Cathleen, sitting cross-legged in a swivel chair, stands up to look closer at the ring. "That's mine," she says.

I hold on to the ring and preface the reading. "Cathleen, stay with me on this, okay, because there's positive news at the end."

Cathleen smiles, "Go for it!"

"I feel that you are finding a way through the sadness or gut-feeling of frustration. Sometimes feelings may be hard for us to identify. That's ok. Feel it in your body first in order to release it. Mental awareness is not always necessary. Try holding your solar plexus and send healing to yourself. The powerful being you are can do much more than you think. In this next part, I heard the lyrics to a song, 'Down by the boardwalk, down by the sea,' so take that for whatever it's worth."

"I wrote down, 'Take a mental vacation at least.' I also had the sense that it would be good for you to 'clear your mind and let your imagination go.' Letting your imagination go is actually your key to manifestation (getting out of your head and into freeing your spirit to create)!"

I continue, "'I see you opening double doors to the outside—letting the air in—freeing your spirit to a new phase. All this comes in at the same level—wherever you are—but a new sense of relief and peace comes in. Cherish this opportunity."

"Put yourself first for a change. You are a divine spirit who has transformed so much of her life and affected others in their own transformations—supporting them and helping them release blocks. You have accomplished more than you contracted to do and it's time to breathe and take this in. We congratulate you and celebrate your success."

"The new phase you wondered about calls for you to JUST BE. Vibrate your natural way, the frequency of who you really are. Nothing more is needed . . . Karma is done. Hooray! We are here for you—call upon us and we will answer."

"What I received at the end seemed really comforting—as if what you just heard about karma wasn't already a relief. 'Love goes beyond itself—always growing as its natural state. Because we are love, our expansion is endless.'"

Finding a way through the
sadness or gut-feeling of frustration. Sometimes
feelings may be hard for us to identify —
That's ok. Feel it in your body first in order to
release it. Mental awareness is not always
necessary. Try holding your solar plexus + send
healing to yourself. The powerful being you are
can do much more than you think!

"Down by the boardwalk" Down by the
Sea or"

Take a mental vacation at least — clear your
mind + let your imagination go! This is your
key to manifestation (getting out of your head +
into freeing your mind to create!)

I see you opening double doors to the outside — letting the
air in — freeing your spirit to a new phase.
Same level but a sense of relief + peace
comes in. Cherish this opportunity. Put yourself
1st for a change.

a You are a divine spirit who has transformed
so much of her life + affected others in their own

transformations — supporting them & helping them release blocks. You have accomplished more than you contracted to do & it's time to breathe & take this in. We congratulate you & celebrate your success. The new phase you wondered about calls for you to JUST BE. Vibrate your natural way, the frequency of who you really are. Nothing more is needed... Karma is done. HOORAY!

We are here for you — call upon us & we will answer.

"Love goes beyond itself — always growing as its natural state. Because we are love, our expansion is endless. "

Kim

My reading for Cathleen, June 2019

When I finish reading what I had written, I hand the page and ring to Cathleen. She hugs me, thanks me, and makes a joke: "Well, my karma may be finished at the moment, but after my drive home, that might be a different story."

While everyone laughs, she expresses her thanks and explains that she is certainly learning how to "just be" and give herself permission for that.

Cathleen's Reading for Maritza

Cathleen then holds up a black stone. "Who is claiming this amazing piece of obsidian, or jet, or—what is it?"

Maritza raises her hand, "It's mine, and it's obsidian."

"The theme that keeps coming up around this stone is 'create a solid foundation.'" Cathleen puts on her glasses and raises the paper to read:

"The heaviness and density of rocks and minerals serve many purposes and have multi-purposed meanings depending on which perspective you choose to view it from. Building a sound and solid belief system— different from what you have known or have been taught will serve you moving forward in ways you never thought possible. Opening the door to new potentials and new possibilities will not only allow you to grow spiritually but will allow you to stand strong in your values and anchor your worthiness, gratitude, and honoring of yourself. How are stones and rocks born? Where do they come from? How are they created? Do they grow? Who or what brought them into creation? It seems a mystery . . . Perhaps they are eventuated, no beginning and no end. Rocks just live their 'rock-ness'—no opinions and no judgment. Wouldn't it be wonderful to be a rock? Solid, free, and rooted. Be still and know."

"It's signed, 'Love always, Your solid rock.'"

As Cathleen finishes the reading and puts the paper down, she holds up the rock again for us to see. "I could feel the power and importance of this stone. The energy pattern emanating from it seems to be more than just what normally comes from a solid, lifeless stone," Cathleen announces. She looks at Maritza. "It seems full of joy and protection. It also feels like it's very special to you."

Maritza nods in approval. "Yes, it's very important to me, and it's part of my Shaman's training. To use it for healing, you cup the stone in your hand and blow into it three times, giving it the breath of life, 'Aliento de vida.' I've been practicing blowing into the rock and telling it to become light. The rock and the act of blowing into it also represents me in the sense that I am both master and rock. My purpose defines who I am, and who I am becoming."

A few people want to see the stone, and while it is being passed around, I remind everyone that "some people don't believe that stones or crystals can 'talk' or carry messages, but any object can be a conduit for a message. With a stone or crystal, however, the process is a little more complex. When we become fascinated with a stone, something ancient within those layers of compacted Earth seems to wake a message within us—it's as if the stone is a seed that grows and bears fruit in the fertile soil of our consciousness. It's possible that particular stones can convey common messages. I'm not sure, but we all have our favorites, don't we?"

Spontaneously, Lynda pulls a small river rock from her pocket, "Yes, indeed."

A couple people ask Maritza about her Shaman's training, but they keep their questions short, minding the clock, because there are several more readings to share.

I ask, "Since Maritza has already given a reading, who wants to jump in next?"

Laura's Reading for Eileen

Laura speaks up and raises her paper. "I loved the images in this reading. They were so clear. Now whose is this?" She holds up a wolf keychain.

"That's mine," says Eileen, adjusting herself in the chair.

Laura begins, "I saw an image of a person with a facial tattoo, a tribal leader or healer standing in front of a dwelling with a basket that needed to be woven. People were walking to a yellow field, a tribal gathering place. Some were escorted to birthing houses. Families and members of the tribe joined together in weaving the basket together until it was finished. This part is the most important, though: 'The weaving cannot only be done by one person. It must be woven cooperatively, shared with others in the family or in the community.'"

"Eileen, this felt so real." Laura gave the keychain back to Eileen.

"Thanks," Eileen says as they hug. "You know, this reminds me of a reading Suman gave me a while ago, telling me that I had been a Shaman in a previous life."

Suman adds, "Yes, I remember that. You were conducting tribal ceremonies around meeting the sun."

I ask, "Laura, was the Shaman in your vision male or female?"

"Hmm. I'm not sure. But does it really matter? I mean our spirits are not specifically identified as male or female, are they?"

"Our souls are composites of all-encompassing energies that include more than whether we are just male or female—in this life or any other life," Suman adds, looking at the rest of the group who are also nodding in agreement.

"My question was from a sense of curiosity about ancient Shamans who were female. History is just starting to uncover more about them. But you both make an important clarification. What we see in spirit can come from a deeper level than what we can see just on the outside."

Eileen's Reading for Pat

After some brief discussion, Eileen shows the object she picked to the group, a small broach.

"That's mine," Pat says.

Eileen reads what she has written on the page. "Your guides are omnipresent and are always in communication with you. They have a lot to tell you and show you. Be ready. Be open. Take care of yourself first so that you can take care of others. Know it in yourself. The frantic energy of last week has run its course."

Pat, who is the oldest person in the group, raises her hands and looks at Eileen, "Oh my God, if you had only known what I went through last week. I had a yard sale and did so much work inside and outside the house. My family came by to help, and I just can't tell you everything and can't remember it all. Oh, and I worked in the kitchen at church, too, and after all that, I'm just exhausted."

Pat laughs, making us all smile.

A few versions of "Pat, I don't know how you do it!" and a few "wows" are voiced around the circle.

She adds, "And I really appreciate what you said about my guides and also taking care of myself. Thank you. I will." Pat closes her eyes for a moment and looks as if the reading means more to her than she can express.

Pat's Reading for Laura

Pat then pulls out her reading along with the object she picked from the bowl. "Whose ring is this?"

Laura nods and says, "Oh, Pat, that's mine."

Pat says, "I can't help what I received, and I hope this makes sense to you."

"I feel some sadness around something for you but know that 'This too shall pass.' New people are waiting to appear in your life, multi-talented people, talented beyond your expectations. I see a large snake, an anaconda, but it's a positive sign because there is bright light all around it. I see Medicine Men, ancestors who were responsible for ancient drawings, possibly Egyptian. There is also a sense of Deja Vu for you with these images."

As Laura's eyes widen, she says, "I have always felt an affinity with Egypt," and she shows us the Egyptian earrings and necklace she happened to be wearing that evening.

"And remind me, what does the snake symbol represent?"

Someone says, "Transmutation, I think."

And Laura agrees, "Yes, I have been going through a lot physically, changing my diet and detaching from the toxicity I've been experiencing with some of the people in my life." As she walks toward Pat and accepts the ring with the written copy of the reading, they hug. "I will meditate to see what else these symbols might mean for me, Pat. Thank you."

Closing the Circle

At this point, Lynda offers to play a flute, allowing us to get quiet and absorb the energy of the night. While she plays, the music seems to expand how grateful I am for each person.

We all place our readings to the side and get ready to stand in a circle once again.

I ask everyone to hold hands, and then I say, "Thank you for being here. May the love in our hearts and the energy of our meeting extend outward throughout our weeks ahead. And so it is! Now let's send the energy of the circle to your left, moving clockwise, to close the circle. Thank you all for being here."

Afterward

Small tangential discussions form while a few of us stretch or grab some leftover snacks. More discussions follow as people catch up from last month or last week, depending on how frequently they see each other. This part of the evening is always light-hearted, with lots of laughter and personal updates.

We snack again on some delicious treats, laugh with good humor, and share lingering goodbyes. As each person or carpool of friends leaves to return home, they take with them a little piece of us all.

Later, as I retire to bed, I review the reading I received that night. Although every one is unique, each time, I feel as if the page I'm holding is a little miracle.

CHAPTER 5

A Bookstore Circle Changed My Life

Psychometry discovered me a couple decades ago when my life was in turmoil over a 15-year on-again/off-again "entanglement" with my first female partner. I thought for sure we were in love, but I had been clinging to my need for the relationship to change. Couples counseling helped for a while, but I had lost myself in trying over and over again to repair a relationship that should have ended long ago. I had been walking on eggshells every day, never knowing when something I said or did would cause a blow up. She felt frustrated, too, and we were both stuck in a sense of despair.

During this period of questioning and doubting, I had been traveling out of state for a couple months to see my mother, who had been receiving hospice care in her home. As these events occurred, my full-time teaching contract would be expiring at the end of spring term. My mother died in February, and her death started a chain reaction that caught my attention and helped me change my life. Initially, the mourning process froze all other emotions except my sorrow; I could see myself, my partner, and my relationship without any of my former rose-colored idealism. Knowing that I would soon need a place of my own, I looked for alternative ways to spend my evenings and steer clear of the drama at home.

I had driven by the Cosmic Bookstore over a dozen times until I couldn't ignore it anymore. The old, yellowing sign seemed to call out to me one afternoon, but even so, I needed to clear my head before going in. I took a deep breath before getting out of my car and stayed a few minutes in the bookstore parking lot. At mid-day in Florida, though, the heat would only allow me a few moments. Glancing around, I could see a small house attached, like an add-on. Only one other car was in the driveway, so it took a bit of extra courage to walk in since it looked as if I would be the only customer.

The glass-paned door had a bell on it that jingled when it opened—for some reason reminding me of my favorite movie, *It's a Wonderful Life*. Ruth, tall and thin, white hair in a teased bee-hive style, greeted me with such warmth that my anxiety began to fall away. Owner and operator of the bookstore, Ruth was an astrologer as well as a former New Thought minister. Her demeanor had an extra sense of quiet joy woven into it, and her eyes twinkled on the edge of wonder or laughter.

I felt comfortable enough to browse for a while. After I found a book to purchase, I read a bulletin board by the cash register. Ruth noticed and explained, "That's our psychometry group, the Thot-watchers. You're welcome to join us. We meet here at the bookstore every Tuesday night at 7:30, after closing."

"What is a psychometry group?"

"Well, psychometry is giving a reading with an object as the conduit. To start, each person puts a small object in a bowl. Then after we meditate as a group, I pass the bowl around for everybody to pick out an object for their reading. You write down what you receive from Spirit and then give the reading to the one who brought the object."

I must have stared blankly for a moment with my mouth slightly open.

"Sounds easy, huh?" she said with a chuckle.

My first thought was, NO, that does NOT sound easy, but I ended up saying, "Would you accept a beginner?"

"Of course! It must be something you need to try. Otherwise, you wouldn't have noticed the bulletin board or come into the store, right?"

As I paid for the book, she mentioned that whatever object I choose to bring, it's best if it's something that can be held within a closed hand.

"Decide what you'll bring and put your energy into it during the week. Also, we try not to let each other see what we bring so that the process is as anonymous as possible."

Looking back, I'm convinced that the Universe conspires to help us—whether we are aware of it or not. I had certainly been off track, lacking self-confidence and focus. In the previous year, I had been working part-time as a babysitter while trying to finish my dissertation. I needed to get on my feet again. As soon as my transcripts showed evidence of my doctorate in composition and rhetoric, I had a full-time teaching job offer at a local community college. Teaching gave me purpose.

A month or so later when I talked with my partner about my need to leave and get a place of my own, her demeanor changed gear so fast from neutral to rage that it scared me. She threw books off their shelves and ripped picture frames off the wall, smashing them onto the floor. In the past when she had been upset enough to throw a dish at the wall, I retreated, leaving the house temporarily. This time, her anger seemed wild. I remember feeling frozen as I tiptoed through broken glass and promised myself this would never happen to me again.

Having to move in a hurry, I ended up at a new colleague's house for a few days until I found a studio apartment, one with a Murphy bed and tiny kitchen. It was the only thing I could afford but just right as a fresh start. Coincidentally, it was only two miles from the Cosmic Bookstore.

Throughout this crazy time, I had been attending the weekly "Thot-watchers" group as often as I could. I didn't talk about how things ended with my partner, but I expressed how I felt lucky to have found an available and affordable apartment. Walking into the store on Tuesday nights, I felt as if I were entering a different world where everything magically fell into place, one that offered genuine acceptance and moments of joy. Even though they were just acquaintances, everyone who joined in at Ruth's helped me find a sense of home within myself at a time when I needed it most.

But it wasn't just weekly meditation or focusing more on my intuition that helped me change my life. Psychometry group meetings included a "healing circle" component. The Cosmic Bookstore group typically sat in a circle with a low, round table in the center. Ruth told me that when the group started, a few decades ago, people got to know each other well and started chatting quite a bit at the beginning, so she initiated a new routine, asking each person to say their name along with an affirmation. This process helped visitors get to know others and balanced the communication between new attendees and regulars.

The affirmations focused on the positive, helping everyone drop their energy down from their heads to their hearts. So to begin the group, Ruth, a strict timekeeper, hushed the chatter by announcing, "It's time to start."

So as the meeting began, she welcomed new people, briefly explained the process of giving a reading, and answered any related questions. After this, she started with her own affirmation, for example, "I am Ruth, and I am always in the right place at the right time." Around the circle, beginning with the person sitting beside Ruth, others would follow.

After we finished the affirmations, everyone in the group stood in a circle. It was a reverent moment, and one of the group, usually Charlotte, said an affirmative prayer focused on clearing our individual energetic fields and opening us to the group healing circle.[19] She asked each of us to connect to the energy of the Earth below our feet and bring it upward through our body until we felt it begin to balance. Then she asked us to hold our hands out without touching each other, with left palm up, right palm facing downward. People next to each other hovered their palms over each other's hands. Charlotte continued, asking for us to pass our positive, loving vibrations to the person on our right. During this process, the energy between our hands gained even more substance—the heat and electromagnetic pulse of what we were giving and receiving was usually quite powerful.

Next, Charlotte opened the healing circle, "Now put forward the names of those who need healing. You can say each person's name either aloud or silently and remember to include yourself."

Spontaneously, across the circle, people would whisper a few names, pausing at the end for a few moments of silence.

Charlotte then said, "I saw rainbows of healing light extending to each person and situation that needs support, going to wherever they need it most. Now let's all hold hands and repeat our healing affirmation together."

At this moment, it wasn't unusual to hear a deep sigh or two, a few "mmmmms and ahhhhhs" as people opened their eyes and gently reached for each other's hands.

"Healing rays . . . (the group repeats after Charlotte) from the Divine Source of all power . . . are penetrating my body . . . making me perfectly whole."

---

[19] If you are interested in starting your own group, I outline all of this in detail in Part 5.

The sense of hope after this part of the meeting was just as palpable as the energy, which I believe are linked together anyway. Without question, these weekly healing intentions helped me believe in myself again and that the healing process would continue—not just for me, but for my loved ones and others with their extended connections, too.

I attended weekly meetings at the bookstore as often as I could, and always felt a sense of cohesion with everyone there, even those I had never met who popped in to attend occasionally. I've kept most of the readings from those years as well as those I've received since beginning my own group. One reading from Charlotte appeared for me after I had moved a hundred miles away for a new job. This job, as Charlotte affirms in the message below, was stressful in terms of administrative politics but relatively smooth in its everyday management.

Below is the text of her reading, followed by an image of it:

11/3/09

Kitchen—cooking cleaning—butcher block top. Sunlight filtered through the air. Quiet time. Very important to take time for yourself. Help neck and stress. Many books. Study. Read for fun more. It is a time for reflection. Look to new and different possibilities. Open mind. Work— Stressful, but really is smooth. Keep doing what you are doing, it will all work out.

Dog is love.

All is in divine right order. In a year, you will look back and be amazed!!!

11/3/09

Kitchen - Cooking cleaning - butcher
block top. Sunlight filtered
through the air. Quiet time.
Very important to take time
for yourself. Help neck?
stress. Many books.
Study. Read for fun more.
It is a time for reflection
Look to new & different
possiblities. Open mind.
Work - Stressful, but
really is smooth. Keep
doing what you are doing,
it will all work out.
Dog is love
All is in divine right order.
In a year you will look back
& be amazed!!!

Charlotte's Reading for Me in 2009

Although Charlotte had no awareness of what my kitchen looked like when she gave me the reading, I had moved to an apartment that indeed had a butcher-block countertop, and since I had no TV, I had started reading quite a bit. Although I don't like to take prescription pain medications, it was necessary for me to take some so that I could function at work. The pain grew to be so rough that I started taking depression medications as well, which was highly unusual for me. About that time someone I worked with referred me to an excellent acupuncturist who helped me heal from the neck pain I had been experiencing. During that year of treatment, my healing proved to be so complete that I no longer needed pain pills or depression medication.

The phrase "dog is love" didn't seem anything unique with me at the time because I had an aging dachshund who was the most loving dog I had ever had. But surprisingly, later that month, I spent Thanksgiving with friends who had inherited a Rat Terrier they couldn't keep. This new addition to my family, a bright, sweet, terrier, stole my heart. Charlotte was right that I could look back in amazement. That year was quite powerful for me because I started looking for a different position and eventually found one two years later, in 2011. Just a few months after that, I started the journey to having my own psychometry group.

CHAPTER 6

New Place, New Peeps

The weekly psychometry meetings in Tampa had meant so much to me that when I eventually moved elsewhere in Florida a few years later, I felt the need to create my own group. It took a while, though, for me to come to that realization. It seemed so natural for others to lead something like that, yet not for me. I felt comfortable in a college classroom, but it was intimidating to think of leading even a small group of strangers through the intuitive process of a "reading." I didn't feel skilled enough in that process yet. Besides, the group in Tampa was familiar to me, some had become dear friends, and "Psychometry Tuesdays" had their familiar identities woven throughout my memories of it.

After two years, I finally felt settled in my new area and had begun to find my "tribe." I had started attending a local Metropolitan Community Church, and through those connections, met a spiritually focused women's group, SOFEA (an Acronym for "Sisters of Faith Encouraging Another"). Some women in the group attended a Unity Church, so I began attending SOFEA meetings and varied between visiting MCC and Unity. I felt comfortable and welcome among them. Their lives were rich with activity, generosity, community, and they had a strong desire to grow spiritually. Many of the women in the group are among my closest friends today, including others who arrived through what seemed to be divine appointment through word of mouth, the Unity church Reiki Circle, or my new, expanding, psychometry group.

I decided to meet monthly rather than weekly, which was important to me because I had been so busy with a new job, and I knew I would be hosting the group on my own. So, I initiated the first psychometry/meditation group meeting in my living room in the apartment complex where I lived. I soon realized, though, that by the third or fourth meeting, the clubhouse would have more room for a dozen or so folks to mingle and snack. The space wasn't as cozy, but it worked for almost a year until I bought my own home. After that, the group started to meld and match the energy we all held for the space.

It takes several months to build a routine for the group and for word-of-mouth to spread. I started by using the same format that was familiar to me from the Tampa group: using affirmations, then a healing circle, meditation, then readings. Just as the Tampa group set Tuesday nights at 7:30 as a permanent meeting time, I created "third Fridays" at 7:00 pm for our meetings. The more people connected with the meeting itself and especially the bond we created with each other during the readings, the more each person looked forward to the monthly group.

I was single at the time I started my own group. A few years later, I met my wife, Rita. Because the group has been so important to me, we probably wouldn't have become a couple if she had been opposed to it. In fact, Rita accepted me and even loved me more because hosting this group not only made me feel more alive but helped me live according to what I valued in my heart. Now, we open our home each month to the group because it's important to both of us.

Of course, not everyone is able to attend every meeting, and sometimes people move away, become extremely busy or temporarily ill. Rita and I are sometimes unable to host every month due to family emergencies or travel, so a few different people have led the group over the years. I always provide the dates two months in advance with each monthly reminder, and when others host, I include the location address and phone number, just in case.

But I realize that my audience for this book may be more interested in how to give readings than in how to start their own group. With this in mind, the next section includes specifics about the intuitive process from published writers as well as members of the group.

PART 3

Advice for Giving Psychometry Readings

"A reading is actually much easier to <u>do</u> than it is to <u>explain</u>."
— *Charlotte, Psychometry Group Member*

CHAPTER 7

Intuition, Energy, and Spiritual Development

Your Own Intuitive Patterns and Codes

Whether intentionally or by accident, we've all had the experience of "reading" energy, whether it's emanating from an object, location, or a person.

To become aware of the difference between what we're picking up on and our own energy, though, we need to know what our own energy feels like first. Sensing the tips of our fingers and toes and then focusing on the "center" of our being, or our heart, is a good start. Energy medicine practitioner Donna Eden recommends the "Cook's Posture" pose for relieving anxiety and centering. It's easy to find instructions or videos of this on the Internet, but basically it consists of a figure-eight: crossing the ankles, hands, and arms and holding that space for about a minute. Energy follows the posture, drawing everything in. It is an excellent centering technique for those who have difficulty distinguishing between their own energy and the energy of the others around them. In terms of giving readings, once we know what our own energy feels like, whatever differences we then begin to notice inform the message.

When I work with clients in energy healing sessions, specific intuitive indicators help me assess areas of the person's well-being so that we can address those areas during that session. For example, let's say my hand picks up some prickly energy in the air above the person's left thigh. When this occurs, my intuition calls my attention to something symbolic (other practitioners may have similar systems for this too). In my case, prickly energy over my client's thigh points to family issues, and the left side identifies the issue as related to a female (or someone identifying as such). Putting those symbolic indicators together can indicate the need for healing a challenge with a female in a close family unit (wife, mother, daughter, sister, aunt, etc.). Note that I am only recognizing a pattern in my client's energy field. Although I can provide energetic support for their healing process, the choice to activate that further, in whatever way is best, depends upon my clients' willingness to apply what they learned from the session.

Patterns or codes might surface while giving any kind of reading because our intuition uses personal associations, symbols, experiences, and emotions. For example, I had a reading once from a psychic who told me that she had an image of lots of black birds flying near me. She said that this represented the possibility of losing loved ones soon—from months to a year, perhaps. At the time, I knew that my stepdad and also another dear family member were both dying, and I had not mentioned that to her. She was right, and those were not my images or symbols, but hers. It's rare for me to hear something like that, especially news related to the loss of a loved one, but I trusted that I needed to hear it.

More likely, we may interpret seeing a cardinal as a "hello" from a lost loved one or a feather as an angelic sign. Even if many people share a common association with a symbol, like the cardinal for instance, we need to remember that each person has a compilation of their own, specific experiences regarding what they see and how they interpret it.

Just as symbols and patterns can vary depending on each person's sensibilities, the process varies as well. Each person is also different in how they receive messages, and because of this, sometimes the Universe speaks to us in a code designed specifically for us—keyed to our dreams, memories, and personal symbols. Once I started a reading for Eileen that began with the word, "Aho," a Native American greeting. I heard the greeting in my mind the moment I began to listen to my inner guidance, so I wrote it down. I hadn't heard that word in well over a decade, but when I read it aloud to Eileen, she told me that the previous weekend, she and Elizabeth had attended a Powwow.

Note that I did not title this section, "How to Give a Psychometry Reading." Although I will be breaking the process down into steps, providing context from professionals, and listing some do's and don'ts, remember that you are unique and have a process of your own that you can learn how to access and develop.

The Universe in Every Object

As I mentioned in a previous chapter, William Denton described psychometry in 1871 as "the soul of things," a phrase that sounds quite mystical coming from a geologist. Extending that point even further, he said, "I am sometimes inclined to think that the universe is contained in every pebble, and it only needs the all-compelling soul to call it forth."[20]

When we read a statement like that, we might assume that only gifted individuals—the "all-compelling souls"—Denton mentions, could be capable of calling forth vast information from a source as tiny as a pebble, so it's even more baffling to consider how it's possible for us to retrieve, organize, and decipher a universe full of information and then put it into an understandable reading.

We really do have access to a whole universe of information within every object as well as inside of us. Our wide-ranging intuitive minds can take us anywhere—which shows how inspiring and miraculous the process can be. Because—as Ether Hicks repeats so often in her workshops—"we have access to the energy that has created worlds," giving a reading is easier than it sounds, and the results are extraordinary.

Let me repeat that thought; giving a reading is easier than you might think. Denton's work provides an example and provides a key to the whole process. His sister, Mrs. Cridge, depicted the precise setting that surrounded a piece of lava from Hawaii. She had no specific training in how to do what she did. What she sensed was in direct response to Denton's question to her about the object's origin. His question provided a target, and this points to something very important that I learned from Laura Day: using a target as a guide is a crucial step when giving any kind of reading.

---

[20] Denton and Denton, *The Soul of Things*, 103.

When we give a reading for someone else, it's helpful to trust, relax, and open our hearts. As we do, we can't help but feel our own indwelling compassion surfacing because the goal is to provide support. That's when a flow of information starts streaming in. Overall, that's the process, but I can see how anyone reading this would need more specifics. Although I will go into further detail later on, first I think it's important to hear from those who are far more experienced than I am.

What the Professionals Say About Giving Readings

Several modern-day intuitives have taught workshops and written books about how to give readings. Among them are Nina Ashby, Sophy Burnham, Sonia Choquette, Laura Day, Debra Katz, Belleruth Naparstek, Penney Peirce, Rebecca Rosen, and Gordon Smith. Day says, "everyone is intuitive," and that we all have the ability to sense energy. In her book, *The Circle: How the Power of a Single Wish Can Change Your Life*, Day insists on centering first and then creating an atmosphere of positive energy all our own before we even begin the process of giving a reading. She describes this as creating a "New Reality," an intention or image we hold in our minds of a feeling, event, or situation that we want to manifest.[21] The energy of embodying this New Reality creates a sacred space where negative thinking dissipates, and positive outcomes take shape. She tells us to focus on that positive vision—to embody it—because it's the jumping off point before starting any reading or manifesting what we need.

Similarly, Belleruth Naparstek suggests a process that focuses on heart-centered visualization, one that can also support healing. Sonia Choquette asks us to trust our intuitive instincts, our "vibes," which is the title of one of her books, and Penney Peirce reminds us that intuition stems from compassion. Peirce and Day provide exercises in their books as well as in-person workshops that can teach anyone how to access and amplify their natural, intuitive skills.

I am particularly struck by each author's unwavering belief that we are all capable of giving an accurate and helpful reading. From their workshops

---

[21] Laura Day, *The Circle: How the Power of a Single Wish Can Change Your Life* (New York: Jeremy P. Tarcher, 2001), 20.

and books, I've learned that even someone with an analytical mind like mine—a retired academic who is certainly more left-brain dominant than right—can learn to access her inner guidance. If I learned how to do it, anyone can. Once we let go of our fears, it's much easier to access an enlightened state of consciousness or even subconscious patterns that somehow, through a sense of higher will or heart coherence, organically form into a meaningful message.

Edgar Cayce on Intuition and Psychic Development

An expert at accessing inner guidance organically and subconsciously, Edgar Cayce was known as "the sleeping prophet" and was one of the most prolific psychics in American history. While he was in a trance-like state, Cayce faced curious questions about psychic development even from his conservatively minded, church-going acquaintances in the southern United States. In the digital archive of Edgar Cayce's 14,306 readings from the early 1900s to 1945, there are nearly 200 that mention intuition and over 400 that talk about psychic development. Cayce was a Protestant Sunday School teacher within the Disciples of Christ, and although many of his readings mention subjects that are far outside of that realm, his discussions of psychic development and intuition primarily have a spiritual focus. Although several readings in the database would apply here, two stand out as having similar approaches to those I've just discussed from Choquette, Day, Peirce, and others.

In Reading #239-1, Cayce is asked to advise a person on how to "best gain control of himself and utilize his abilities to best advantage." In his answer, Cayce says, "Depend more upon the intuitive forces from within and not harken so much to that of outside influences":

> [I]n the still small voice from within does the impelling influence come to life in an individual that gives for that which must be the basis of human endeavor; for without the ability to constantly hold before self the ideal as is attempted to be accomplished, man becomes one as adrift, pulled hither and yon by the various calls and cries of those who would give of this world's pleasure in fame,

fortune, or what not. Let these be the outcome of a life spent in listening to the divine from within, and not the purpose of the life.[22]

In addition to listening to the "divine from within," Cayce advises his client to develop the ability to hold to an ideal. This concept of embracing an ideal aligns with Day's emphasis of affirmative embodiment or "New Reality."

In another reading, Cayce explains that intuition, psychic forces, and psychic development "are so often misunderstood" and should be associated with a "soul mind" or "soul body" rather than separately in terms of soul, mind, or body.[23] Sonia Choquette makes these points throughout her work, emphasizing the importance of connecting to the guidance from our souls. In *Trust Your Vibes at Work*, she says,

> When I ask people why they didn't follow their intuition, most say that they killed these notions by dismissing them as fantasy before they were even born. Unfortunately, soul direction from a higher plane is ignored all the time, yet you can't follow your vibes to greater things if you're constantly squelching your inner voice. You have to be open to guidance to benefit from it . . . .[24]

In the same reading that Cayce says intuition and psychic development are so misunderstood, the client, a housewife, asks him to explain how to study and "train" her "intuitive sense." Cayce's answer is firm:

> Train intuition? Then, how would you train electricity, save as to how it may be governed! By keeping in self those thoughts, those activities of the mental mind, those activities of the body that allow spiritual truths to emanate

---

[22] Edgar Cayce, "Reading #239-1," Association for Research and Enlightenment, Member Database, Nov 23, 1933, https://www.edgarcayce.org.

[23] Edgar Cayce, "Reading #255-12," Association for Research and Enlightenment, Member Database, Nov 23, 1933, https://www.edgarcayce.org.

[24] Sonia Choquette, *How to Trust Your Vibes at Work and Let Them Work for You* (Carlsbad, CA: Hay House, 2005), 49-50.

through . . . [K]eep the body, the mind, the soul, in attune with the spheres of celestial forces, rather than of earthly forces.[25]

The "celestial forces" that Cayce mentions could be literal, but it also carries symbolic meaning in relation to what is generally associated with our better selves—the loving part of us that seeks to help others, treat them with kindness, and strive for outcomes in our lives that are best for all involved. Having open hearts in a state of attunement while seeking the best possible outcome seems to be the most effective way to start a reading. The conditions, however, are not only emotional and mental, but physiological, too.

When I worked with my spiritual mentor, Lila Underwood, many years ago, she told me something I will never forget: "People often have the goal of wanting to be more psychic, but it's much more important to grow spiritually. That's the better goal. Insight that many call 'psychic' is just a side effect of a deeper, more active spiritual life." For her, an active spiritual life included meditation, prayer, maintaining a healthy body, having the heart of a servant, living with gratitude, and paying attention to her own inner guidance.

It's interesting that what she taught me more than thirty years ago aligns with current research on meditation and gamma waves.

The Link Between Intuition, Compassion, Meditation, and Brain Frequencies

Recently I heard author and scientist Dawson Church discuss categories of brain waves, and what he says about gamma waves relates to the meditative mindset we create in preparation for giving readings.[26] Church noted that the lowest frequencies of brain waves, delta and theta, are associated with sleep, dreams, and a trance-like state that supports super-learning. The next level is a characteristic of conscious thought,

---

[25] Cayce, "Reading #255-12."

[26] Dawson Church, "Sculpting Your Creative Brain," Oct18, 2023, in Art2Life, produced by Nicholas Wilton, podcast, audio, 54:47, https://www.art2life. com/2023/10/18/sculpting-your-creative-brain-dawson-church-ep-104.

consisting primarily of alpha and beta states, which have a much faster frequency.

An even higher state, what Church calls, "top of the range," is gamma. Characteristics of gamma waves, he says, include "compassion, insight, and creative brilliance."[27]

Recalling one research study, Dawson explains that some advanced meditators put out 25 times the gamma frequencies of ordinary people.[28]

Another study of gamma waves published in 2017 illustrates "an increase in high-gamma 60-110 Hz associated with meditation expertise."[29] From this research, as well as from my own personal experience, meditation enhances insight and expands a person's capacity for compassion.

Extending this point, neurologists Richard Mendius and Rick Hanson discuss in detail how "the meditation activity itself activates frontal lobe structures that sustain intention for wholesome states of being."[30] According to their research, meditation activates an area of the brain called the insula, which corresponds to increases in a person's capacity for empathy.[31]

From these recent studies and from what professional psychics have said in their books, we've learned that

- Intuition is a natural part of everyone.
- Our intuitive capacity is linked to specific psychological, emotional, and physical conditions.
- Meditation, purpose, and compassion reinforce intuition.
- We can learn to improve our intuition when we are focused on being our best selves and also helping others to do the same.

---

[27] Church, "Sculpting Your Creative Brain."

[28] Church, "Sculpting Your Creative Brain."

[29] Claire Braboszcz et al, "Increased Gamma Brainwave Amplitude Compared to Control in Three Different Meditation Traditions," *Public Library of Science* 12, no. 1 (January 2017), https://link.gale.com/apps/doc/A478747194/STOM?u=29577_wppl&sid=bookmark- STOM&xid=4a909b1f.

[30] Richard Mendius and Rick Hanson, *Seven Guided Practices to R"ebuild" Your Brain for Lasting Joy and Fulfillment,"* on Sounds True/AW01357W, 2009, Digital Audio.

[31] Mendius and Hanson "Practices."

The Importance of Meditation and Prayer

Since research has proven that meditation and mindfulness can change a person's heart rate, lower blood pressure, and reduce stress, the importance of it has been popping up everywhere—from a pamphlet at the doctor's office to a class at the YMCA. Today, the app Insight Timer lists over 20 million members and provides over 150,000 free meditation tracks ranging, on average, from 5 to 60 minutes each. The creators of Calm, another meditation app, boast that their site exists in over 190 different countries with over 100 million downloads and over 1.5 million 5-star reviews. Amazon lists over 70,000 books on the topic.

As a practice, meditation extends far beyond the basics of inner relaxation to include subcategories such as "contemplation" or "centering prayer." In my own spiritual practice, prayer and meditation blend into each other. For me, prayer does not usually consist of words I utter to a holy being outside myself, a "please help me with _____ or help someone else with ___" kind of approach. Although I believe that all approaches to prayer have value, I learned long ago that prayer and meditation are an intrinsic part of who we are in terms of our emotions, our thoughts, and also our bodies. When I meditate, the boundary between myself and God—or Spirit—can become as indistinguishable as a drop of water from the ocean. Eric Butterworth describes this much better in his book, *The Universe is Calling*:

> "God is an allness in which you exist as an eachness. As I say in *Discover the Power Within You*, 'God is not in you in the same sense that a raisin is in a bun. That is not unity. God is in you as the ocean is in a wave. The wave is nothing more or less than the ocean expressing as a wave."[32]

If I set a deep intention for my prayers—for healing, clarification, guidance, or whatever—the energy of that intention connects me to more than the thoughts I hold in my mind; it extends also to my emotions and senses. I feel gratitude for something ahead of time, imagining it, feeling

---

[32] Eric Butterworth, *The Universe is Calling* (New York: HarperSanFrancisco, 1993), 22.

the healing and movement toward outcome (even though I have no idea what that might look like for myself or for another). Again, let me defer to Butterworth who describes it this way:

> Your prayer is not for God to listen to. True prayer is words that God may utter through you . . . that you voice, or feel in the silence . . . . In our praying, we do not cause God to spring into action. Rather, in our praying, we are hearing the call of the universe and responding to it.[33]

Similar to personal counseling at its best, prayer and meditation are inward processes that transform our consciousness and our behavior. When we change ourselves and retrain our thought patterns toward appreciation and self-awareness, our perspective of the world opens, helping us adapt and discover much more than we did before. We begin to see that instead of relying on others to give us what we need, our focus reorients toward self-improvement, creative problem-solving, and unconditional positive regard toward others. As a result, we appreciate and enjoy our inner and outer lives more and more.

Perhaps this sounds as if I'm assuming meditation and prayer will erase life's difficulties. Nothing can wipe those away, but as Ariana Huffington says in her book, *Thrive*, "Mindfulness, yoga, prayer, meditation, and contemplation aren't just tools reserved for retreats over long weekends anymore—they are the ultimate everyday performance enhancers."[34] In a series of articles in *Time Magazine* on mindfulness and meditation, researchers explain that mindfulness enhances resiliency by lowering heart rate, breathing rate, inflammation, and by activating "the region of the brain associated with emotional reactions." In another article in the same magazine titled, "The Meditation Miracle," research shows that the "more experienced the meditator, the more quickly the brain recovers from stress."[35]

In contrast to mindful breathing exercises, guided meditations that focus on love and compassion have proven to be more helpful to people

---

[33] Butterworth, *Universe*, 8-9.

[34] Ariana Huffington, *Thrive: The Third Metric to Redefining Success and Creating a Life of Well-being, Success, and Wonder* (New York: Harmony Books, 2014), 93.

[35] Mandy Oakland, "The Science of Bouncing Back," *Time*, May 21, 2015, https://time.com/3892044/the-science-of-bouncing-back.

seeking emotional healing and intuitive development. Citing research from the HeartMath Institute, Naparstek explains that at the Institute people are invited to "direct attention to their hearts and to deliberately and consciously generate and hold feelings of love, care, compassion, and appreciation there for several minutes."[36] The Institute measures these frequencies, and as the meditation continues, it creates "one coherent internal rhythm pattern of low-frequency, amplified peace."[37]

In her own work, Naparstek uses guided imagery to produce "this heart-focused state."[38] "Meditation and heart-based imagery slow our brain waves down," she says, which "produces in us an expanded perception during our still points, the points of rest at which we expand out into all points in the universe at infinite speed. In this state of expanded subjective time, we can better absorb and bring back to our manifest world the information we collect out there."[39] All of this is important because it is the state of mind which is most conducive to giving a reading.

Giving a Reading in Ten Steps

Ten may seem like a lot of steps to remember, but after just a little practice, most of the items on this list become subconscious. It's a lot like learning to drive when much of what we do becomes so routine that it seems automatic.

Generally, it happens like this: in the psychometry group, as the bowl of objects makes its way to us, we lift the scarf that covers everything just enough to reach in, then pick something, not knowing whose it is. After choosing it, we hold it, silently ask our target question, and allow the energy to unfold into a message.

My wife Rita says that it's helpful if she isn't wearing any rings or other jewelry that might distract her from the energy of the object. She told me that she centers herself by focusing on her breathing. She sits with her hands cupped around the object and waits for whatever information comes through.

---

[36] Belleruth Naparstek, *Your Sixth Sense: Activating Your Psychic Potential* (New York: HarperCollins, 1997), 107.

[37] Naparstek, *Sixth Sense*, 107.

[38] Naparstek, *Sixth Sense*, 108.

[39] Naparstek, *Sixth Sense*, 110.

If she gets stuck, she asks her target question like a prayer, "What can I say to help this person?" Then she breathes into it, without thinking or analyzing, and just focuses on her breathing. After this, she told me that the information flows to her in images, words, music, or feelings, and she writes it down.

When giving a reading—or making sense of intuitive information in whatever form—it's important to clear your mind with the goal of being as open and objective as possible. Naparstek provides more details about this in her book, *Your Sixth Sense*, a compilation of her interviews with 43 highly intuitive people. When she asked each one about how they process psychic information, she noticed some important commonalities:

> Along with a receptive mind state and an inward focus, the experience of receiving psychic information also has two related critical features: first, a quality of very alert attention to the subtlest and most fleeting of inner impressions; and second, an acceptance of those impressions as is, without assessing, interpreting, embellishing, or noodling with them in any way.[40]

She explains that the problem of interpreting information after receiving it is a "natural tendency of the mind to make assumptions, interpretations," but is, nonetheless, a "common cause for error and distortion."[41] Naparstek cites a research study conducted by Charles Puthoff and Russell Targ which uses the Louisiana superdome stadium as an example of this. The stadium is "a huge, circular silvery building with metal sides and a white dome that gleams in the sun."[42] From this description, it would be easy to misinterpret it as a giant spaceship.[43] A way to avoid this kind of "secondary elaboration" would be to report the image as it appears rather than to label it as a spaceship or stadium.[44]

Naparstek reiterates another important point from Puthoff and Targ's study, explaining that they "broke new ground" when they described how the subjects of their study were best able to use their intuition:

---

[40] Naparstek, *Sixth Sense*, 82.

[41] Naparstek, *Sixth Sense*, 83.

[42] Naparstek, *Sixth Sense*, 83.

[43] Naparstek, *Sixth Sense*, 83.

[44] Naparstek, *Sixth Sense*, 83.

First, they underlined the importance of paying attention to easily ignored, subtle fragments of impressions, regardless of how vague and momentary they were. In addition, they found that scores improved when subjects gave more weight to certain impressions: to their first impressions; to their more spontaneous and surprising impressions; to impressions that were multisensory as opposed to merely visual; and to impressions that carried an emotional component.[45]

I can't overemphasize the importance of what Naparstek explains here. Paying attention to first impressions heightens our ability to receive intuitive information—especially the spontaneous, multisensory, surprising ones that are accompanied by emotion.

Holding an object can often distract our overactive minds, distancing us just enough to allow those first impressions to surge. Usually, our aim in the psychometry group is to sense the energy imprint of the object (rather than trace its history) in effort to provide supportive information for the person who brought it. When I hold an object for the purpose of giving a reading, sometimes an image, feeling, sound, or phrase surfaces that I can write down immediately. If the flow stops, I clear my mind again and wait for more. Throughout, I make the conscious choice to trust that the information a recipient needs most will come through.

Taking all this into account, let's sum up this information into those ten steps I mentioned:

1. Create a sacred space and relax through meditation, contemplative prayer, or gentle breathing.
2. Check in with your senses to provide a baseline. In other words, before you begin, know what it feels like to be yourself so that it's clear to you when you encounter a "new sensation" that might be part of the reading.
3. Open your heart and cultivate a sense of compassion (meditation helps with this).
4. Trust the Divine (or the Universe or yourself) knowing that you are safe.

---

[45] Naparstek, *Sixth Sense*, 83.

5. Set your best intentions, embody them—feel them manifesting around you even if it's just for a moment. By doing this, you are inviting the most positive emotions you can imagine while you also connect to the loving, nonjudgmental energy of the group.

6. Specify your target. Intuitive information is vast, so getting to specifics can help a lot. Try asking, "What does this person need to know or hear now? What can I say now that will help this person?"

7. Be willing to be wrong. It's ok if you're afraid that you are making it up—remember, when you are in what Naparstek calls that "state of expanded subjective time" first impressions from your intuition work faster than your imagination.

8. Wait for information. Observe. The flow of it may come to you in lots of different ways, through one, a few, or all of your senses. Note any emotions that pop up. Intuition doesn't feel the same all the time. Sometimes it feels insistent or like a loud boom; other times, it's light and breezy like a whisper or a wild guess that twinkles underneath your conscious mind.

9. Seek to report rather than interpret or label. Write everything down quickly without worrying about spelling—be as specific as you can be in terms of colors, sounds, feelings, and images.

10. Finally, after you feel the flow has stopped and the message has finished, take a peek at what you wrote (if this is on paper). It's okay for your linear mind to gear up again while you think about how you are framing the message. Instead of lapsing into secondary elaboration, check on whether the information is positive or helpful. If not, think about how you will verbalize the message in a way that will be objective and truthful yet also compassionate . . . and then trust that all is well.

My First Experience Giving Readings

To be honest, my first efforts in giving a reading were awkward. I tended to reach outside of myself for a message, which felt as if I were an explorer all alone in a vast vacuum of empty space. I kept searching, looking even deeper for information, but had no idea what I was trying to find. Another analogy for this problem of looking outside myself is that instead of being the bait on a fishing pole, I swam among the fish. Although I've improved quite a bit, sometimes a reading can still be a bit hard for me to do. When that happens, the result contains random words and thoughts that are difficult for me to string together.

It's natural for anyone to experience a disjointed reading once in a while, and a few of the women in the group have talked about some of the reasons why that might be. One night, several of us had difficulty getting our usual informative "vibes" while holding our chosen objects, so we discussed it among ourselves and discovered that, coincidentally, several of us had chosen something that we had not worn for very long. In each case, it was either a ring that had been forgotten in a drawer or a necklace that someone only wore occasionally—so the imprint from those objects happened to be weak.

Comparing my own energy healing work to psychometry, when I have sessions with clients and hold my hands above parts of their body, I can more readily receive imprints of what might be happening in their energy systems and what might help them begin the healing process. I am not sure why this is. Perhaps it's compassion combined with adrenaline—having a client in front of me who needs something immediate, or it could be as simple as the energy being stronger because it's more direct—flowing unimpeded by an object acting as an intermediary.

I also discovered that when I meditate, pray silently, or send healing to someone, I can sometimes receive messages. Through practice, I found that for me, tethering outward for information isn't the best way to proceed with the process of giving a reading. What's best for me is to focus on feeling compassion and then waiting to receive whatever impressions come my way.

Also, it's not unusual for me to just "know" something—I won't understand how I know it, but I do . . . and when others don't agree with me or understand, I can become insistent and uncharacteristically forceful—especially when it feels really important. The term for this is claircognizance. (Some might say, instead, that it's bullheadedness or the fact that I'm an only child. Maybe so, as I'm not always aware of how strong this inner forcefulness is until afterward when I take time to stop, close my eyes, and check in with myself).

Above all, my intention for any reading is for my words to be helpful, but it takes courage to let go and trust the process. Some examples of how I do that are in the next three sections.

The Importance of Filling up Your "Positive Energy Tank"

For almost two decades now, when I give psychometry readings, I follow the standard advice I give to others: I sit with the object, ask a target question, and wait to receive information.

To minimize doubts and overthinking, I follow Laura Day's advice as much as I can. First, I center myself, then I think of my "New Reality," part of the manifestation formula Day mentions in her book, *The Circle*. It just takes a few seconds of imagining me becoming my best self in that moment. It's not the same as getting into my ego. Instead, it's more like feeling the bliss of everything flowing well for myself and others—like filling up my "energy tank" with positive feelings. Sometimes I imagine an epic moment on a mountaintop, breathing fresh air, feeling free, and soaking up the best possible vibes sent my way from the Universe.

If I don't do that first, I fall into that awkward searchlight mode, seeking whatever random information pops into my head that I can put on the page. It's not that the reading will be "wrong," only that it might have more of my mental meanderings in it. As a result, the words might lack context, timing, or clarity. When this happens, I recognize it as a need to rebalance and plug myself back into Source. Doing a reading by that seek-and-find method feels like putting my hand in a glove that's too big. Symbolically-speaking, when my fingers or my "energy" doesn't fill what I identify as "me," I won't be able to be myself in my day-to-day world. My hand (and, thus my "reading") will feel clunky and awkward.

In other words, when we fill ourselves with our own, positive energy and presence, it completely fits and fills our inner spirit or, metaphorically speaking, each fingertip of our "glove" with no extra space to absorb anything belonging to anyone else. This way, nothing from anyone or anything can attach to us and drain our energy. Essentially, the goal is to fill *your* "aura," *your* "energy glove," with the most positive vibes you can muster. The purpose is to embody our best selves so that we can be of service and live more fully in alignment with the spirit within.

Let's look at this New Reality idea from a different angle. What if, out of the blue, without any context, something negative pops up in the midst of what you are receiving in a reading for someone, and you start to worry? Worry and over-analyzing depletes energy. In such cases, embodying a dream—feeling it as it manifests in our senses—will re-engage us and, as Day's teaching illustrates, re-situate us in an empowering place.

Focusing on a Target Question

After embodying my "New Reality," I focus on a question that Day calls a "target," something like, "What helpful information does this person need to know at this time?" It's stated positively, in present tense, and has a time frame. I could phrase the question more specifically if I wish and ask for suggestions regarding health, career, relationships, or self-empowerment. Generally, I only start asking for specifics if nothing seems to be happening right away or if what I'm receiving seems too vague. Although generic information can be helpful, I might receive a "feeling"— something like a sudden heaviness in my heart or stomach upon touching the object. In such cases, I switch to new questions and ask, "Where is this heaviness coming from, and what be helpful for this person to know about it in order to heal?"

If I wrote down "heaviness," left it alone, and moved on in my reading without asking follow-up questions, it would be okay, but would leave that part of the message unfinished, blurry, or under-developed. My belief is that I wouldn't receive a feeling or a word like that unless it has a purpose. That's why the target question is so important; it filters out what's unnecessary, leaving what is.

Sometimes I need to go back and forth between my mental mind and my intuitive mind, and that has required some practice. Within the scope of doing a reading, the onus is on me. Who knows whether I need to contextualize what I am receiving as an opportunity, a confirmation of something, or route the energy of whatever it is toward healing. I would never know unless I pay close attention, stay with the words and feeling within that moment, and, best of all—hope for the best—which goes back to relying on positive outcomes and knowing that Spirit or Source has our best interests in mind.

Letting Go

Whenever we give a reading, we must be willing to consider that we could be wrong, which helps in at least three ways:

1) Thinking we always need to be "right" stems from ego and is from our head rather than our heart.
2) The need to be right makes it much harder to remain detached. When we get in the way, the power of our reading for another person can suffer.
3) Remaining detached allows for the reading to unfold in its own way—according to divine guidance—rather than how we, in our limited ways of understanding such things, might want it to go.

The importance of detachment is the major reason we cover everyone's object with a scarf when we hold psychometry meetings. We would rather not know whose object we're choosing because when we give a reading to someone we know, it's extremely difficult to detach from our own internal thoughts and memories about that person. As a result, we can either lapse into giving advice (from our heads) or seem as if we are, even if we miraculously get past the familiarity barrier and share the genuine guidance we receive. So, essentially, we prefer "blind" readings because they allow us to let go of our assumptions and remain as detached as possible—making it so much easier to ask the necessary questions and trust what comes forward.

As I mentioned earlier, learning to distinguish between leaving something seemingly "negative" alone or staying with it and asking more questions comes with practice. Our intuition works faster than our imagination, so after asking the target question, trust that whatever is necessary for you to share will flow into your thoughts and then go from there. This allows you to write whatever comes and then let it go. We don't have to understand it or sugar-coat anything because when a person needs to hear the gritty whole truth, prettying it up can dilute the message and make it appear less important.

In the next chapter, I will illustrate what I've tried to explain here because it happened to me one evening when I hosted the group.

CHAPTER 8

Nydia's Envelope

After I finished leading the meditation for the group, people stretched, opened their eyes, shifted their bodies, and wiggled their toes. I passed the bowl to my right, so that each one of us could choose another person's object for the reading. Before now, no one had ever placed an envelope in the psychometry bowl, but a small, sealed, white one lay hidden below the rest of the objects. As the host and the last one to pick an object from the bowl, it was mine to read by default.

As I reached for it, my mind immediately pictured the minster of a metaphysical church I attended in Tampa. A few times a year, Reverend D.J. would ask the congregation to write their question, sign their name on a piece of paper, and then slip it into a sealed envelope. These sparsely attended services occurred in the evening, and in the soft candlelight, church volunteers collected the envelopes in offering plates. With plates in hand, the volunteers stood silently while Reverend D.J. said a prayer, then sat down in reverence while she started her billet readings from the pulpit. With her predictable dramatic flair and knowing smile—taking advantage of the spotlight—she would hold the envelope over her third eye and announce whatever she received from Spirit: "Spirit says, Dear Heart, that a trip is coming for you, overseas, with family . . . a happy trip. Don't worry, the money for it is in God's hands and an opportunity will present itself so that you will know when the time is right."

It would be typical for her look directly into the pews and add a P.S. with a wink, "No need to keep buying lottery tickets to afford this." After laughter subsided, she would then read the name—if the person wished it—and then begin a new reading with the next envelope. The messages weren't always upbeat, of course, which depended on what kind of question a person asked or what emotions were involved. For example, she might say, "Dear One, take heart, for although Spirit understands your disappointment in hearing this, know that it's best to wait for this next step. Trust and know that everything is in God's hands and that you have something better coming after this is over."

With Reverend D.J.'s offering plate readings as my only context, I picked up the envelope, held it in both hands, and stared. It was blank and so lightweight that it didn't feel as if anything was inside. Before my mind could step in and remind me that I've never "read" an envelope before, I could feel my heart and stomach sinking like a heavy weight. I didn't want to share this kind of feeling with the group because I could only feel deep sadness. What I received from this envelope was unlike anything I felt in giving a reading before. The depth of pain emanating from it transcended my capacity to convey in words. I admit to being shocked and a bit stuck, but I tried not to doubt what I received. I stayed with it. I waited for the heaviness to change into a lighter feeling, words I could hear, or an image I could see. I waited, and I waited. And when nothing else presented itself after a couple minutes . . . with no words, no other feelings, I panicked inside.

At that point I prayed in desperation, silent tears welling up under my eyelids, "Oh please Divine Source, help me write something useful for this person. Push aside my fears. Reveal to me what is here for me to share so that I can be a clear messenger of truth and light."

I opened my eyes, put my pen on the blank paper, and, once again, waited in a long stretch of silence for the message to surface. This time, the sadness began to fade, and I saw a seed germinating in the Earth, sprouting upward to the light. The feeling behind it was clear: after a period of heaviness, sadness, and waiting for those feelings to fade, there would be light and hope. A seed that was planted would grow, and new life would begin.

I felt my body returning to normal, especially as the heaviness left my chest. I sighed deeply, knowing that the envelope had conveyed its message. As I looked down at the piece of paper in front of me and re-read it, I wondered if I needed to add anything else. It was, after all, only a few sentences, and what came out seemed confusing. How could an image of a little sprouting plant hold any coherent meaning for the woman who brought the envelope, especially when it was so hard to shake that initial gut-wrenching feeling? Regardless, I felt relieved and grateful for the answer to prayer. I just had to let go and trust that the reading would be helpful and . . . maybe . . . since the heaviness lifted as part of the message, it might, despite its short, illogical appearance, even be healing for her to hear.

The room remained quiet and almost everyone had finished writing down their particular messages. A few women still had their eyes closed; others surveyed the room, re-situated themselves on the sofa, or re-read the paper in their hands. Typically, some tend to wait until their paper fills with words before they open their closed hand and peek at the small object prompting the message. It's also not unusual for the readers to add snippets of information at the end in an effort to convey as much helpful information as possible.

After the last pencil stopped, the sharing began, one at a time. Normally, as each woman shares her reading and the person who brought the object shares her reaction, I'm riveted to every word. This time, all I remember about the sharing session is that my heart pounded in my ears. When it was time for me to share, the lively conversation between the last exchange had grown quiet and everyone looked at me. I'm sure that the other readings were just as important, but the envelope seemed to be on everyone's mind from the beginning.

I held it up and looked around. My eyes met the reading's recipient halfway around the room. Nydia was new to the group, invited by her friend, Maritza. My next thought was, "Oh no! She's new to the group, so I hope this reading doesn't make what we do sound crazy."

Still holding the envelope with one hand shaking a bit, I explained the context of what I hoped would be a helpful message: "As I picked up the envelope, I felt heaviness and sadness. I waited for more information, but the waiting seemed to be part of the message. After a while, the heavy feeling began to fade and, in its place, I saw an image of a seed sprouting and growing. So, overall, I sense that from this heaviness and sadness, new life will begin."

Nydia and Maritza glanced at each other with a knowing look, whispering in each other's ear. I saw Nydia's face turning pink and her eyes welling up with tears. She turned to me and said, "Open it."

"Are you sure?"

She nodded yes.

When I opened the seal, I saw a black and white picture and slowly pulled it out. A tiny baby lay curled up as if it was sleeping. Something about the baby seemed different, and I looked at Nydia, who had tears running down her face.

"It's a picture of my stillborn son."

All of us felt a crystallized sense of time in that moment, a sense of the world stopping in unified grief.

I think I put the picture on my lap at that point because along with everyone else in the group, I started to cry. Maritza hugged Nydia tightly while she sobbed.

Nydia told us about her grief and that she could relate to the heaviness of it. "I hold on to the hope that, someday, I will be able to have another child. This reading helps me believe that."

When all of the readings were finished, Nydia embraced all of us, some in a group hug of three or four at a time. Before we started the after-group snacking, women sniffled and pulled tissues from every Kleenex box in the house.

That night, everyone left with an even greater awareness of how supportive and extraordinary our little psychometry group could truly be. Sometimes readings take us by surprise, and in my case, that reading felt like a miracle.

Nydia didn't come back to the group for a long time, but I happened to see her at a restaurant a year or two later. She waved and asked if she could come over to where we were sitting and pulled up a chair.

We greeted each other and as she hugged me, she said, "I am so happy. My husband and I never gave up trying to have a baby. Look!" Immediately, she reached into her purse and showed me a picture of her six-month old son, his eyes and smile gleaming as bright as could be. "I just wanted you to know. Thank you for helping me have hope again."

"Nydia, all I did was pray for the answer to help you. I admit that I was afraid to share what came up, but I'm so glad I paid attention to what the Universe showed me. I hope you can join us again. It would give the others such joy to hear about your new baby."

Reflecting once again on a few of Reverend D.J.'s "not-so-upbeat" envelope readings, what can seem like a "negative" message may not truly be negative at all. Editing-out parts of what we don't think a listener would want to hear blocks our own as well as another's path to wisdom. We are all human, after all, and we go through many ups and downs. The important thing is to keep growing into our better selves (minus our fears and controlling tendencies) and keep learning better ways of helping others do the same.

Also, as we remember Denton's idea of the universe being contained within a pebble, it's important to consider that I did not end my reading after sensing the deep level of grief associated with Nydia's envelope. If I were just reading the object itself and writing a description (like the lava rock from Hawaii), the message would not have been helpful. In fact, it would only show what I could do as a reader—as if it came from my ego rather than what Divinity could do through me. The Universe contained within that photograph had much more to share through psychometry than just a description of who, what, when, and where. Although we can all learn how to use our intuition and how to read an object, opening our hearts and bridging that intuitive space with compassion is what truly changes our lives, and others' lives, for the better.

CHAPTER 9

Objects as Energy Conduits

Advice for giving psychometry readings would not be complete without discussing what we use as a conduit—our objects. Choosing one may not seem to be important by comparison, especially since what we need to know will surface regardless, but the energy of the object can matter more than we might expect.

The objects everyone brings to the meetings do not always translate the precise message a person seems to want or from the spirit of someone who previously owned it. For example, a wedding ring may not always signal a message about a person's spouse, or a father's military medal may not convey a message from him or about anything related to his lifetime. We may have some influence regarding the focus of the messages we receive, but, generally, the Universe delivers what messages we need to hear.

Any intense emotion can create a strong imprint on an object. If the object is an antique or has had multiple ownership, its energy, and any messages associated with it, become more difficult to discern. It's also difficult to read an object that has very little energy imprinted in it. For example, a stone carried in someone's pocket for a several days will have a stronger imprint than one picked up in a store, left in a drawer for months, and then placed in the psychometry bowl for a reading. Objects with some metal attached, such as a pendant or ring, are also easier to read because metal is more conductive than plastic, ceramic, or most crystals.

In one of our meetings, a reading focused on an object that Claudia found. She said she wasn't necessarily fond of the object and felt funny when she wore it. Since the object didn't carry any significance to her, it's important for us to consider her experience with it as a lesson about connection and what people choose to bring to the psychometry group. If a person shares no bond with an object, then the vibration from it may not be appropriate for a reading. An object could, in fact, open up the person and/or the group to a message that is not in anyone's best interests. In this case, when Suman picked Claudia's "found object" out of the bowl, she felt an odd antagonism coming from it. As she lifted her reading to share, she stopped to make a comment: "The object is talking. It's saying, 'I am a powerful energy.' It needs to be cleansed, though, because it claims to be sweet and it's not. Perhaps it's time for you to release it. Actually, this may be among a family of objects that may need to be released together."

If the purpose of our psychometry group focused on developing the kind of clairvoyance that could determine where an object is from, what circumstances surrounded it, or who previously owned it, then the whole structure of the evening could change into cerebral puzzle-solving exercises and, possibly, one-upping attempts to improve our psychic accuracy. However, that is not what happens and would make the group much less appealing for everyone. Our circle thrives because the meditations, conversations, and readings focus on supporting each other. Our hearts are involved because the way we use our intuition relies on compassion.

When each of us chooses an object to bring to the meeting, that object is something that has meaning; it resonates with us or speaks to us in some way—either our own object, or a friend's or relative's. Overall, if we are in a positive mindset and attracted to a particular object energetically, then what we bring will most likely align with the energy of the rest of the group and, as a result, will help whoever chooses it to communicate something helpful.

CHAPTER 10

Framing the Message

Providing a helpful message can sometimes be a challenge to write down on paper. It's difficult to decide whether it's helpful, for example, to be direct and say, "I saw a spider spinning a web in a corner," or "I saw a spider spinning a web in a corner and sense this is symbolic. Perhaps reflect on this or research what this symbol might suggest for you." Of course, when reading it aloud, the added information could be verbal rather than written down, but how the message is framed makes a big difference in how it's received.

One of the women in the group told me that she wished she could improve how she expressed her messages: "I wish I could express or write in a better way, but sometimes I think that I don't know how to say a message without being blunt. It makes me feel bad thinking I would hurt somebody's feelings." In response, all I could say is that communicating the message in a way that is positive and affirming can be challenging, but it becomes easier through practice and intention. At times, we all need a direct, no-buts-about-it message, but that's different from making a negative judgment. As we all grow, we begin to feel the differences in how we frame messages, and the more we practice psychometry, the more we train our thoughts to distinguish between the two without having to think much about it.

I asked Charlotte, who has been practicing psychometry for over thirty years, whether she filters information in favor of positive outcomes in her readings. She said, "When I started psychometry, we always talked about that as one of the first things we tell a group before they start the readings, saying that we wouldn't have negative messages. And I think it just became part of what I asked for. Because of this intention, I never really received any negative information. And that's just how it has flowed."

Being positive carries its own benefits. In his book, *The Energy Bus*, Jon Gordon maintains that "positive people live longer, happier and healthier lives."[46] Being positive in a moment of bliss is easy, but consistently learning to become more positive takes months if not years of practice. Because none of us is perfect, we can get depressed or frustrated or even angry at times. After reading Wayne Dyer's books and hearing him say many times in his audio presentations, "What you focus on expands," I have learned to become more self-aware when something bothers me. It might take me a while, but sometimes I can intentionally shift my thinking to a broader way of understanding and then my feelings begin to shift, too.

Focusing on something, whether it's positive or negative, according to the Abraham teachings of Esther and Jerry Hicks, is like sending a signal to the Universe that attracts more of the same. They call this your "point of attraction."[47] With practice, they explain, a challenge that previously might have kept us in a negative spiral suddenly "looks like an opportunity; like something that's interesting; like something that you'd like to think about."[48] Gordon, Dyer, and Hicks are not the only ones emphasizing the benefits of positive thinking. Norman Vincent Peale, Dale Carnegie, Stephen Covey, Rhonda Byrne, Napoleon Hill, Eckart Tolle, Bill Teague, Mike Dooley, and many others teach this principle.

Perhaps all of this underlies why we believe that each reading will in some way be helpful to the person who receives it. From the very beginning, we've set that intention as a group.

Even when something within a reading might express sadness, there's usually a silver lining that people can focus on without being fake. Discussing whatever shows up stirs a sense of compassion in the group. For example, one night Allie had brought a friend and Maritza gave a reading for one of them that mentioned "the angel of death." It was unusual, yes, and surprising for sure. But it didn't put off anyone in the group in

---

[46] Jon Gordon, *The Energy Bus* (Hoboken, NJ: John Wiley and Sons, 2007), xvi.

[47] Wayne Dyer and Esther Hicks, *Co-Creating at Its Best: A Conversation Between Master Teachers,* (Carlsbad, CA: Hay House, 2014), 40-45.

[48] Dyer and Hicks, *Co-Creating*, 45.

a negative way. The recipient could see that what Maritza said was quite powerful and needed to be heard. Afterward, in the feedback from the reading, some people cried because the message provided support even after the heartbreaking loss of a loved one.

So, overall, when people in the group give readings, they tend to focus on using the object as a bridge to giving a personal message to someone instead of tuning into the object's history and recounting various events—some of which could be quite sad. Although how we view the past is subjective, too, the energy that carries through from it can often be harsh and unforgiving, so asking for helpful or positive information—and expecting it—is the most important component in how to frame a message.

CHAPTER 11

How Others in the Group Give Readings

Most of the participants vary in the ways that they receive messages. Some seem to connect with past lives during a reading; others receive intuitive information in terms of what they hear, see, or feel (or all the above). And even for the same person, messages don't always surface in the same way. We might hear words or a particular sound, taste or smell something, feel a tightness in our chests, or have a queasy feeling in our stomachs. All of this varies and can translate onto the page as pieces of intuitive information. Each reader can take it further and ask questions, wait for answers, then write down whatever impressions follow, being careful to avoid overthinking.

Of course, as I've mentioned before, no one who gives a reading is always right. On the other hand, it could also be true that a reading may seem off when it isn't. Perhaps the message is correct, but we don't recognize that yet. The past/present/future part of it could potentially be off (timing is difficult to pinpoint in a reading, anyway) because we all make at least a thousand conscious choices per day, and nothing is pre-determined. But given how we've learned to function in our society today, it's natural for anyone to become over-analytical and second-guess his or her intuition. Overall, it's best to temporarily minimize the worry of whether what we're writing down will be valuable to the person who brought the object. Then, as we step aside, we learn to keep an open mind, stay positive, and trust.

Let's Try an Experiment

Picture for a moment that you are present, right now, in the group. Although I know this requires repositioning your readerly point of view, try to imagine yourself as being Eileen, one of the women in the circle. Although what appeared in Eileen's mind during her reading will likely have been entirely different, I hope you will follow along with me as if you are experiencing this on your own.

When you reach into the collective "psychometry bowl," you happen to pull out a tiny ceramic object, a sculpted llama. At this point, what might you be thinking? Try to picture yourself holding the little llama. Your eyes are closed, and in the quietness, you push out all doubt from your mind, like clearing a slate. You wait a little longer, imagining that you *can* do this, making the way clear in your mind so that you will be aware when your senses alert you to a message that you can write down.

In the stillness behind your thoughts, you see indigo light that feels all-encompassing, as if it's wrapped around someone. You sense that it's surrounding the person who brought the object. You sense that this indigo light represents this person's third eye, and as you wait for more, you also feel it straining, as if this person's sixth sense has been working very hard. For several moments—what feels like a long time—you are left with only that image.

In the quiet, you ask yourself, "What does this person need to know now?" And as you wait, you hear, "Others depend on your light, your inner guidance, and upon you. Don't sit in its shadow."

Following the directions you heard about giving readings, you write this down on the blank sheet of paper in your lap. While staying open, you continue to wait for other messages, so you write down other impressions, including what you feel or see, whether they seem related or not. You hear, "Sometimes you've got to cry to get through." You see everything become clear and then write, "Tears can bring clarity." Next, you feel a breeze blowing through this person's hair. You write that down and also the word, "Enjoy."

The thought comes over you that this person needs to access another life. You write this down, too. You feel as if they receive whispers from the other side.

A doubt begins to swim in your head. "Did I get it right?" "What if this makes no sense and is too sad?" But you write it down anyway and keep writing whatever comes up. The last thing that comes to you is, "You are in the flow. As one cycle closes, another begins."

As you attempt to suppress your fears, the readings around the circle begin. The first person starts. You listen to their words and watch the reactions around the group. Your intention now focuses on others' readings, often enraptured by them, pulled away from your own doubts about what you wrote. For a moment, your attention snaps back and forth, comparing your reading with what you're hearing around the circle. Your left brain second-guesses what you wrote, "Maybe I need to add more detail or rephrase it a different way? What if the recipient doesn't believe in past lives?"

Perfection Is Not the Goal

Stepping back now from this scene, perhaps you have a clearer understanding that second-guessing is normal. It's actually a side-effect of wanting to do our best, so it comes from a good place. However, it's possible to worry too much; when that happens, the fear of disappointing someone can interfere with the wholly beautiful, powerful, and comforting experience of the circle itself. When the analytical wheels start turning, they can disrupt the natural flow of intuition. The key is to remember that the group's focus is not on ourselves, but each other.

The reading I just described was written by Eileen for Helen, but the text of the reading itself is from Eileen. I inserted some fictional imaginings in order to illustrate some of the typical thoughts that pop up during this phase of giving a reading.

Although each person is free to just say "thank you" without providing feedback, Helen wanted to confirm what Eileen had written:

> I haven't been meditating, but I know that it would help.
> I've been going though a tough time and, yes, I have been
> crying. I know that others rely on me, too, and I've been
> journaling to sort all of this out. The other day I wrote
> about a breeze that I felt from another life.

Amazing exchanges like this happen all the time. As a reader, we may sense something is coming through and part of us doubts whether it's correct, but it's important to express it, regardless. We never know what part of a reading might resonate the most with someone. Learning to trust comes with practice, and the more we practice, the more comfortable we become with whatever we just seem to "know."

In *The Book of Love and Creation*, Paul Selig says, "This is simply about knowing, and being in your knowing means accessing information, and how you hear your knowing, how you understand it, is a God-given ability."[49] Selig goes further to explain how we can set our intentions to receive the best possible information[50]: "Now we want to make a distinction between high hearing and low hearing, and this is actually important," he says. "When one begins to develop his senses as a clairaudient," Selig writes, "one is able to access information at different levels of consciousness."[51] As this happens, it's "imperative," he says, to stand in "protection as a Divine Being and only access that information which is of the highest source available . . . for the highest good of all around me."[52]

In such cases, we tend to assume that each person is doing their best to grow in their own way as all of us try to make the world a better place. As Brené Brown mentions in at least one of her podcasts, it feels like a better world when we imagine each person striving to do their best. That's also the frame of mind we apply as we allow ourselves to receive information for each reading. Filling our energy tank with positive feelings can function like a radio dial tuning in that "high hearing" Selig mentions.

Some Examples of Different Experiences

Let's listen to a few of the women in the group describe their process in their own words.

---

[49] Paul Selig, *The Book of Love and Creation: A Channeled Text* (New York: Jeremy P. Tarcher, 2012), 59.

[50] I want to make a distinction here based on something Suman told us in the group: "Rather than stating an intention, it's more powerful to become it," which makes a powerful difference.

[51] Selig, *Love and Creation*, 59.

[52] Selig, *Love and Creation*, 59-60.

Amy

Each of us chooses an object and "taps in" to its energy, writing or drawing whatever comes to mind.

As I hold my chosen object, I do my best to delineate between what my mind chatters and what "comes through" or is "shown to me." It's not always easy for me; I desire very much for my reading to be a gift to the receiver.

I continue to recall my friend's coaching words: "Don't judge what comes through, just write it down – it may mean something to the other person."

Charlotte

Charlotte has been participating in the Tampa psychometry group since 1976 and relates how the intuitive process begins prior to choosing the object from the bowl:

Once we've done a meditation, I'm already in that place where I feel connected to the flow of Spirit, so broadening that connection to the object seems easier. I try to not only just sense it . . . It seems like I almost go into the object. And I just ask for any messages, and then it goes from there. I just write, and not only do I hear, but I see, I feel. And over the years, I think it's shifted a little bit. It flows a little better than it used to. I used to get short messages, but now I get longer ones, a little bit more information into each message the guides want me to give.

If I were to give others advice, I would say that with enough practice you can understand the messages that you are receiving; you learn to trust yourself that you're hearing them, and your life follows from there.

Dee

When I participate in psychometry with the group, I hold the item, breathe diaphragmatically, and think about my expansiveness as a divine human, acknowledging that I am listening . . . then, I do. I write down what comes up through me.

Eileen

Eileen says she stills her mind as best she can and then asks, "What does this person need to know?" and/or "What does this person need to hear?" Then, she says, "I just write whatever comes into my head and try not to think too much about what I'm writing."

As she continues, she emphasizes a few other points:

We all had to learn to trust the process. From the first visit onward, anyone can feel the loving energy within the circle, but it takes a little practice to be able to let go, trust, feel confident that the underlying template of non-judgment within the group is unconditional, consistent, and compassionate.

The unifying bond we all share is that we truly want to offer clear messages that help each other, whether or not they are from a spirit guide, the Universe, God, an angel, a tree or crystal, or the object itself—which, by the way, is rarely just "the object itself" because when we set our intentions, God-energy, Christ consciousness, or Spirit conspires through whatever means necessary in order to provide us with a helpful message.

Elizabeth

When I first started attending the monthly psychometry and meditation sessions with Kim, I wasn't so sure how to do any of it. Psychometry was totally foreign to me. I had never experienced it before or even heard of the word. After three sessions or so, I began to really understand what was happening.

Psychometry is nothing to fear; it is the Universe speaking loud and clear. It is a gift that we can give each other. It is easier than you think, and we all can use as much insight and support as possible. Sometimes when I usually sit and hold it in my hand, I don't look at it. And when I receive, sometimes it's visions . . . sometimes it's a voice . . . sometimes it's a thought. And then as I'm going through the process, I keep clearing my mind. I close my eyes, feel the energy, ask the question, "What does this person need to know?" and write.

How simple is this? You hold an object, you let go of yourself, you try to imagine the person whose object you're holding, you grab a pen, and you let it flow knowing that everything on that paper, for that person, is the correct thing for them right now. It is such a comfort to know there are no judgments and no right or wrong readings. How beautiful is that? If I can do this, anybody can; it is as easy as it sounds. Am I preaching to the choir?

Laura

My method starts with connecting to the object and the energy attached to it. I need to breathe first, consciously inhale/exhale, and walk myself out of the monkey mind. In doing so, I can discern what could be my emotional state of mind, whether I'm sitting with fear or worry and could project that in the reading. Once I let go of the "I," images, words, and messages come to me. Not judging the experience is the key for me.

I normally don't write much when I give a reading. Most of my readings leave me with a full heart, and we know a reading isn't just for the person to whom we are giving the reading for.

Pat

Pat uses the word "automatic" in her description of how most of her readings seem to just "happen." Pat has given many readings throughout her lifetime, but rather than putting herself on a pedestal and telling everyone in the group what to do, each month she sits back and appreciates all of the messages each person receives. She sees us all as peers (even people who are first-timers) because of the energy we've all created within the group.

When I asked her to explain a bit more about what she does, this is what she said:

When I pick up the object, it seems that God, my Spirit Guides—or whatever—start talking to me immediately. I pick up the person's vibrations, it seems like, almost effortlessly. I don't have to think about it. In fact, that's the last thing we want to do is think about it. You just hold it and wait to receive Spirit's message. Once we start thinking about it, it's not really good because that influences the message.

A message just tends to happen whether I'm sitting in the group or not. We were in church one day, and I saw Kim and Rita. And I said to Rita, "Are you diversifying or buying new companies?" and she was shocked. She told me, "I've been thinking about it." That's an example of how it "just happens," and when it does, I always want to share it.

But what I did want to tell you that a long time ago someone told me that when people get psychic messages, it's as if they have suddenly become schizophrenic, and it's hard to explain that to somebody. When the messages come in, it's like someone talks to you or you have a knowing, but it's not a verbal conversation, and it's not a mental disease. The thoughts just come—we're not asking for them—although sometimes we are asking for the information, for example, when someone else wants to know the answer to a question. It is very clear, usually.

Rita

My process, number one, is thinking of how a reading can help the other person. Whenever Kim explains that, I always go to that reference point of, "How can this reading help the other person?" So that's very, very much the case. The preparation of the meditation and the healing circle beforehand set the canvas, set the right atmosphere. The fellowship and friendship of our group is very important, and the loving nature of everyone comes with the intent to help each other.

So I sit with the object in my hand. I close my eyes, and I trust and let go. It's an emptying . . . a sense of breathing in, letting go, and letting my intuition work. You can pause to ask yourself, "What do I feel?" "What am I sensing?" Sometimes I can start getting a sense even before I have the object. Sometimes even before the group comes. Sometimes I can get a sense of an energy or images, which I find very interesting.

But once I hold the object, I usually put both my hands together, and I just let that message come over me, really, and it happens pretty quickly. Usually for me, nearly immediately I get a message, and I start writing it down for what it is, and it's very strong. And I certainly get very clear. Sometimes I can get sounds, images, like of mountains or rivers, and words flow. And as I reflect on how this happens, it's a combination of pictures, feelings, words, and sound . . . sometimes I hear singing. So it's a powerful experience, and it feels good to be helping someone else.

What Do These Approaches Have In Common?

Even though everyone has a different method, similar approaches unfold so that we can learn from each.

For example, Dee, Laura, and Rita use breath prior to giving a reading. Rita calls this "an emptying."

Perhaps this is similar to what Amy, Elizabeth, Laura, and Pat do in terms of letting go of what is in their mind. It's helpful, as these women explain, to connect with the loving energy of the group—to release judgement and think of the reading they are giving another as a "gift."

Most of all, though, the common thread for each is connectedness to a larger awareness than their physical senses typically provide. Dee describes it as thinking about her "expansiveness as a divine human," and Charlotte says it's being "connected to the flow of Spirit." Eileen calls it "God-energy" or "Christ consciousness," and Pat refers to this energy as "God" or "Spirit guides."

All of this came about through practice. In the next chapter, we will explore what some of their initial experiences were like.

CHAPTER 12

What It's Like to Experience Psychometry for the First Time

Our group's regular attendees were first-timers at one point. They stayed in the group despite their lack of familiarity with giving readings. In fact, several had to talk to themselves, release their fears, and trust. I hope it will help other newcomers to hear these women explain, in their own words, what their first meeting was like.

Elizabeth

At Kim's invitation I attended one of her first meetings that offered meditation and psychometry. At that time, we met in the clubhouse of her apartment complex, which was a very nice and comfortable setting. Kim made it very clear that the space created for this was very sacred and safe, and we trusted it to be so. I could tell that night that there were ladies that had previously done something similar, yet there were a few there like me who had never participated in anything like this before.

It was a great psychometry meditation. I think about the details of it now which are a blur, but I do remember feeling that it was very special. I was looking forward to going back again the following month. When I walked out of there, I felt light and terrific. The meditation and psychometry reading really gave me an adjustment, and I wanted more. I remember hoping that Eileen would find this as valuable as I felt it might be.

Cathleen

January 2012, I was invited to the first psychometry group held by Kim through a mutual friend who thought this type of group was in alignment with other material I had been studying. I wasn't familiar with psychometry, nor did I have any idea what it entailed, but it sounded intriguing and "woo woo" enough for me to say, "Yes, I will check it out."

When I arrived, it was a small gathering with unfamiliar faces. Still, the energy in the room felt comfortable. After introductions, Kim provided a description of psychometry and kindly directed everyone to place a small personal object into a covered bowl.

Even though I had been integrating metaphysical teachings into my life for a few years, my initial reaction was that of self-doubt. I had never practiced "reading" people's energy or the energy of any material object for that matter. I remember thinking to myself, "Oh no, how am I going to pull this off and avoid a heap of embarrassment?" I was sure my friend who invited me had described many delightfully peculiar and mystical things about me, and so, I began to surrender to the fact that my outlandish reputation was about to be nullified in a moment's time!

Following a meditation exercise, each person quietly chose an object as we passed around this mysterious covered bowl. As I picked one and held this stranger's object, I set my intentions of letting go of all judgments and resistance and simply allowed myself to be in observance and feel whatever energy I perceived coming from and/or through this object. Despite all the self-doubt and fear I was accustomed to creating within my own private world, I somehow began to intuitively know Spirit was gently guiding me through this process. I delivered my message with confidence and a knowing that it was truly Spirit conveying their message for that person. I felt the experience anchored a newfound awareness that has nurtured my spiritual growth for which I will always be grateful.

Amy

As I think back to the first time I attended psychometry, I recall experiencing a mix of emotions. I was invited to join the group by my friend and decided rather quickly that, schedule permitting, I would participate. Having a brief experience practicing psychometry in a workshop previously, reading the energy of objects was not completely foreign to me and I wanted to learn more.

As my first psychometry evening approached, I was excited—and a little nervous. My higher self knew Kim had assembled a safe and loving group, and that the meeting would be orchestrated divinely. On the other hand, attending an evening with a group of those unfamiliar to me drew out my tentative introverted nature. Add to this the vulnerability of giving (or receiving) an inaccurate (or accurate) reading, my shyness crossed into uneasiness. As the night progressed, however, the ease of the group calmed me; the opening affirmation acquainted me with the others, the meditation drew me into alignment with my higher power, and the generous offering of loving energy through a nonjudgmental presence provided great safety.

Angel

I was invited to the psychometry group by a friend who briefly described the process and said it was a fulfilling experience each time she participated. I happily went along, allowing excitement to win out over fear. Even though I felt excited and apprehensive at the same time, I looked forward to a new way of experiencing a connection to "Spirit" in a group setting. I also felt a little fear because I didn't know how or if I could "do it right." I decided to just let go, go with the flow, and see what would happen.

During the session I felt a wonderful shift in energy and a feeling of upliftment! I realized that yes, there was definitely something going on here. I don't remember the specifics of the reading I received although I do remember thinking, "Wow that struck me in a way I didn't expect." I heard simple words that sort of gently prodded me to take the next step on my journey. Afterwards I felt very refreshed. I knew this group had developed a special connection and a sacred space for sharing spiritual insights, and I was "hooked!"

Helen

I was very nervous coming to the group for the first time. I didn't really know what to expect. What I knew was that I felt comfortable and connected with Kim and Rita at the retreat we attended together. The email I received explaining the group and the process really helped me.

I could see that this was a place without judgment, a place where I could practice opening myself up without fear of criticism.

Lynda

I am sure, like many first-timers, I was nervous due to doubts in my ability to give a reading or to discern what was me simply applying meaning to something, not being able to stay out of my head or questioning what was meant for the receiver or what I was just "making up." I was intrigued by the premise of the gathering, so it was easy to say yes to the invitation, and my soon-to-be partner knew me well enough to know I would stand to gain a wonderful spiritual experience and connection with other like-minded people.[53]

Eileen

The first time I went to the psychometry group, I felt nervous and a little unsettled. The entire concept was unfamiliar to me, so I had no idea what to expect. At the same time, I was intrigued by what little I did know. The two main factors in my deciding to go that first time were that I knew several people who would be there and, most importantly, that I knew and trusted the moderator of the group. She is a woman of great integrity and intelligence balanced with a kind heart.

Alex

Alex was still a teenager in high school when she attended her first meeting. Even though she only attended once, she was willing to write about her experience:

My first time being asked to attend a psychometry group felt a little nerve-wracking because I didn't exactly know what to expect. Being that I was one of the youngest people there, I definitely had doubts before attending. I questioned if I would do the reading correctly, or if I would receive the message that I needed to move me forward on my spiritual journey. I wondered if the item I was bringing was even readable. I knew

---

[53] Lynda and Amy are now married, but at the time Lynda first attended the group, they had just started dating.

that I wasn't as spiritual or on the same wavelength as the other women who meditate practically every day. The only thing that kept me from turning down this opportunity was that there was hope of someday being on a higher vibration.

Once I arrived, I was assured I wasn't the only newcomer. There were two other women that were new to the group as well, which made me feel a little less worried. We were required to place the items we brought into a bowl with everyone else's items in it. The bowl was covered with a white cloth in order to not let anyone visualize the items of others—which, in my opinion, I thought was beautiful to know—your item would be read by the memories that are held inside. It's like getting to know someone before you see them . . . like falling in love with their heart and not their appearance.

When we started, we began with a meditation that took us deep into an open mind and higher vibration. Our hands were hovering over one another in a circle. I could feel the energy shift within the circle—combining our energy together is what it felt like. Shortly, after the bowl was passed around and everyone picked the item they felt first, each woman began to get quiet and read their object. Whatever they felt or saw, they wrote down on a piece of paper that eventually was read out loud in the group to the person who brought it. What was written on the paper is supposed to be a message for the other person to take with them.

I received an object from a woman named Lindsey. It was a bracelet that was given to her by her partner. I remember feeling a sense of joy and children, which she said meant something to her. When it was my turn to claim my object that was read, I received a message about the love and support I receive and give to others. I remember it being an emotional thing to hear because at the time, I felt as if I didn't give as much love to others nor was I feeling that I was receiving any. My experience, I can honestly say, was an eye opener to realize that there is enough love to go around and that I am also returning it to the world.

Maribel

Alex's stepsister, Maribel, who was a year or two younger, also attended the group and uses the same word, "nerve-wracking," to describe how she felt her first time:

The first time I went to psychometry, it was a bit nerve-wracking. But I was really open, or it wasn't that hard. I was scared mostly as to what I would be receiving in my reading.

As we began the process, it was very welcoming, and it was all explained. So that was comforting. When we picked our objects, I remembered mine feeling so hot and filled with the owner's energy. I let all the thoughts flow through me as I read this person's object, and it was the greatest experience ever. Once I was finished, I didn't think any of it made sense, but when I started reading it to the other person, it all matched up with her. The woman was deeply moved by my reading and said it helped her on her journey.

So many of my readings have been a huge part of my life, whether it was guiding me down the way I was unsure about or giving me insight into a problem, it's all so helpful. And very empowering. This is an experience anyone could have. It's comforting, loving insightful, and life-changing. I am humbled by it all.

CHAPTER 13

Tips for Newcomers

A regular meeting among the seasoned group members becomes a bit more nuanced, however, when a newcomer arrives. It's challenging to help a new person feel comfortable doing a reading for the first time—especially in front of several people they've never met. That's the first hurdle, and the second hurdle can come from fearing that they don't know how, won't do it right, or will write down something that sounds like nonsense.

One of my friends attended a meeting soon after I formed the group and recently told me that it would have eased her fear to know more details about what to expect and how to do a reading. For instance, she said it would have helped her to know that the purpose is to connect to her compassionate, intuitive senses and then ask, "What can I write that would help this person right now?" I was just starting the group and wasn't sure how to explain the process just yet, so she felt uncertain about the whole purpose—whether to write about the object itself, how it felt in her hand, whether to guess what it was, or look at the object and try to write a message from that.

I feel awful that I wasn't more in tune with what first-timers needed to know before attending and trying to "read" on the spot. Since it's been at least a decade down the road now, I am more experienced about how to introduce psychometry to someone who has never tried it before.

When we have newcomers, I try to help put them at ease by offering some general advice about giving a reading. I like to remind everyone that giving a reading is much easier than we might think. We just let go of worrying about it and allow ourselves to receive the information from our senses. Typically, I welcome first-timers with a speech something like this:

Try to put aside your nervousness because we are happy that you're here, and no one will be judging what you write. The purpose of the reading is learning how to connect to your own inner guidance while giving someone a message that will be helpful. The more you can focus on practicing that, while also helping someone else, the less you will feel the fear.

Also, when you connect with your heart and give your intuition a job to do, then the more it will respond with information. Try not to go into your analytical mind and reach for information, though. Just turn on your senses and wait for a message to come to you. Often, there's an energetic lightness to this rather than heaviness. It won't be long. In fact, your intuition works faster than your imagination, so write down the first things that pop in your head—whether it's a word, a song, an image, a feeling, or even a scent. It always ends up being what the other person needs to hear, even if it's just a few words.

Usually, some women in the group chime in here, either agreeing or adding their own explanation to what I just described. At this point, the atmosphere is so welcoming and nonjudgmental that it helps reduce any anxiety.

In her nearly 50 years of participating in weekly psychometry sessions, Charlotte has had a lot of experience with first-timers in the Tampa group. When I asked about how they ease these kinds of fears, she told me that they have thought a lot about how to put beginners at ease, so she has some ideas about what a new person needs to know:

In the first place, it's a little bit intimidating because people think they have to produce a "reading" for somebody else before we even get started. We try to explain—especially to a new person coming in—that it's really not that at all. I mean, we do a reading, but it's more about learning how to open up your senses and being able to read that object, even if it's just a couple of words or a whole page. It's not about giving a "psychic reading" to somebody. I think it's intimidating. It makes them nervous. My daughter came once, and it made her so nervous, she won't ever come back again. Because she just felt like she had to come up with something, and her mind just sort of froze up. I really think that's what happens to a lot of people. It makes them so nervous that they won't even attempt it.

New people need to know that it's not about them giving someone a reading but about the benefits they will derive from practicing, and in turn, that will grow to help the next person or next few people who receive the reading. It's not about being accurate or giving a super fabulous reading. It's more about sharing, learning, compassion, and love.

Yes, the performance anxiety a first-time reader can feel is real, which is why disarming any newcomers' fears before the meeting starts is so important. As Charlotte suggests, focusing on the benefits of practicing and connecting with their inner light is helpful; it keeps them from worrying so much about how others will view them or how the reading will be received. By its very nature, learning through self-development is more likely to displace the idea of anyone judging the outcome. It frees rather than freezes our intuition. Over time, as beginners attend the group, their judgments and fears eventually disippate. Concerns about what others think eventually subside. The true joy group psychometry is in feeling the aliveness of connecting to our inner voices, part of the infinite intelligence many of us call God.

CHAPTER 14

When You are the Recipient of a Reading

Remember, You Are The Expert On Your Own Life

At the most basic level, we also rely our own inner guidance when we are the recipient of a reading. If Nydia had interpreted my reading for her only as an indication that eventually she would heal from grief, that would have been her choice. What if she didn't want another child? She could have resigned herself to a much different interpretation than hoping that the new life I mentioned meant having another baby.

Likewise, in the example experiment I provided, Eileen used the phrase "another life" and described a breeze blowing through her hair; both could have represented something completely different to Helen.

Images in a reading can be literal, symbolic, or both. They can be prominent or subtle, and if the illustration or wording is vague, it's up to the recipient to interpret. Over the years, the readings I've been given range from specific to wide-ranging in their focus. I may not understand everything in them right away, but as I continue to review their words in the days and, possibly, weeks that follow, whatever I needed to know seems to surface at just the right time.

Remember, though, even if a renowned psychic warns you about something that might happen in your future, it doesn't mean it will. We all have freedom of choice, and perhaps a warning is just that—a precaution so that you can alter your course and find a better way.

It's Possible For a Reading To Be "Off"

Sometimes a reading misfires. Perhaps its timing is off. As I mentioned before, it could be that the reader senses something far off in the future or something remote in your past. Either way, even though it might not seem off target to the one giving the reading, it could feel quite off for you because it doesn't resonate.

I've done readings for people who have been so deeply touched—and surprised by how much they needed it—that they cry. I've also done readings for others and, the moment I give it, I sense that the other person felt like it wasn't helpful, no matter how much I went into my heart and tried to connect with what they needed. Recipients can also be so protective of their energy that it makes them hard to read. Maybe I'll claim that as an excuse in such cases, or, more likely, I'll just chalk it up as my own mistake. No one is perfect, and it's helpful to know that—because who wants that kind of pressure?

Listen With An Open Mind—Consider Looking At Things In A Different Way

You might come with the hope of hearing a message about selling your house, but instead, hear about a challenge between you and your sister that needs to be resolved. The Universe—and the reading you receive—has its own set of priorities. It's important to keep in mind that the reader's goal is to be helpful. Elizabeth explains this in terms of "little nuggets from Spirit." She says that the information often shows up a little differently depending on the circumstance—whether it's "brushing the dandruff off your shoulder or your suit, or telling you that your son would be happy working as an EMT."

So if a message doesn't resonate at first, look deeper. Perhaps nothing is going on in your life at the moment that needs the support of a reading. Or the opposite might occur—overanalyzing too much. Didn't Sigmund Freud say that "sometimes a cigar is just a cigar?"

It's also important to be ready to hear something you might need to know but from an angle you don't quite understand or didn't expect. A reader sees things through his or her own lens, so what you hear or read in a message can often come from a perspective that wouldn't normally occur to you.

We don't always consider the chain reaction a message might create, but if we trust that it's what we need to know, and accept that with grace, we might become a better person because of it. Isn't that the overall point—growing spiritually and finding better ways to help others and ourselves? Esther, one of the women in the group, shared how she appreciates what she learns from the others: "I listen with joy to each and every one and learn about so many different ways of love." That's really the key to developing the frame of mind for receiving a message—being grateful and seeing joy in all of the exchanges.

PART 4

The Benefits of Being in a Psychometry Group

"Perhaps it wasn't always the messages or the content of the information channeled. But it awakened an inner knowing to the people receiving them. Hopefully they realized we never walk alone."

— Pat, Psychometry Group Member

CHAPTER 15

Why Meet in a Group?

In his book, *How to Develop and Use Psychometry*, Andrews lists seven benefits that result from "developing clairsentience, and specifically psychometry." Overall, he says, it helps us become more aware of our feelings and reactions, improve our ability to concentrate and pay attention to details, and increase our capacity to be more open and creative.[54] In *Your Sixth Sense: Activating Your Psychic Potential*, Belleruth Naparstek emphasizes how using our intuition can open our hearts and even make us better people:

> Even if you're a pretty terrific person to start with, engaging in this process might make an even better human being of you, because it will ask you to open your heart in order to gain access to psi.[55] . . . . Very simply put, when the heart is opened to its own boundless, compassionate, loving energy, boundaries dissolve and intuitive information starts showing up.[56]

What Andrews refers to as becoming aware of feelings and also being more open and creative, Naparstek calls opening the heart. Sharing a similar point of view in *The Intuitive Way*, author and teacher Penney Peirce says that "Compassion produces the highest, most efficient level

---

[54] Andrews, *Psychometry*, 17.
[55] "Psi" refers to psychic ability, ESP, intuition, etc.
[56] Naparstek, *Sixth Sense*, 3-4.

of intuition."[57] Developing our natural intuition, however, is not merely an individual, isolated experience. Although we can open our hearts and feel compassion for ourselves, the intuitive experience does not typically occur in a vacuum and must, by necessity, involve our relationships with others—our families, friends, colleagues, and those we meet in our daily activities.

Practicing on Your Own Versus Working With Others

The exercises that appear in most books designed to teach intuitive or psychic development speak to one person at a time, urging the reader to practice on his or her own. It's often difficult for a reader to feel successful when completing one of the suggested assignments due to a lack of existing feedback.[58] Day has tried to remedy this in *Practical Intuition* by asking readers to complete an exercise using their intuition and then check the "answers" printed upside-down on the next page. It's also possible to develop these skills through journaling, reading, learning, then experimenting, then trying over and over again. Indeed, many people can improve their ability this way. But practicing together with others, in a group, is not only more beneficial, but more fun.[59]

One way to participate with a group is by attending a workshop on intuition. Afterward, attendees have opportunities to reach out to each other regularly in order to hone their skills. It's helpful, but once the workshop ends, practice is usually maintained one-to-one through email or phone calls and cannot truly be compared to the magic and communal spirit of in-person meetings.

---

[57] Penney Peirce, *The Intuitive Way: A Guide to Living From Inner Wisdom* (Hillsboro, OR: Beyond Words Publishing, Inc., 1997), 84.

[58] *Receiving* feedback is different than *needing* feedback. From Laura Day's teaching, I've learned that as we develop a relationship with our intuition, we start to trust the process and work in such a way that we let go after giving a reading. In my opinion, as intuitives learn, they hone their discerning ability. Practicing this way helps them become more confident so that they are less dependent on hearing whether a reading was on target.

[59] Day works with groups also. She teaches live and online intuitive training in groups a few times a year. Many other professionals teach live classes as well.

Looking back through the last decade of hosting my own psychometry group, I can honestly say that it's changed my life and others' lives for the better—which is what most of this book is about. Pat, who is the most senior member of our group and also the most experienced with psychometry, told me a few years ago that she believed that the group has become "more powerful," and that she thinks "the messages are more clear, and more in depth." "I might be mistaken," she said, "but the people that keep coming are all opening up more each time." Another woman in the group, Sabrina, said something similar:

> It is an amazing experience when you're in that circle. Each time is different—it's always a different experience for me. The more I went, the more powerful the circle became—whether it was a small or big group, the energy was always different and always radiating with light.

When I interviewed members of the group and asked them to talk about their experiences, their answers encompassed more than I expected to hear. They reflected on readings they had given and received, but most of all, emphasized what being part of the group has meant to them and how it's helped them grow.

Even though individual readings are wide-ranging and unique, overall, group member responses relate to how psychometry gave them the opportunity to . . .

1) Be part of a supportive, heart-centered community
2) Help others
3) Build self-confidence
4) Open their heart
5) Practice self-awareness and trust
6) Connect to Divine energy
7) Experience a sense of joy and wonder about life

Although practicing psychometry on your own can produce many of the outcomes Andrews lists, the difference between that and group participation is vast due to the potential for growth within a highly supportive, heart-centered community of people who learn from each other. Frankly, even without practicing psychometry, regular participation in a community naturally supports stronger communication skills because people listen to each other, feel empathy, provide encouragement, laugh together, and become more self-aware. In a church community, temple, or synagogue, congregants can experience all of this and, of course, feel connected spiritually, too.

But if people can receive all of this in their own spiritual communities, then what makes what we've been doing so special? I believe that group psychometry fills a growing need: more people are searching for a perceptible experience of their inner light in a way that can be healing and helpful to themselves and others. According to Laura, one of the women who attends the group regularly, "For me, the benefit of being in the group is that one light shines where we are at the moment, but more lights together reveal the path."

That still, small voice within, if we pay attention to it, starts to expand our inner landscape and opens us to a life that can be more balanced, peaceful, confident, and compassionate. Consequently, our friendships gradually shift toward a preference to be around those who share similar values and beliefs despite coming from different religious traditions. It's not easy for those who are developing spiritually to discover a safe space where they can openly speak from their "still, small voice" within, and conventional religious practice provides almost no opportunities for that. If a person should discuss something he or she sensed intuitively within a traditional church setting, it could be looked upon suspiciously, as if the individual is irrational, "airy-fairy," or had lost contact with reality.

But haven't we all had our occasional "ah-ha" moments while driving, walking, or standing in the shower? How can creative thinking that results in fresh ideas be so different from what we may receive through our own dreams, prayers, or meditations? Being internally focused on receiving messages in these ways could, instead, be viewed positively, as we embrace our intuition as a helpful—if not sacred—resource.

Hearing words that we are not intentionally speaking to ourselves or seeing visions we didn't consciously invent does not automatically mean a person is psychologically abnormal. Experiencing flashes of insight— whether through prayer, meditation, or otherwise—could mean that we have become more open to receiving intuitive information. Or, as some believe, it could be that our inner voice is from a higher vibration of ourselves—our "higher self," inspiration from the muses, a teacher or guide from the other side, an angel, or even the voice of what we perceive as God. Because I have been used to hearing so many argue against this point of view, it was eye-opening for me to read Richard Rohr's thoughts on this subject:

> If God wants to speak to us, God usually speaks in words that first feel like our own thoughts. How else could God come to us? We have to be taught how to honor and allow that, how to give it authority, and to recognize that *sometimes our thoughts are God's thoughts.* Contemplation helps train such awareness in us.[60]

My grandmother, who was a staunch Southern Baptist, worried that guidance from an inner voice—through ourselves or others—was a sure sign of false prophecy or some kind of demonic possession. To her, the gift of sharing messages from the world of spirit only occurred in the Old and New Testaments. For most congregationalists—and I believe for most people—the time for prophecy occurred in the past. According to that frame of reference, modern day prophets, psychics, and spiritualists cannot be trusted. Perhaps some can't be, which is why relying on our own wisdom and practicing our own sense of intuitive discernment is so crucial.

Even when everything falls into place and advice from a spiritual medium feels real, people will still tend to doubt what they hear. Day describes it this way:

> People always want to know how something works, believing that every result must be comprehensible and have a "logical" explanation. How mediumship works is a mystery. I don't think anybody really knows if it's the spirit actually speaking an energy that has been left

---

[60] Richard Rohr, "Inner Authority," Center for Action and Contemplation, Daily Meditations, November 21, 2021, https://cac.org/daily-meditations/inner-authority-2021-11-21.

behind or an intuitive's ability to enter a state in which he or she has access to information about things we normally don't perceive, at least not consciously. (I can tell you from firsthand experience, however, that genuine mediumship does exist.)[61]

It's natural to question how intuition, mediumship, psychic readings, and psychometry work. Quite often, though, other kinds of questions arise. When some of my church-going family members and acquaintances discover that I teach energy healing and host a group that does psychometry readings, they are polite about asking questions without becoming too confrontational. It feels like a discussion at a family dinner in which Republicans and Democrats are trying to keep the peace by avoiding fractious topics. Spirituality and politics are intensely personal issues, yet we all know that extremism and unquestioned complacency exist in both. Even among Christians, we still witness divisiveness between Catholics and Protestants or between those who have faith that Spirit can speak through anyone (even a non-Christian) versus those whose faith tells them that Spirit speaks only to certain people in certain situations—the "chosen" ones.

One question I've heard a couple times seems important enough to share here, and it goes like this: "What you do sounds good, but is it Christian?" The short answer is that it's universal; it transcends what we normally think of as Christianity and is within the larger realm of the sacred. A longer answer is to explore the question itself. What if we take away the judgments and beliefs that anything needs to be Christian in order for it to be spiritually beneficial?

Author and speaker Caroline Myss ponders something similar to this in terms of the chakras. In her book, *Anatomy of the Spirit*, she says that for years, she questioned why there were no Christian equivalents to such a predominant and valuable Hindu teaching. In a chapter called, "Made in the Image of God," she recalls that while teaching a workshop and drawing the seven circles of these power centers on the board, she suddenly began to recognize "congruencies" between the Eastern chakras and Judeo-Christian traditions. According to Myss,

---

[61] Day, *Practical Intuition*, 89-90.

The seven sacred truths of the Kabbalah, the Christian sacraments, and the Hindu chakras support our gradual transformation into conscious spiritual adults. These literal and symbolic teachings redefine spiritual and biological health and help us understand what keeps us healthy, what makes us ill and what helps us heal.[62]

In the following chart, I list the common concepts about the chakras on the left, and the sacrament Myss associates with each is on the right, along with connections to the Kabbalah.[63]

Chakra Number and Name	Trait	Sacrament	Kabbalah
1st - Base	Security/connection to our family, home, or "tribe"	Baptism	Yesod
2nd - Sacral	Relationships	Communion	Hod-Nezah
3rd - Solar Plexus	Self-empowerment	Confirmation	Tiferet
4th - Heart	Love/openness	Marriage	Gevurah-Hesed
5th - Throat	Willpower, truth	Confession	Da'at
6th - Third eye	Wisdom, inner guidance	Ordination	Binah-Hokhmah
7th - Crown	Life purpose, enlightenment, living in the present	Last rites	Keter

Myss calls attention to these congruencies, explaining that "Because our biological design is also a spiritual design, the language of energy and spirit used together crosses a variety of belief systems."[64] She says that this "opens avenues of communication between faiths and even allows people to return to religious cultures they formerly rejected, unburdened

---

[62] Caroline Myss, *Anatomy of the Spirit* (New York: Three Rivers Press, 1996), 67.

[63] Rebekah Kenton, "A Kabbalistic View of the Chakras," Kabbalah Society, published November 26, 2022, http://www.kabbalahsociety.org/wp/articles/a-kabbalistic-view-of-the-chakras.

[64] Myss, *Anatomy*, 64.

by religious dogma."[65] I believe that what our psychometry group does is metaphysical and inclusive, and that each individual can discern whether their takeaways from a meditation or a reading are spiritual, psychological, or physiological. Each person applies their own beliefs to what we do—whether they are Buddhist, Christian, Hindu, Jewish, Muslim, Wiccan, or anything else. Respecting each others' spiritual principles allows us to benefit and learn from different perspectives.

But the kind of spiritual growth our group supports extends beyond respecting each other's beliefs. Myss emphasizes that many people today are searching for "a heightened consciousness of the sacred" and that living according to this level of consciousness helps us move from a "parent-child relationship to God and move into spiritual adulthood."[66] Our psychometry/meditation group provides this—each meeting allows us the unique opportunity to connect our spirits, our energy, and our consciousness, to something greater than ourselves.

I wish I had learned the principles of open-mindedness, acceptance, and non-judgment much earlier in my religious upbringing. It's long overdue for traditional religious practices to embrace that mystical awareness is not just for prophets and saints from ancient times. By saying these things, I'm not trying to discourage people from going to church. There is no denying the benefits of church attendance, as it's changed so many people's lives for the better. Quite often, when I attend a church service or Mass with my family, I feel connected to them, to God, and to the sacred part of me that dwells within. I admit, though, that I would not be able to progress spiritually though church services alone because conventional churches are seldom inclusive and rarely offer opportunities for people like me to feel accepted or connected to our inner voices.

Charlotte, my friend from the Tampa psychometry group, told me that Patricc, who has attended their weekly group almost as long as she has, "always says" that "the psychometry group was his 'church'—every Tuesday night was his church. In fact, he said it was better than his church." Except for time spent in nature or the occasional service that somehow—though music, message, or both—touches my soul, I could say the same thing about psychometry meetings being my "church," too.

---

65 Myss, *Anatomy*, 64.
66 Myss, *Anatomy*, 66.

Our group is egalitarian and accepting; it requires us to be cooperatively engaged with each other and to "God," the Universe, or to whatever we call our inner guidance. We base this upon a relationship of collaboration and connection (power *with*) rather than a system that relies on hierarchy (power *over*). As I grow, I pay more attention to communicating with my inner guidance as a co-creator. If we believe that there is more to being human than our physical body, then why not be open to whatever we name this inner voice to be, as long as the guidance is wise and compassionate?

Throughout this book, I include copies of more than a dozen actual readings written during group meetings. Each one stands on its own, evidencing that such wise and compassionate guidance is accessible, available, and beneficial.

CHAPTER 16

First Benefit: A Sacred and Inclusive Community

Being Spiritually Diverse and Socially Inclusive

Among the core group of thirteen who have attended at least a dozen times over the last eight years, seven are first-generation immigrants—coming from Columbia, England, Guatemala, Italy, Hungary, India, and Ireland. The entire group also represents a variety of professions, including two international business executives, customer service employees, teachers, property managers, a banker, University administrators, massage therapists, an executive travel coordinator, a retired county accountant, executive office manager, a social worker, a hospice minister, a medical translator, a counselor, a psychotherapist, an exotic pet sanctuary owner, a financial consultant, a real estate professional, a couple teenagers, and a few who just refer to themselves as retirees. Only one woman, Pat, has ever worked as a psychic—the only person besides Charlotte and me to have had prior experience giving any sort of intuitive readings to others.

Those participating in the group vary in their religious backgrounds and spiritual practices. Over half would call themselves Christians, having grown up Catholic or Protestant, yet currently embracing a form of spirituality that is "non-traditional." About half are currently attending or have regularly attended either Unity or Metropolitan Community Church (MCC) Sunday services. Others attend worship services occasionally with their families, but a few would prefer to avoid church meetings altogether, preferring walks in nature, individual meditations, retreats, or their own varied approaches to spiritual stewardship and self-awareness.

Everyone in the group—even those who regularly attend Sunday services—express that they are open-minded about alternative spiritual approaches. Several in the group seem quite comfortable with the idea of past lives and the term "seeker," but in general, all try to avoid oversimplifying what each other believes. We tend to align with common terminology such as God, Christ, Christ consciousness, Higher Self, chakras, guides, angels, prayer, Spirit, inner guidance, auras, energy body, etc., even though we may not always perceive the complexities of each in the same way. It's not surprising that we also welcome affirmative perspectives from a wide range of mystical or nature-based philosophies, including ancient Hindu traditions, Buddhism, Wiccan, indigenous and Native American belief systems. We don't have to de-emphasize labels because everyone's spiritual beliefs blend in such a way that multiple approaches can be just as real and truthful as any single one.

Being spiritually inclusive is essential to creating a welcoming atmosphere. Each person has the opportunity to be part of a sacred circle, a community that offers a safe space for sharing and growth. In their interviews with me, nearly all of the women said that they felt welcome and safe. For example, Eileen said, "Knowing, not just intellectually, but also in my heart that the group is a safe, supportive, judgment-free space full of people who truly seek to uplift one another is one reason I keep coming back." Pat said this, too: "As I walked through the door, I felt safe, loved, and welcomed beyond belief. The meeting was awe-inspiring (as every meeting is)." Several others expressed similar sentiments, saying they felt uplifted and that even on their first meeting, expressed how it felt like being with a group of old friends. After even just a few meetings together, people started creating a lasting connection with each other. "Everyone is always genuinely glad to see everyone else," Eileen explained, and "it doesn't matter if you come every month or twice a year—the sense of welcome and the freedom to just 'be' are the same." This freedom, mutual caring, and respect, she said, "allows us to be more open to each other and to whatever the universe decides we all need to hear."

There's also a sense of comfort in the fact that we are all women. Sabrina told me that, for her, this was part of what makes it so special: "I felt as if I was becoming part of a sister group—soul sisters—and it was amazing every time we got together. It was like I was 'home' in a sense, and it was just so peaceful, each time."

By the way, I didn't start the group thinking, "I won't invite men." I originally invited people I knew who were interested in spiritual growth, meditation, and intuition, some of whom were former clients. Most of the group, however, consisted of friends from work and church—both lesbian and heterosexual, some coming with partners and some solo. Because I had started attending the local gay- and lesbian-friendly Metropolitan Community Church, I had already met some like-minded women who had a monthly book study on spiritual topics. This is the SOFEA group I mentioned in an earlier chapter, and I really enjoyed going to their meetings. Naturally, since the group consisted of women, and since many of them became friends, my initial psychometry meeting ended up being 100% female.

We had a couple men inquire about joining us, and I was open to that. The timing never seemed to work out for one of them. Another came for a few of the meetings and wanted to keep coming, but his partner wasn't interested in attending. Both were very busy. Since we usually meet on a Friday night, sometimes that can also cut into a couples' time together. During high school football season, one mother of a teen supported her daughter's cheerleading, so attending Fridays wasn't possible for her. The same was true for another with a young child who had difficulty finding a babysitter. I'm aware that these things happen, yet being inclusive also means that once in a while we offer a Saturday or Sunday afternoon group meeting instead of Friday nights. Whenever it feels right to offer a weekend meeting, I tend to give advance notice of at least a month or two.

All of this spiritual and cultural diversity has occurred naturally— unplanned but not unintentional. In the early days, the psychometry group varied in terms of each person's level of comfort with giving readings. At the time, Eileen referred to this as "being on a spiritual learning curve, and the fact that we're not all in exactly the same place on that curve, makes the whole experience more impactful and interesting."

As I've grown spiritually over the years, it's become my intent to be accepting and open in my thinking and in my social circle. However, at the same time, I notice more similarities than differences among us, including a strong sense of shared values. We share sacred moments as witnesses to each other's wide-eyed amazement, laughter, and tears, and especially as we share our desire to connect with divine guidance.

No Drama, No Judgment

Because the group has connected so well, my job as the host requires protecting the sanctity we've created. I ask the others to let me know if they're interested in inviting someone else, and I pray about it. I check my inner guidance. Sometimes I've had to say "no" for reasons that have nothing to do with who is doing the inviting or how wonderful a person is.[67]

Pat explained to me that she believes that our group cohesion receives an extra layer of divine protection: "The ones whose vibrations are aligned with the group keep coming back, but those who are not aligned usually are not ready, so they don't return." I've witnessed this happening, especially during the first few years. I also think it's one of the reasons why the group has been successful. Sabrina described the women who attend as "radiant with light and love," and emphasizes that "there was no drama, no animosity toward anything—just this peaceful, family-like group that sticks together no matter what, and the bond that they share is amazing."

The lack of drama evidences how we have all sought to grow and improve ourselves—inwardly, that is, by being more loving, forgiving, more vulnerable yet more confident and strong. I think it's safe to say that the group members continue to work on practicing non-judgment—about others, themselves, religious beliefs, and about the readings each person offers. Suman, who comes to the group regularly, explains her point of view this way:

> Judgment is a way of shrinking the world down. There is no judgment in Hinduism, and, really, no "ism" in it. It says in the Gita, "I have God, but I have no religion." The word "Namaste" means "The Divine in me acknowledges the Divinity in you." But people only tend to use it when

---

[67] I'll say more about this in Part 5.

they are impressed with someone. It's interesting that people use that phrase to make a judgment, but it comes from a belief system that tries to avoid all that. Actually, there is no such thing as a "wrong" thing, and there's nothing anyone can do to you that you don't already have within you. The Divine spark is not limited only to what we consider "good." There is nothing that we cannot learn or create from.

During those initial nights of hosting everyone, I emphasized the importance of non-judgment in light of all that we are giving and receiving within the group. I think it's natural to assume that it would be detrimental—if not devastating—to someone if we were to judge any reading we might receive, yet somehow it seems culturally appropriate for us to judge and second-guess ourselves. Why is that?

Suman's reminder during one of our group discussions took this idea to a whole new level. A reading that evening mentioned how our lives can become stunted when we judge ourselves or others. She discussed how it's like falling into a trap that forces us to see only limitations. Beginners who give a reading for the first time can be too hard on themselves if they fear writing (or omitting) something that could possibly be wrong or disappoint someone. Instead, as Charlotte explained, it's more helpful to treat the practice of giving a reading as a means of spiritual growth, a way of connecting to inner guidance.

Growing Beyond Fear to Freedom

So, besides offering the opportunity to visit and support each other, many of the women explained how the group functions as a space for spiritual growth and intuitive practice. Diana settled into the group during her first visit because, as she explains, she was able to connect with her heart, her sense of curiosity, and her ability to trust the others who attended:

> I don't exactly recall the date I first attended the psychometry group. What I can tell you is that it was a heart-opening experience in total, but initially, it was a

bit of a challenge for my ego to be concerned if I could even do it. I was so curious and wanted to give myself a chance to experience this. Since I have been growing my intuition for quite some time, it made sense to check this out. The connectedness with all the intuitive, spiritual people there helped ease my discomfort. Then as the readings were shared, my heart was engaged to find out more, so I made the decision to attend as often as possible with the intention of learning more and experiencing and exercising my "intuitive muscle" in a safe and sweet environment, which is what this group has provided.

It's wonderful to hear Diana say that after her first visit she wanted to give herself a chance and that her "heart was engaged to find out more." It's clear that excitement and connectedness outweighed her fear.

Like Diana, Laura was initially curious, too. She was raised in Milan, Italy, and compares her initial experience with psychometry to her arrival in America:

Just like coming to the U.S., going to psychometry has opened my eyes. Although I started going because I trusted, unconditionally, what I call this "League of Extraordinary Women" (yes, like the movie), I was also curious.

That sense of eye-opening wonder and gratitude for the group supported her expansion, and her trust in the group began to mirror inward.

According to Laura, "I did not believe much in myself and my gifts, yet this powerful circle of women continued to believe in me until I started believing in myself, something I can honestly say is still in progress."

Repeatedly, each of these women said that they felt supported while they practiced in a judgment-free setting. Expressing that they felt "welcomed," "safe," "at home," and among "soul sisters" allowed them to let go of having to meet a particular standard in giving a reading.

Another woman in the group, Phyllis, explained that before giving her first reading, she felt a sense of belonging first and then the freedom to write whatever came through:

> Feeling like I was exactly where I was supposed to be, I totally embraced my intuitive training wheels. Kim encouraged us to "allow" and not judge what we were getting, to just write whatever came to us. I remember feeling the room was full of loving energy throughout the evening. Afterwards, a sense of validation was present within me—maybe I really can tap into my intuition!

Community provided not only the opportunity, but the foundation and, more importantly, the validation for Phyllis to believe that she could connect with her inner guidance.

But sometimes, just feeling a sense of belonging isn't enough for someone to connect with their inner voice. Anyone could be conditioned to hide his or her intuitive gifts or feel disempowered based on particularly challenging experiences. Laura told me that when she grew up in southern Italy, people "were very superstitious," which reinforced a sense of fear:

> They say, "Don't drop oil, salt, and please don't break a mirror!" If and when we got "chain letters," we were supposed to make copies and deliver them religiously to neighbors' mailboxes. I hated spreading this sort of fear and ignorance into other people lives.
>
> In my late teens, I put my foot down and told my mom that we had to stop doing these things. I believed that those letters could cause harm if we gave power to them, and for me, the key was to stop reinforcing such fears. Ignorance is generationally taught, ingrained in people's DNA, and it takes time to clear those layers and get rid of patterns that no longer serve us.

About this time, my family discovered Tarot card reading. About once a year, my mom and I went for a reading and met with a lady who lived in Milan. She was a friend of my mom's sister, and when we saw her, I was very intrigued by her abilities . . . such a power, which, we believed, of course, was reserved only for those with special gifts. Also, I had a few friends who participated in a few group sessions that featured a psychic medium, and one did not go well. Being raised Catholic, I feared the devil, and anything that was occult related. Ahh dogma, another way of paralyzing the masses. Coming to the States was my ticket to freedom from bondage to the many levels of my belief system.

Laura's actions—wanting to stop spreading fear—was, as she says, one of the layers in the patterns she learned growing up. Releasing one pattern, then, revealed other layers and beliefs that she eventually discovered were holding her back. Laura believed only those with special gifts could receive intuitive messages, so she didn't even consider that it's possible for everyone, including herself.

Throughout my 67 plus years, I've known many Catholics, Baptists, Muslims, Jews, Buddhists, and Hindus who were open-minded about life—spiritually mature and also politically and culturally open-minded, too. But if we are raised to fear something, no matter what religion we come from, it's very hard to stop thinking in terms of black and white, good and evil. Like Laura says, ignorance can be "generationally taught, ingrained in people's DNA."

Also immigrating to the US from another country, Maritza came to the U.S. from Colombia in 1980. Like Laura, it took a long time for her to let go of her fears. Maritza grew up Catholic and still observes that but respects the beliefs of others and incorporates some indigenous native spirituality in her life as well. When I asked her about her spiritual background, she told me that she has been interested in spiritual things since she was a child. From the time she was four or five years old, she said that she was seeing things that "nobody else saw," and this scared her:

I would see things that normal people don't see, like ghosts, figures, stuff that can be scary. Because of that and having no way to communicate or ask anybody, I used to be really afraid and shy. I remember when I was about six in the house where we lived, there were always these lights—not from the lamps or houselights—but lights that would appear on the ceiling, so I would just look at them. I also had a sense about when something was going to happen. This also created a feeling of fear because I didn't know what that was until I started learning more about it. I used to read a lot, trying to find answers.

So when I turned twelve, I started meditating and from meditation and doing the breathing exercises that I learned in books, my senses started to open in an even bigger and bigger way. At that time, I started having premonitions, and I became more afraid because I was seeing so much more that I didn't quite understand. There was a point when I was so afraid that I told myself, "I don't want to feel it. I don't want to feel anymore. I don't want to see anymore." So I closed myself to it. I stopped meditating, stopped doing everything related to that, and then gradually, it all went away. But I was never happy after I closed myself because I missed that part of my life.

And then, when I came to the U.S., I started trying to gain that back, and eventually it did come back but in a much different way. I started sensing what what is going on in a person's body. I could tell when and where a client had pain. It's like I became an empath. So that was my whole life until I met you ten years ago.

Besides Maritza, other women in the group expressed having fear and uncertainty about their own intuitive senses. Claudia, who was also raised as a devout Catholic, said that she remembers questioning her faith a lot as a little girl in Guatemala.

There was really no room for an inquisitive, truth-seeking child, so I was silenced at a very young age. At six years old I remember my grandma saying to me that I had a gift (probably because I knew she had it). I remember getting premonitions through dreams and because I was not allowed to speak about them, I got scared and disconnected from the ability to receive messages in my sleep. My whole life I felt like I was unique in the way I related to the world, and I continued to experience life in a very empathic way but under the impression that I was the only one.

When I came to the US in my early twenties, I continued to seek spirituality on my own. I never felt connected to any religion, and whenever I would "receive" messages through my dreams, I discounted them as "coincidences." Being able to be part of this psychometry group was a true gift. To be surrounded by likeminded, powerful, kind women was something I had been missing my whole life. I felt connected, seen, understood.

Cultural judgments about the appropriateness or validity of their visions as young girls caused Maritza and Claudia to question and even fear their own gifts, so they closed their hearts. I can't help but wonder how much different their lives would have been if they had found a community much earlier in life, one in which—to use Claudia's words, they felt "connected," "seen," and "understood."

"You are Safe Here, Rest a Bit"

During my last dozen or so years of hosting the group, nearly everyone has faced a major challenge of some kind. At least two women have healed from cancer, and some have had loved ones pass or suffer from debilitating illnesses. In each case, the spiritual nature of the group offered a degree of comfort and protection. An example of this is the support Pat received after her husband had passed:

Shortly after I attended for the first time, my husband was diagnosed with Stage 4 throat cancer, and I didn't come back for quite a while. When I returned to the meetings after Al's death, everyone picked up on my sadness and grief. The messages I gave and received after I returned were inspiring, comforting, and without exception, full of joy and love. Each and every one had an impact on me. They supported my will to carry on.

One of the messages in psychometry that I received and loved was the poem Cathleen wrote to me:

It's not so much the things you say as that which you intend,
And whoever you are calling up is at the other end.
It's not how rough or paved the road or how they twist and wind,
But whether it will lead you to the goal you hope to find.
It's not the manner of your smile, nor yet how hard you strive,
It's all the special things in life that make us feel alive.
It's not how much we've laughed or cried, but only that we cared,
Along with all the memories that we have kept and shared.
It's not the color of thy sky, nor the glimmer of a star,
It's not what things appear to be . . . but what they really are.

It's quite rare for anyone to write a poem as a reading or even part of one, so this verse from Cathleen was very special. Pat explains that almost all the readings she has received have been inspirational, uplifting, and nonjudgmental. "How else could it have been?" she asks. "We never know whose item we were writing our message for."

Although the readings we give and receive are often vital and full of life, they are not the only reason people keep coming back; they also reinforce rapport and friendship. In Elizabeth's words, "I have grown fond of everyone in the group and look forward every month to the meeting. We all laugh together and cry together—with and for each other. We speak on a soul level with each other. We recognize that our group is no accident. We are indeed drawn together."

When I asked another woman in the group, Esther, about why she comes to psychometry, she answered with a glowing explanation of the sense of community I've been trying to describe:

> I attend, not as much for my reading, but to be with mesmerizing people. To me, last evening felt like beautiful people coming together to shine on each other. Sometimes we do not know who we are and what to do, but there is a light in us that knows. Then your wonderful meditation brought peace, togetherness, and such protection. The room was soothing, and I was thinking, "Esther, you are safe here. Rest a bit . . . and I received such beauty."

In writing this book, I've read Esther's words again and again. Each time I read them, my heart overflows, and I'm tempted to cry. Although I don't consider myself to be "mesmerizing," I agree with Esther that "mesmerizing," "shine," and "beauty" are good words for what the group meetings feel like.

In this chapter I've touched on the loving support all of us offered to Pat and others while they were going through difficult times. The next chapter illustrates ways we have helped each other in terms of specific readings.

CHAPTER 17

Second Benefit: Helping Others

Earlier, I mentioned seven benefits of group psychometry. Being involved with a sacred, like-minded community was the first and most obvious one. The second benefit is that it offers us the opportunity to help each other. Throughout the book, I have many examples of this happening within our circle since nearly every reading is helpful to another person in some way. However, this chapter focuses on readings that stand out—something treasured in the words, impact, or timing of a message, a confirmation received, or an uplifting feeling that offered support through a difficult situation.

Impactful Messages Occurring at the Perfect Time

The timing of a message can be so perfect that it appears like a surprise. It can also serve as a confirmation of an action or goal, like receiving guidance that the Universe sees us walking our path and says, "We're cheering for you. Keep going!"

The reading Rita and I received from Suman that uncovered the secret that we were building a new home, and also the one that Eileen gave me about "ignoring the loud" are both examples of messages that came at the perfect time.

Just a few months ago, Elizabeth delivered a message that applied to a big decision Rita and I had been considering. She said, "When in doubt— DON'T. You have everything you need. Believe it." Further down the page, she wrote, "Spending $$—important purchase—Take your time. It may take a while for it to come together. Patience." Once again, we had been looking at real estate for a vacation spot in Asheville, but had told no one in the group. Elizabeth's reading confirmed that, yes, it was a big purchase and would cost a lot of money. I received this reading from her in May 2024. Just four months later, Rita was scheduled to fly to Asheville to look at some property. Her flight was cancelled, which happened to be the day before Hurricane Helene devastated so many people's lives in the Southeast.

Many times, as we considered Elizabeth's reading, we talked about slowing down our search, grateful for her advice but not completely understanding its context. Never in a million years would we have thought the reason for such a pause would have been a hurricane that devastated so many people's lives.

The timing of readings like these tend to reverberate in our minds, reminding us that it is one of the many ways we are able to help each other. In another example, Phyllis shared several impacts and insights with me in her reaction to a message from Amy in the summer of 2014.

In Phyllis's reading, Amy said, "Careful is not the way. This is a time of plenty. Your life is unfolding and all of the clarity you have asked for is coming to you now." Phyllis calls this "Impact #1" because she says, "Clarity was my white stone word for 2014." To add context for this, the Unity church that a few of us attend provides a "white stone" service as part of the first Sunday in January. Every congregant is given a small, blank, white stone that originates from quarries in Jerusalem. During meditation, each person becomes open to receiving their "word" for the year, something that represents a recurring theme for this period of their lives or a specific message the word carries for that person.[68] As Phyllis mentions, her white stone word was "clarity," and Amy's reading confirmed the importance of this word for her.

---

[68] A passage in Revelation 2:17 mentions a white stone: "The one who has an ear, let him hear what the Spirit says to the churches. To the one who overcomes, I will give some of the hidden manna, and I will give him a white stone, and a new name written on the stone which no one knows except the one who receives *it.*" *(NAS Version).* Several Unity churches note that in the ancient world, a white stone had multiple symbolic meanings, including innocence, freedom, or authority. If a freed slave or prisoner was given a white stone with a new name on it, they could use it as proof that they were free or no longer considered guilty, so symbolically their new name offered a clean slate for a new life.

"Impact #2" for Phyllis came through the next part of Amy's message: "You are a healer for many. Your presence is needed in the lives of those who are with you on this journey. Be sure to love with the purest of light that you are." Phyllis said that her "intent has always been to be the conduit of love and light." She has also taken several healing classes and, at the time, was currently a primary caregiver for her father, who lived on the same street and was in his late nineties. At the time of the reading, Phyllis was going through the day-to-day care for her father by taking him food and checking on him a few times each day. Although we all know that we decline as we age, it's difficult for anyone to predict how much care an aging parent might need in the future. Amy's reading cautioned her that her presence was needed and reminded her to "be sure to love with the purest of light that you are."

The next part of Amy's reading for Phyllis is a short sentence full of impact: "Care for the child in your life. Her path is shadowed. You are her light." Phyllis calls this "Impact #3," exclaiming, "My child is buried so deeply!" While sharing this with me, tears began to well up in Phyllis's eyes as she recalled the passage that brought "Impact #4": "The source of your knowledge is beyond this realm of being. You may transmit that which is unknown on this plane to help others who are confused. This is a call (your call)." After reading this again, Phyllis says, "I start to cry at this Truth that I know from my core." The rest of Amy's reading re-emphasizes that message:

Careful is not the way.

Purple light - healing energy.

You are so loved. Lighten the world with your love and light. Continue to push and be vibrant.

Careful is not the way.

"This reading from Amy completely engulfed my soul," Phyllis said. "It washed over me with powerful energy that I still feel to this day . . . . So piercing was its message, so pure was its intent. My commitment to spiritual growth was accelerated as I embraced my Divinity more fully."

The timing of a reading that Lissette gave to Suman supported a recent change for her at work. Lissette wrote that Suman was creating her own map—"for herself and for all." Lissette reiterated the words, "My map, my dance, my walk . . . detach from outcomes, and enjoy the walk." When Suman responded to the message, she explained that she had been told that she had fulfilled the responsibilities of her position and was asked by her supervisors to create a new role for herself—a new job that she could outline, or "map," so to speak. Lissette's reading confirmed this.

In addition to the messages, though, Lissette told me, "The most impactful moments in the group for me have not been the personal readings I've given or received but the ones I've witnessed others receiving":

> I remember when Pat said that she was depressed after attending a specific place. She cried and affirmed that she felt "something" was attached to her. Afterwards the group stood in a circle around her to send her healing energy. Pat cried because she felt so grateful and relieved.

Lynda recalled this as well because she had given the reading to Pat that night. Lynda said,

> I could feel the consumption of negative energy. Pat confirmed that something had "attached" to her after a trip to a retreat center in NC, and she could not get rid of it. I don't even remember the reading, but I certainly recall what happened afterwards. Amy sat on one side of me and Helen on the other. After we were done with our readings, I spoke up and asked if Pat would allow us to gather around her and assist in ridding her of the negative energy. We did. We chanted . . . we prayed and banished the energy, telling it to leave Pat. It was an incredibly powerful experience.

When I asked Pat to talk about that experience from her perspective, this is what she said:

> I had gone with a friend to a place in North Carolina and felt really good about going there. When we first arrived, we met the manager of the center, Michael, and

something strange happened to me at that moment. I am not totally sure what it was.

During the retreat, my friend and I would walk together sometimes, and other times would take different paths. When Michael saw me walking by myself, he said, "When are you leaving?" instead of, you know, "How are you enjoying this day?" And I thought, "Well that's kind of an odd question." I didn't say anything.

And then when I got home, I kept feeling a sense of depression and darkness within myself. It was a really bad feeling that wouldn't go away. Sometimes I think, as lightworkers, we don't protect ourselves like we should, and I hadn't, because I had felt safe at the retreat.

But later on when we had psychometry, Lynda wrote a message for me that started out by saying, "I see you in a dark room …" Immediately, I started crying. I was just beside myself because she had defined my situation so clearly.

That's when I thought that I had brought something negative with me from that retreat center, something I would not define as spiritual. After the readings ended that evening, I think it was Lynda that said, "I think you should sit in the middle of our circle, and we'll all pray for you." So I said, "yes." And when that happened, everybody got around me, and their prayers were like a bright light shining. I knew that whatever had been affecting me was lifted. It was gone. And I felt clear after that. I've never, ever had a feeling like that before.

Afterward, Cathleen said whatever it was that attached to me came to me because I was strong enough to remove it. Well, I'm not sure about that, but I thank God for the psychometry group that night because they took it from me.

Although a circumstance like Pat's is unusual, it's natural for people in the group to notice when someone is in need of support, whether it's for healing or a listening ear as someone shares a personal challenge. Without reader or recipient even realizing it, this level of support can occur just through a reading, as is the next example with one that Rita gave Helen.

When it was Rita's turn to share what she received with Helen, Rita sat forward in her seat, turned her head toward Helen sitting in the chair next to her, and said, "This came through very strong! Usually, I write on the back of the page as well, but this message was just on the front and quite direct."

Rita held up the reading and spoke: "I am of the mountain. My strength flows through you. Fear not the unknown. Fear not . . . Fear not, for you have unbreakable strength."

As she gave the reading to Helen along with her object, a keychain, Helen looked at Rita and the rest of the group.

"This is so perfect. Thank you." As Helen looked at the page and back to the group, she said, "This emphasizes how I have needed to release some of my fears, and actually, this very thing has been my focus lately—to feel the opposite of fear, spreading my arms wide open in acceptance of life and all that it brings. In fact, as I drove over here tonight in my car, I actually told myself, 'You are unbreakable. You are unbreakable.' I used the same word: 'unbreakable.'"

Perfectly timed readings like these actually occur quite often, and when they do, the timing is a message in itself, alerting us to the miracle of how our lives matter and that—through these messages and in so many other ways—we can make a difference in others' lives.

Messages as Confirmation

The theme of being on the right path occurs again and again as people discuss their satisfaction with some of their most memorable readings. Life offers us so many choices, and receiving confirmation that the choices we've made are wise ones can not only clear away those nagging cobwebs of doubt but strengthen our resolve.

Allie shared an example of this with me, saying that one of the readings that had the greatest meaning for her was from Eileen:

She wrote several paragraphs about how I am the persona of love. It meant so much because I know myself to be self-absorbed, and yet I trust God daily to change my heart to become more focused on others. It was a confirmation that I'm on the right path.

Another example comes from Adrienne, who mentioned feeling uplifted by a reading reminding her that something she had been seeking is on the way. "The message talked about taking care of myself, being quiet, and taking life slowly because I needed to find myself first," she said. It stated that what she was seeking was coming, "but at the moment, it was still hidden, almost ready to surface from the well within," which she described as hopeful: "I love this message because it helped me know that progress is happening, and I was on the right path."

In many cases, the person who provides a reading for someone else can tune into these qualities because both reader and recipient share them.[69] For example, when I asked Maritza to talk with me about readings that had the most impact for her, she described one that featured a message to Suman from Suman's departed mother, and the other one focused on Rita. In the first one, she said she loved the reading she gave Suman because the words and meaning came through so clearly. Maritza spoke highly of Suman's mother, whose spirit conveyed both love and strength, and Maritza also said something similar in her reading for Rita, referring to Rita as having power "within her," like "backbone":

> When seeing Rita, the power she has within her. How do you say that word? Being so "herself"— like her backbone . . . her . . . her strength. That reading I remember. It gave me a good sense of what a person should be, what a woman should be.

This reading occurred in 2016, three years before we went on a trip to Peru. Looking back, a couple of the symbols that Maritza drew appeared during our trip, especially the round image she labels "Nacar,"

---

[69] I discuss more about this economical quality of readings in the chapter titled, "Seventh Benefit: Connecting to Divine Energy."

or mother-of-pearl, and a wheel, which describes one of the necklaces Rita bought without even recalling the reading three years prior.

Continuing the text of the reading, Maritza describes Rita as:

> Strong at heart, very alert, ferocious, secure, proud, who just knows how and what to do, goes through life being happy looking at flowers, beautiful flowers, who enjoys a ride on a bike, the freedom of the wind, the Earth . . . who is just happy. I heard the sound of a door closing, but she has many windows through which she can look at the beauty of the pastures, the gardens. This woman is comfortable in her own skin, this woman whose heart is bright as the sun who shines in her glow . . . satisfaction, empowerment, strength. It was comforting to feel that. Beautiful.

Rita loves being in nature, feeling the wind on her skin, riding a bike, and, yes, she is strong and comfortable with herself. Maritza's reading confirmed all of that and more. However, when Maritza says, "It was comforting to feel that," I have to emphasize that one of the wonderful experiences of doing a reading includes feeling the joy of another person's inner light. This inner light is also reflected in the reader herself, which is why she could witness it. This explains how Maritza could feel the love and strength in the message from Suman's mother. Like Rita, Maritza is strong, too—she loves nature, has a rich inner spirit, and shares her joy generously with others.[70]

The next example is also about Rita, from Pat. Rita told me that this particular reading stood out for her because some of the details were shockingly accurate.

---

[70] Later in the book, I discuss how a message can often apply to both reader and receiver (See Chapter 22).

Nov 13, 2015 - Friday 13th Pat   For Rita
I saw an instant rainbow. You are
truly heaven sent their is a small
bird sitting on your left shoulder. It
tells you all the secrets of the
world. It sings the most melodious
songs to you. Music that has
yet to be written. Everyone that
meets you admires you for your
strength, love, compassion, your
willingness to listen to an
opposing idea & you take it
into consideration & realize you
don't have all the answers. You
are definately a family orented
person entho' you moved to a
foreign land - you knew it
was here you would find true
happiness. Your lite shines so
bright it encompasses all who
come into your vibration. You can
heal the sick & minester the
needy - You give them something
to carry on - You give them hope
love & joy & peace in their
lives & yours. I see a purple

heart it is almost like a tatoo or birthmark — this is a special symbol — from a tribe long ago; it was a symbol of the Chosen One. You are very close to St Frances. He sent you his dove.

Pat's Reading for Rita

The text of Pat's message reads as follows:

November 13, 2015, Friday the 13th, Pat

> I saw an instant rainbow. You are truly heaven sent. There
> is a small bird sitting on your left shoulder. It tells you
> all the secrets of the world. It sings the most melodious
> songs to you—music that has yet to be written. Everyone
> that meets you admires you for your strength, love,
> compassion, for your willingness to listen to an opposing
> idea, and you take it into consideration and realize you
> don't have all the answers. You are definitely a family-
> oriented person even though you moved to a foreign land.
> You knew it was here you would find true happiness. Your
> light shines so bright that it encompasses all who come
> into your vibration. You can heal the sick and minister to
> the needy—you give them something to carry on—you
> give them hope, love and joy and peace, in their lives and
> yours. I see a purple heart. It is almost like a tattoo or
> birthmark. This is a special symbol from a tribe long ago.
> It was a symbol of the Chosen One. You are very close to
> St. Francis. He sent you his love.

Rita told me that it's difficult for her to think of herself as a "chosen
one," feeling a little embarrassed for me to put a reading saying all this
in the book. But after reflecting on it, she looked at me and said, "Well, I
guess I'm the chosen one for you!"

In light of this theme of confirmation, several parts of the reading very
much align with who Rita is. For example, she is highly family-oriented,
being one of nine siblings and is certainly an immigrant, having moved
from Ireland to a "foreign land," as Pat mentions. She also has a birthmark
on her eyelid.

One of Rita's primary goals in life and in her work is to find "a
third way" between two extreme choices or positions. She respects others'
viewpoints and is a very good listener. From my own perspective, as her
wife, I have witnessed many times in which she has also helped many

family members and friends with her healing compassion, generosity, and support. In terms of the little bird on her shoulder, at times it does feel as if she knows "the secrets of the world" because out of the blue, she will think of a new idea that solves a particular problem—mostly business-related ones, but also in our everyday life at home.

These readings may have made Rita blush, but overall they affirm the strength of her spirit and celebrate her uniqueness. We could say the same for Allie, Phyllis, Suman, Adrienne, and others, including Elizabeth, who like Rita, expresses how difficult it is to absorb the glowing compliments we sometimes hear from our spirit messengers.

In preparation for this book, Elizabeth reviewed all her readings and thanked me for giving her an excuse to study them. This is what she discovered:

> I have several readings that I have saved over the last three years now. I wish I had them all. There is so much information in all of my readings and so many common threads as well; trying to sum it up is not easy. It feels like I am barely scratching the surface of the contents of the readings given to me. However, in reading through them, I started to hear some of the same things over and over again, so the statistical side of me decided to count it up. I have 19 of them, and these are the commonalities I found:
>
> - 5 mention healing or healer
> - 5 mention love
> - 2 mention cabin
> - 2 mention diet
> - 2 mention need for meditation
> - 2 mention "do not take no for an answer"
> - 2 mention the color purple
> - Several of them speak of a unity with God and universe and of being the light.

Elizabeth says, "Some of the words in the readings blow me away, like 'recognizing my divine wisdom and purpose' or 'you can heal the sick and feed the masses' or 'God is your guide, you are divine.'" I'm not sure what to do with some of the statements, they can be a little uncomfortable, but I trust it is what I need to hear."

Given Rita's reactions and Elizabeth's sentiments, I'm sure others have been "blown away" as well, but there's no denying the importance of a message when it's extremely specific or repeated several times.

Confirmation that Inspires Healing

Angel has been attending our group meetings for several years, and her readings continue to emphasize the positive feelings she felt when she first arrived. In March 2018, she wrote a beautiful, and uplifting reading for Pat, who is one of our most beloved "truth tellers" because it's obvious that we treasure her unfiltered and often hilarious comments in our day-to-day conversations.

Below is the text of her reading, followed by an image of it:

> Temple of Gold. Light pours out of this temple. You are welcome here. Have you visited this temple in your dreams, your guides will take you there if you so desire it, once again. Life is showing you many challenges at the moment, but these are only temporary. You will soon be on the other side walking along a golden path into the golden temple. It's not a physical place, but a state of being. A state where your beingness activates a positive vibration to everyone around you. You are a truth teller and a bringer of light. You have a true gift that will radiate out into the world and transform it. You are dearly loved and blessed by many in spirit. You speak the language of love, and it blesses many. You are a treasure dear one! God Bless You!

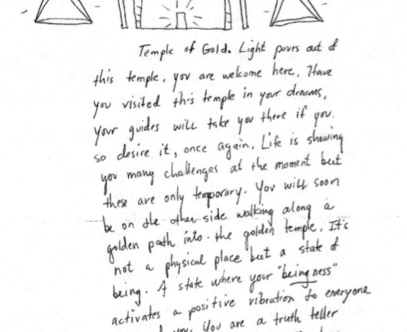

Temple of Gold. Light pours out of this temple, you are welcome here. Have you visited this temple in your dreams, your guides will take you there if you so desire it, once again. Life is showing you many challenges at the moment but these are only temporary. You will soon be on the other side walking along a golden path into the golden temple. It's not a physical place but a state of being. A state where your "being ness" activates a positive vibration to everyone around you. You are a truth teller and a bringer of light, You have a true gift that will radiate out into the world and transform it. You are dearly loved + blessed by many in spirit. You speak the language of love and it blesses many, you are a treasure dear one!
God bless you!

Angel's Reading for Pat, March 2018

Angel's drawing illustrates light pouring out of everything. In the message, she explains that Pat may have been going through temporary challenges but that she would be on her way to a more profound state of being, one that spreads light, love, and transformation to those around her. Pat confirmed to us that she had been going through a rough time and appreciated hearing that this sense of light and hope was on its way.

Confirmation of Life Changes

Somehow the Universe picks Pat to provide some of the most jaw-dropping messages for people. She recalled two that stand out for her, but there are certainly many, many more:

> Of the messages that I wrote, a few stand out in my memory. In one reading, I started out writing to Jaye, "How Great Thou Art." Just those words made a believer out of her because a minister that was making a guest appearance at a local church had asked her to sing that song the next weekend. Then there was the lady whose husband had asked for a divorce, and her message started out, "The house that Jack built is crumbling down."

No one in the group knew beforehand that the woman's husband had asked for a divorce, but it came through in the message as confirmation—a painful one, but evidently necessary for her to hear.

Regarding the reading mentioning the song, "How Great Thou Art," Jaye said, "When I received my reading, I became a true believer in psychometry. It was as if the person giving me the reading had known me my entire life—and especially what was going on in my life at that particular time." After that, Jaye decided to come to the group as often as she could.

Confirmation Across Several Readings

The readings Diana received were not jaw-dropping one-liners from Pat, but they provided helpful confirmation of some important changes in her life. Diana's messages occurred across four months. She says, "During

2015, all the readings I received had a common thread of love, validation, and encouragement of my current path":

> In January, my reading spoke of fear of the unknown, releasing old patterns, and moving into unknown territory. This validated the right choices I had made to let go of what no longer served me. In my life, both my career and relationship paths have taken on a whole new and unknown direction. Also, this unknown territory included the unseen world. My guides are with me, and I know that now. New energy was coming forth as well so that I could begin to see myself as a vessel flowing with healing love and energy.

The healing energy mentioned in January's reading recurs for her again in March, with images shining with light and reaching out her hand with a flame of healing energy in it:

> Accomplishment and healing were the themes for my reading in March. It started with an image of me going through a basket, doing an inventory of all that was in it and feeling good about my accomplishments. I interpreted this as a sense of both present and future— the manifestation of all that has yet to transpire, which felt so good to hear. The words, "You are feeling very good about your life," confirmed all of that. The second theme, healing, was emphasized: "A new gift is coming—you are so uplifted. You just shine with light. You put your hand out and it has a flame in it—healing energy." Also, "green Archangel Raphael" was mentioned as well as "tiny green orbs floating around you."

February's reading spoke of looking intensely into the horizon "like a hunter but without a gun," conducting and orchestrating. This is my work now, being a "hunter" for the insurance business that I am doing and then taking care of that need. This was such validation, and I am grateful for that. I felt such love and comfort from the words, "We treasure your commitment to growth."

Also in March and April, both messages mention a beautiful sense of nature and being at peace. One describes "looking down on the lights of the town and then up at the stars in the dark sky," and the other talks about, "new horizons, dawn, a view of Earth with the sun peeking from the atmosphere."

These moments of peace contrast with the next part of her reading in April, which conveys a sense of urgency: "Time moving faster—not a minute to waste, sense of urgency to move ahead, guided to do so. All is well in this." Diana adds, "Such was the case, because I had been trying to get the flow of income coming in while at the same time allowing my gift to blossom." The last line of her reading in April says, "You are blossoming/ blooming. Can you witness this within yourself?" Diana told me that she said "Yes" to that: "Again, such a validation of my path. I am so grateful for all these readings, which I treasure very much."

Generational Healing

As in Diana's example, healing can occur as a theme across several readings and, in Elizabeth's case, across generations. Elizabeth told me that she has received some unforgettable readings, including the one from Esther that helped her express how she felt about her daughter's move to the West coast. Another one that Elizabeth described as "spot on," helped her navigate challenges with her mother. At these crucial times, she said, "Pat's readings were particularly helpful." The gift from these experiences, she told me, is that "I've learned you can't hide in psychometry. It will speak your truth, so be ready for it."

A specific example of this is from 2015 in which Pat mentions a previous lifetime when Elizabeth had been childless, and the longing for a mother/child connection carried over into this life. Even though this statement was just a small part of the reading itself, it brought up a lot of emotion for her:

> I had one reading recently that recalled another lifetime
> for me where I was childless, and it carried over to this
> one. That was very true and although it was very painful,

it did come to pass, and I did end up having my daughter. Wanting a child so badly and not being able to have one was so painful. I was shocked that it showed up in a psychometry reading. So, psychometry also reminds me of the miracles in my life.

Also in alignment with this reading, Elizabeth described having a strong connection to a doll in her childhood, one that she still kept and had not been able to detach from or donate. However, as a mother now, she told us how she has been able to heal this pain through her own inner work and through the close relationship with her daughter.

Generational healing also occurred when Lynda received a reading from Maritza. Lynda's son was going through a difficult time, and what Maritza wrote supported her, inspiring a sense of peace. Lynda describes this message as "profound and meaningful":

> The first reading I ever received was from Maritza, and she drew masks and described the person as a traveler. A person who traveled on the wisps of breath. I had brought a stone that was my son's that he had drawn a compass on. At the time my son was in a dark place, and I was very concerned for his well-being. I believe my son is gifted but does not know how to see his gift, and that seems to torment him. I learned that this stone is what grounds him but allows him to travel. He is a traveler. There was something so profound and meaningful about this reading that I can't even really put it in words. What I do know is it brought me great peace and the ability to let go of my need to try and control what he was going through.

Messages with Repeated Themes

As Cathleen reviewed the pages she kept between July and December in 2017, she noted a progression of threads, from surrender to freedom and, finally, to expansion. "At the time," Cathleen explains, "It had been a year since my partner of 27 years and I had separated, and I was still adjusting to my new life." She says that "these readings really touched my heart and gave me a sense of hope due to the life changes I was experiencing at the time."

This July 28, 2017 reading is from Claudia:

Reading from Claudia, July 2017

The text of Claudia's reading for Cathleen is as follows:

Third eye

An owl looking around

An old gentleman, gray hair with a mustache in a white suit (sailor, captain) on a wooden, long dock.

Sounds of the night, crickets, sprinklers, birds, someone sitting on a white porch swing.

You will take a thousand steps before reaching. Don't despair. I am with you. I will guide you. I am your shelter, your lighthouse.

"Surrender"

Tenacity

A pink cactus flower (almost looked like the inside of a papaya). Develop the subconscious and be enveloped by the light.

The stars are aligning for you, summer is not yet over to do what you need to do.

Persevere, manifest, and the Universe shall respond in return with abundance and peace.

Receive with a joyous heart. Open your palms and just allow them to receive.

You are your own sanctuary. You are my temple, my shining light. I love you!

In this message for Cathleen, the word "surrender" stands by itself. Also the idea of a sanctuary pops up in terms of the phrase, "I am your shelter," and in the last couple sentences, "You are your own sanctuary, you are my temple, my shining light. I love you." After she received this message, Cathleen told me that "It was comforting to feel safe within the solitude of myself since I had experienced a separation followed by a new relationship." She continued, "Claudia also picked up on my daily routine of sitting outside on the 'sanctuary' of my front porch by myself in the evenings and enjoying the sounds of nature."

In September, Cathleen received a reading from me. In it, the word "surrender" is mentioned again, near the end: "tomorrow is the beginning of a new day—surrender?"

Kim's Reading for Cathleen, September 2017

This is the text of the reading:

> "Today is a day that the Lord hath made. Rejoice and be glad in it."
>
> New energy, new purpose—new meanings—manifesting from a blank page of life—full of light and vibration. A new phase, a new level for you—much growth ahead without struggle.
>
> Your choices will come easy—flowing with the energy of life. It arrives like a natural opening—a piece of nature inside and out, like a work of art. This art is you, and your life a masterpiece. What do you want to last? Create.
>
> I see a cabin—woods—your body needs rest, yet your mind needs freedom.
>
> Armchair adventures (through meditation or reading)
>
> Let go—tomorrow is the beginning of a new day — surrender?
>
> Let the energy and vibrations move up from your feet to your head at least once a day.
>
> Open arms to receive many, many, many blessings coming your way. (Included is an image of a stick figure with open arms with an equal sign next to the phrase "the new you"). Bring it on!

Hearing that, symbolically, "a new day" was coming after a sense of surrender "was comforting to hear," Cathleen said, and especially that a new phase or new level was coming "without struggle."

In the next reading, also from me, the word "release" fits into the same theme. The message also re-emphasizes "freedom," and "inner peace":

10/20/17   Kim for Cathleen

Bringer of Peace & Joy, we celebrate you on this journey. Light & healing supports you (and has been). The Heaviness a challenges you've been facing are beginning to make way for your progress. I see arch angel Gabriel wearing white + gold — s/he is with you, helping you release a burden — something that had been holding you back. (It felt like someone's hand on your Rt. shoulder preventing you from stepping forward). Gabriel is telling me that you can fly — only you allow yourself to hesitate now. Free yourself of feeling held back (not necessarily of the person holding you back) — because this is more than that — more than one person — it's a string of other related lessons.... all designed to help you grow. You know all this, but it's time to visualize your freedom. Once you do, the sense of inner knowing + power (self-esteem, confidence, manifesting "juice") will expand!

My Reading for Cathleen, October 2017

This is the text of that reading:

> Bringer of peace and joy, we celebrate you on this journey. Light and healing support you (and have been). The heaviness or challenges you've been facing are beginning to make way for your progress. I see arch angel Gabriel wearing white and gold—s/he is with you, helping you release a burden—something that had been holding you back. (It felt like someone's hand on you. Right shoulder, preventing you from stepping forward). Gabriel is telling me that you can fly—only you allow yourself to hesitate now. Free yourself of feeling held back (not necessarily of the person holding you back) because this is more than that—more than one person—it's a string of other related lessons, all designed to help you grow. You know all this, but it's time to visualize your freedom. Once you do, the sense of inner knowing and power (self-esteem, confidence, "manifesting juice") will expand!

Cathleen reacted to all three of these, saying "I had to let go of what was familiar, routine, or comfortable and surrender to what was going to show up in my life. I had been resistant to change, which may be represented by the symbolic hand holding me back." "The last reading confirmed," she said, "that the heaviness I had been feeling was subsiding and that I was making progress toward an expansive 'new me.'"

All three readings Cathleen received within this time frame also mention "light," and although, symbolically, enlightenment in these messages is something we take for granted, she said, "Those specific words signaled that my path was right for me and that it was supported by the wisdom of Universe."

Sometimes, looking back on the readings we've received, we see details now that we may have missed, made other assumptions about, or, at that time, taken for granted. Many of the women shared with me that they continue to refer to readings they've received through the years in order to look for patterns, repeated guidance, and validation. Adrienne sums it up this way:

All in all, the readings have helped me continue on my path with confidence and gratitude and grace. The group has been great support for me, and I have met some of the nicest women. It's a gift and a blessing. I keep them in a folder and refer to them from time to time because what was given was something I needed to hear.

CHAPTER 18

Third Benefit: Self-Confidence

Generally, most of us are taught to put more faith in institutions and creeds than in ourselves or our intuition. How is it that so many of us, all too often, have felt pushed to accept others' opinions and traditions as more important than our own sense of what is true? Where does this come from? The answer to these questions is not simple, and blaming our established institutions for that gets us nowhere. Although shared beliefs can keep societies from falling into chaos, if we are to live with open hearts and enjoy life and its relationships, we must learn to consult and trust our "sixth sense."

Among the list of benefits that group psychometry provides, self-confidence develops with time and practice. We all have an inner guidance system, and when we connect to that, it brings a feeling of "aliveness," love, and connection to our souls that feels real. That's where deep, transformative healing can change us from the inside out; it's where a healthy sense of self-confidence and spiritual maturity can grow. The following examples from group meetings illustrate this.

The "Surprise" of Giving a Helpful Reading

Receiving a reading that confirms something in our lives boosts our confidence in the choices we've been making, but providing a helpful reading can do so much more! Because it feels almost magical, a successful reading shows us that inner wisdom is not only limited to our physical senses but also stems from our spiritual or extra-sensory systems. It's evidence to us that we can connect to a larger sense of who we are—our souls, or Spirit, or God-consciousness—in a way that feels wondrous.

Nearly everyone in the group mentioned being nervous before, during, and after providing their first reading. At the risk of sounding repetitive or boring, I'm including how each expressed their initial fears. It's important to see because they moved through that challenge as well as others they encountered. All of the participants come from different levels of experience and backgrounds, yet as they witness how amazingly accurate their intuition can be, they feel something new that replaces their fears—joy and surprise.

Suman's First Experience with Psychometry

I'd never heard of psychometry until a friend, Jaye, described the session to me one evening over dinner. She talked about getting messages for people simply by holding an object that belonged to them. I'd never tried anything like it before, but this friend was very excited about it, and she said that the messages came through from Spirit and were very meaningful to the person receiving them. She asked if I would be interested in attending one such session, and I readily agreed.

When the day finally arrived, I remember feeling more than a little excited, but I also wondered – what if it doesn't work? I didn't want the person whose object I would pick to feel deprived! What if my imagination took over and I analyzed the object instead?

I started to relax during the meditation that preceded the object reading and by the time we were done, I was able to completely let go of all my fears and apprehensions and just be.

I wish I could remember the object I picked that day or the reading itself. All I remember is that the moment I selected the object and held it in my hand, I felt bombarded with images and impressions and rather than try to decipher what these meant, I let the words flow as best as I could without getting in the way.

At the end of the session, I was nervous about reading what I had written, but to my pleasant surprise, the message was well received and clearly understood. The reading that I received that day was also amazing. I received the confirmation that I had been seeking and something shifted in me for good.

We all have extra senses that we're either unaware of or dismiss as overactive imaginations! I think that if we are truly spiritual beings on a physical journey, our communications begin in the non-physical plane first, and what we experience by way of words and gestures is only a fraction of what wants to be known by us.

Rita's First Experience in the Group

On the night of my first meeting, I was so warmly welcomed by all the women that I immediately felt at ease with the affection and kindness I felt. As the evening progressed, Kim led a meditation that was wonderful. It put me at ease, and I could feel the connection and positive energy of the other women.

We had all placed a small object in a bowl, which was covered and unknown to each other. As the bowl was passed around the room, each of us quietly and discreetly took an object. I can remember so clearly how it felt to hold that object in my hand. I immediately received a rush of images in my mind. It was so strong and clear. I then had to put any doubts out of my mind and start writing.

When I finished writing the first few phrases, I closed my eyes and quietly listened. To my surprise and delight, I received more images, and more words started to flow. I quickly wrote them down, thinking I might lose them at any moment.

When it came my turn to read, I remember feeling very nervous. I truly wanted my reading to mean something to the person receiving it, and I was delighted that it did.

In the days that followed, I couldn't stop thinking about the whole experience. I could feel a shift in myself, a deeper sense of my intuition. Without a doubt, I could feel a confidence rising in me. I could hear my inner voice; it was stronger than ever before. This experience was life-affirming, and it left me in wondrous anticipation for the next meeting.

Helen's Experience at a Church Retreat

Rita and I met Helen about six years ago at a retreat sponsored by the local Unity church. She ended up sitting at a table with us for one of the classes we shared. Later that day, I taught a class titled, "We are all Healers and Intuitives," which Helen also attended.

During the class, I led the group in some exercises to enhance their spiritual connections and intuitive nature. Then I asked attendees to place a question they wanted to be answered (without using their full names) on an index card and fold it within in an envelope so that no one could see. We put the envelopes in a basket and passed them to the next table. Each person who chose to participate would take a numbered envelope without looking inside, and after connecting with it intuitively and energetically, would write down the answer they received on a separate sheet of paper.

At the end of the exercise, when the numbered envelopes had been redistributed, several people stood up and shared the responses they received. One woman stood up, her eyes welling up in tears as well as amazement. She said, "This reading was so spot on that I can't believe it. I didn't use my name, but I asked a general question about my health. I am still shocked by the accuracy of the answer: 'Your surgery will be successful, and all will be well.' I didn't mention that I was supposed to be having hip surgery, but my answer mentioned the word. I am just so grateful, . . . so grateful." The applause in the room surprised her as well. Everyone looked at each other, asking, "Is that the reading you did?"

As we got to know Helen through our local Unity church, I invited her to attend psychometry because she had enjoyed the retreat so much. Months later, as we got to know Helen, she leaned over to me as if to tell me a secret, whispering, "Remember the woman at the retreat who stood up and cried because she received a reading that really amazed her? Although I never told her, I wrote that."

Both of our eyes widened, and I looked at Helen, "Why didn't you tell me this before?"

Helen smiled sheepishly. "I am still building confidence, I guess. Part of me thinks it was just coincidental, but I'm working on believing in myself."

Confidence-Building Takes Time

Sometimes, however, guests to the group find that their fears are too difficult to overcome. A few women told me weeks after their first and only attempt that they just didn't feel comfortable enough giving readings or judged themselves incapable of providing something they felt only professionals could do. And even when a reading is successful, I've heard many women in the group say that it was difficult for them to believe in themselves.

Helen mentioned that she needed time to build her confidence, which is a healthy attitude, actually. Self-doubt is quite common, especially during the first few readings. As I've mentioned before, the group provides a nurturing atmosphere for spiritual connection and intuitive practice, which naturally builds confidence. But no matter how much I try to convince those who are on the fence that the group's inclination is to appreciate rather than judge, it's difficult for anyone to believe that unless they witness it more than a few times. Below are examples from several women in the group who discuss what helped them work through their self-doubts.

Even though she had some connection with her own intuition, she still thought of herself as a "novice." On her first visit, she told us that her grandmother had the gift of psychic insight and that she felt this could also be true of herself. Claudia's early childhood experiences and messaging did not allow her to claim this for herself like her grandmother did; instead, she kept it quiet, applying her intuition naturally in life as the opportunities arose but never quite trusting it. She tells us more about this, in her own words:

> My dear friend Lynda invited me to attend my first meeting. She described it as "a group of very spiritually-connected women who would give messages to each other based on personal items they would bring to the group." This was so very new to me, so I went and did a little research on it and found some interesting and fascinating information online. I decided to give it a try. That first meeting I felt very nervous and self-conscious. I was very concerned that being a "novice" at it would result in what I considered a "poor" reading. One of the reasons I joined was because as part of my journey at the time, I was trying to connect with my intuition, which I felt had somehow left me.
>
> I remember trying really hard to concentrate, but my thoughts kept circling in my head. I began to doubt my ability to even come up with one sentence. Then I just relaxed and decided not to have any expectations or put any pressure on myself to do it "perfectly." To my surprise I was able to actually "see" messages through very vivid imagery, and I felt a sense of joy but also a little skepticism because part of me (probably my ego) wanted to dismiss the power of my Knowing.
>
> After we went around and I heard the caliber of everyone else's reading, I felt nervous about mine. When it was my turn, to my dismay, the person I was doing the reading for

was one of the hosts! My heart dropped because I thought, "how could I even provide anything worthy?" But Kim was very gracious and received what was of value to her.

As I sit back and reflect about that first experience, I realize how much better I got at receiving messages. It was like exercising a muscle; the more I did it, the easier it got. My readings became very clear, and the imagery very precise as time went by.

Adrienne's Confidence Grew by the Second Try

Having studied healing and mediumship at Arthur Findlay College in England, Adrienne had previous experience with metaphysics. Even so, she talks about how she still felt "nervous" about doing her first psychometry reading for someone:

Being new to the group, I was nervous about giving a message for the first time. I wanted so much to bring in something that had meaning and was understood. I had not done psychometry in years, so I wasn't sure how well I would do with it. Someone in the group described the process of giving the reading as silently asking in our hearts what the person needed. So I did.

All I remember about the message I gave is that I saw a woman like myself going through a change and there were choices she was going to have to make. I saw an older female in spirit who may have been a guide or family member, one who was going to help with these changes. This message was received in a positive manner, and I was given feedback which was helpful for me.

The second time I gave a reading, I felt more confident. As I held another person's object and received information for them, a female presence came through in a way that felt very strong. The presence told me that she was the grandmother, and she showed me several pictures. When it was time for me to share what I had received, I showed the object to the group, a ring, and read the message aloud. The woman who had brought it said that the ring had belonged to her grandmother, and she confirmed everything I had told her. I think I was as happy as she was to get the message and also to know that I was able to receive it so clearly.

In Adrienne's case, she was able to feel more confident on her second visit, which is rare. For most, it takes continued effort as well as quite a bit of courage to give a reading, whether it's the first time or the tenth—even among friends. Feeling safe and believing that whatever we say might be helpful to another person can help alleviate those "performance" fears.

Tammy's Reading of the Pen

One of our most recent members, Tammy, says that the group is "strengthening" her belief in herself and her abilities, "slowly but surely." She explained it this way: "I struggle with remembering/retaining and connecting dots on a lot of things. I have had a lot of self-judgment about the readings I've given but did feel a little better about the last one for Elizabeth and her dad's pen. It kind of surprised me a little bit to be honest."

Again, giving a reading can often feel like a "surprise," because when a person gets comfortable with the process, the easy flow of information feels fresh and new. In the reading Tammy mentions, Elizabeth had put a pen in the bowl. The message Tammy wrote began with

> "Sweet child, you are the master creator of the story of your life. Your words are powerful and sacred, loving and humble—both verbal and written wisdom. Sharing your truth will help others in profound and healing ways. Your heart is pure, and you are loved exactly as you are."

Elizabeth explained that the pen had belonged to her father, but now she uses it daily for journaling each morning. Her ritual includes pulling a Tarot card and then some narrative writing. The key points Tammy mentions seemed to come from Elizabeth's dad, who had just passed the previous year.

When Tammy explained how she felt, she expressed how her confidence began to grow through a combination of inner work on feeling worthiness, focusing on the importance of her own spiritual growth and her courage to join others in the same process. She describes it this way:

> Getting to hang out and know these beautiful ladies has been the biggest gift of all! I had never been a part of such a lovely group of women (or any for that matter). To be honest, the idea terrified me. I remember Lynda and Amy speaking to me about it quite some time ago, and I dismissed it completely. I have done a bit of work on myself since then and am beginning to give myself permission to partake in things I never felt worthy of. This has been an incredible experience in spiritual growth. Everyone is so inspiring that I want to soak up all of their beautiful energies!

A Vivid Experience Can Come as a Surprise

When giving a reading, we can tune into something so real that it stays with us. True, undeniable experience can certainly minimize self-doubt. In Allie's case, she said, "My most vivid experience was when I picked a ring that had belonged to Kim's father. I saw a leather horse saddle. It was the first time seeing something vivid as that picture in my mind. I was so glad when Kim said that her father rode horses. I was glad to be able to make that connection for her."

Initially, Allie told me that she felt a bit of anxiety about giving a reading. On a subsequent visit, in May 2019, she picked my object from the bowl again (of course, without knowing the object was mine), and began the reading by saying, "You have an immense amount of energy!"

The text of her reading is below, followed by an image of it:

> You have an immense amount of energy! I see a kayak moving very fast through a beautiful river with the sun

shining through the trees. You bring joy wherever you go. You are ready to take on a new project or adventure. You don't have to figure out every detail as you go. Trust each step being present in the moment. Those who know you appreciate you more than you know. Saw a dog about the size of a German Shepherd. He or she was barking angrily. After some time, the dog was calm. Trust in source with all your being. Source will direct you in the way in which to go.

Kim's Reading from Allie

Allie's message confirmed what had currently been happening in my life as well as what I had been planning. For example, I had just started renting a clinic space and seeing clients for craniosacral therapy and massage. I was heavily involved in building my business, and, at the same time, Rita and I made the decision to build a house. We were also planning to go to Peru with friends within the next few weeks—the new adventure she mentions. So, yes, I had a lot of energy swirling around all of this in my life. She also mentions a dog the size of a German shepherd, and around that time, our dog, Princess, a Rat Terrier, had been scared by two large dogs similar to German Shepherds in the neighborhood. They were off their leads, running directly toward her. The dogs scared her so much that she jumped waist high into Rita's arms to get away from them. After getting home, Princess calmed down, uninjured.

Sometimes a message can signal an event in the present or future while also confirming the past, which actually is quite helpful because we are more likely, then, to trust the predictions. Allie, who had no previous experience giving readings, was able to pick up on all of this despite her fears. Her experience, however, is not isolated, as so many of these examples illustrate.

Sabrina's Journey from Skepticism to Trust

When I met Sabrina in 2012, for years she had been longing to have another baby. At the time, she had a grown daughter in high school, and even though it took several years for her desire to manifest, she finally had another baby in 2019. Her determination extends to other areas of her life as well, which includes overcoming her fears and saying "yes" to joining the group even though she wasn't completely sure what we did. This is her story:

> I've always known that I had some type of ability to see the future, to kind of predict events, and see Spirit and talk to loved ones on the other side. But when I was younger, I never really tapped into it too much because I was afraid and was taught that it was evil, something people shouldn't do. So I pushed it off and didn't want to really open up to that. I shut it down. For about ten years I had kept it turned off until I met these amazing women through a friend of mine who introduced me to the church.
>
> So I said, "Sure I don't mind trying this group. That would be great. I would love it." It seemed to be a group

of women that I could relate to, and they can relate to me, which was amazing because you don't find many people out there like you—or it's not talked about because it's taboo.

Well, I looked online to see what psychometry was, and when I was doing my research online, I got a little leery because I wondered, "How can someone read an object from someone else?" Or "How is it that these women are practicing this? Are they protecting themselves, are they using light and love and only using positive energy?" I didn't really know these women at the time, and so I was a little concerned for my own safety and for the group's safety—knowing from past experience how people can use these abilities negatively.

I'm open minded even though a little skeptical. I was more skeptical about myself, though, and wondered if I would be able to do this more so than doubting the group—because it had been such a long time that I had used my abilities for anything. And I didn't know I could read an object. That's not my forte. I can only see dead people or things that would potentially happen in the future—but I had not been able to see or read the energy from an object. So I said, "No, I don't think I can do that," but Kim reassured me that I could. Anyone could. She said, "You just sit quietly, trust Spirit, and trust your intuition."

When I had my first reading for someone else, I picked up the object and at first, I didn't feel anything or see anything like I once did before, so that discouraged me a bit. I went into my head and told myself, "See, you can't do this . . . It's not your forte." I had to shut that off and say, "No, let me keep an open mind, and let me go back and really concentrate on this object," and so I did. I think everyone must feel that way in the beginning. And once I started to let go and trust my intuition, trust spirit and let spirit guide me and give me the answers that this person needed to hear, I was able then to see things and feel things. I was amazed by this experience overall and how I was able to help the person I did a reading for.

But then, as I listened to the other readings, I got kind of worried that mine wasn't good enough because everyone else's seemed so elaborate, so beautiful, and so powerful that I thought, "Oh my gosh, mine wasn't all that great." I can see now that I had let myself go too far into my head and didn't let Spirit do its job. Later, though, as I continued to attend, I saw that my readings got much better (in my opinion anyway).

Overall, my experiences with the group have always been positive. In the past when I was reading people and wasn't protecting myself, I was very scared of being energetically vulnerable.

As Sabrina explains, attending the group and giving more readings helped her continue to develop trust in herself and her abilities.

Getting Over the Hurdle of Judging Our Own Readings

Sabrina is not unique in terms of comparing her first psychometry reading to others'. I've heard several of the attendees say the same thing. The best advice we can offer each other for building confidence is patience and continued practice. In Eileen's case, it took about three visits to "trust her gut" that whatever reading she gives—whether the information is a little or a lot—is "just fine."

It's difficult to describe what I felt during that first session. For someone unused to consciously feeling the energy around them, the healing circle was very good and just a little scary simply because it was outside of my prior experience. As for giving my first reading, I was afraid I could do it wrong even though we'd been told we couldn't really be wrong. That feeling increased as a few others gave their readings. Their messages seemed so descriptive and seemingly in-depth. There I was, holding my paper with four or five short sentences, wondering if I had messed up somehow or (even worse) if the person whose object I had would feel short-changed. Of course, those worries were groundless. It still took me about three more meetings to know in my gut that however little or much information that comes through is just fine.

Similar to Eileen, another participant, Dee, expressed that she had some concern about her readings as well: "Each time I give a reading, I have some reservation about its validity; however, the response I receive reminds me that Spirit's guidance is accurate and that I am empowered not only in myself, but in the efficacy of the spirituality of the group." She also mentions another important point: "Once in a while, even the most experienced group participants have difficulty with a reading, for whatever reason." Yes, sometimes even those who have given more readings than others have difficulty occasionally, which can occur for a variety of reasons. I've already mentioned the big one—the uncertainty of discerning and trusting what we're sensing, hearing, and seeing on behalf of another. I'll come back to this again at the end of the chapter, but first, let's explore other reasons for why this could happen.

Situations When Giving a Reading Can Be Particularly Challenging

Every time we give a reading, we connect with "energy," and the quality of this "energy" influences the exchange of information. I prepare our group space beforehand, and I pray for divine protection and wisdom to come through for each person's highest good. Nothing in the group has ever occurred to cause me to doubt that. Given this, whatever "energy" each person picks up from the objects they bring or in terms of what each person discerns, will be exactly whatever is needed. Psychometry, though, not only relies on the quality of energy but on its quantity.

Although I've mentioned this briefly in a prior chapter, I want to re-emphasize that the amount of energy emanating from an object often depends on the frequency of its use or its significance. A ring I've worn day and night for ten years most certainly emanates energy of both quantity and quality. My father's wedding ring, even though it's been sitting in a drawer for over 50 years now, still holds a sense of importance—a sense of love and connection that the Universe can speak through. Perhaps my faith creates the foundation for the energy to come through or perhaps I'm just proving my readiness, and divine timing brings the message through more than anything else. Regardless, there is no question that both the quality and quantity of energy in an object make a difference.

Usually, an object has to have a certain "aliveness" to us—a connection we can relate to—in order to provide enough energetic resonance to register in a reading. If I have only worn a watch a few times, it wouldn't hold much of my imprint and would be difficult to read. A challenge occurred with this during a group meeting about a year ago, and Elizabeth explains it from her point of view:

> When I hold the object, of course, the first thing that pops into my mind is, "What does this person need to know?" But last night, in the group, I was sitting with Pat's bracelet, and I mean, this was very unusual. Nothing was coming. I mean, not even energy . . . nothing, nothing. And I thought, "What the heck is going on?" I didn't look at it, but I had to look at it because I could not imagine why I wasn't getting anything off of this. So I looked at it, and I thought, "Okay."
>
> So then I put the object down on the paper and put my hand over top of it, hoping that that would help provide some energy. Eventually, I was able to feel some things, but that is not typically the way that it works. Typically, I pull it from the bowl. I close my eyes, I sit with it, and it just starts to come and I receive all kinds of things. It just depends upon whatever it is. And this, it was very, very unusual. I really had to sit with it longer. It was like

I had a little fear in there. In fact, it was difficult, actually. So I dug in. In my mind, I sat myself down and thought, "There's got to be something in here regardless . . . there has to be." And so just a few bits and pieces came, but it still didn't feel quite right compared to several other readings that I've done.

In that meeting several people had difficulty starting. As I heard people talk about their experience having a little difficulty, I thought it was fascinating that I had the same experience. I'm like, "Why isn't something coming?" And then you get that little bit of panic. But there's a great reinforcement to your own intuition when you just go back to the feeling of that meditation and let it calm everything. Then I can ask again, "What do I need to tell them?" and let it come through. Something comes through—it may not be a lot, but something will come through. Even if it's just a little bit. Well, we have to figure that whatever we received is all that they needed. And that's what I had to tell myself. That's exactly the road I had to go down because I thought, "there has to be something here, right?"

I just got one piece of information for Sabrina, whereas normally I get several. The more I sat with it, the more the reading kept coming back to the same message, so I thought, "Well, that just must be it." It seemed a simple message, but it really resonated with her. So, afterward, it's like "Wow, that's what it was meant to be then." And it's funny because it felt like I wasn't getting anything.

After we had all given readings and closed the circle, I talked about the difficulty connecting with these objects with Pat and a few of the others. We concluded that in each case, the object didn't hold enough energy. Pat said, "Oh, I've only worn it just a few times and it was in the jewelry box." The same for Rita. She said that she had that object less than a week.

So I think there was just not enough energy built up in a few of the objects for us to ease into a message. But the surprising thing about this is that it really validates what you do. Because you feel so strongly at other times when this kind of challenge doesn't happen. That's the black and white. You think to yourself—that's the reason why the panic that sets in is so great—because this is not what your "typical reading" feels like. Then you realize how much and how important that "typical" has become when you're not able to find it at that moment.

So this was very unusual. But, you know, with this new lesson and everything, I figure that it will happen again, and when it happens again, I will remember this moment and know that it's okay, that it will come up and the second time around will not be near as fearful or as alarming. That was the lesson for me—how I take for granted when I'm able to pick the object up and automatically start going. That's right, you know, I don't even think twice about it, and that sets the bar pretty high.

What Elizabeth expresses here is deep and multi-faceted. From this, we learn that a reading relies not only the energy built up in the object but also upon something even more important—our history as readers, our connection to spiritual resources, the level of our inner confidence, and resilience.

Allowing Doubt and Learning From It

As we move through doubt, the goal is to grow from it rather than let it stifle our questioning mind or natural state of wonder. Elizabeth, for example, worked through her fear of not being able to receive guidance for the person who brought the object by quieting herself, trying a different approach, and being persistent.

On another night, an even more challenging opportunity presented itself to Pat. That evening, she happened to pick out a ring I had placed in the bowl. When it was time for her to speak, she held up the ring and asked whose it was. After I told her that I put it in the bowl, her eyes pointed at me with a laser focus as she said, "This ring isn't yours, is it?" Well, nearly everyone gasped and smiled at this because Pat's directness can sometimes come as a shock.

Pat added, "The first few sentences are for you. They are from *A Course in Miracles*. The rest is about the person who owned the ring."

I explained to her and the group that it was a ring that may have belonged to my mother's mother. I had found it in storage after my stepfather passed. It was a sterling silver band that looked well-loved and felt to me as if it carried some of her energy in it. She died two years before I was born, and I have always wanted to know more about her. But just in case the ring didn't have enough energy in it for a reading, I wore it for almost a week prior to putting it into the bowl.[71]

Pat told us that while she was writing the message, at a certain point near the end, she stopped her pen because she suddenly started to worry that what she was receiving might be wrong. The image of her reading shows this at the point where she wrote, "She/He." Pat explained this to us in the group as she read the message aloud, stopping to insert a comment or two.

I've included the text below, as well as an image of her reading:

There is a place in you where nothing is impossible. There is a place in you where there is perfect peace. There is a place in you that the presence of God abides.

This person loved music and occasionally wrote a piece or two. She loved to bake and was "over the top." She should have entered some baking contest. She always wanted to play the guitar but could never master it. She overcame some hardships that none of you were aware of. Perhaps

---

[71] Of course, receiving a message from a parent or grandparent doesn't require an object with their energy in it. The following month after this, I placed one of my own rings in the bowl, and Angel's reading for me that night included some advice from my grandfather.

you got a hint occasionally but never the whole truth because a happy face was always put on. She/He made an imprint everywhere she went, and it will be carried on always and forever.

There is a place in you where nothing is impossible
There is a place in you where there is perfect peace
There is a place in you that the presence of God abides.
This person loved music & occasionly wrote a piece or two. She loved to bake & was was "over the top". She should have entered some baking contest. She always wanted to play the guitar but could never master it. She overcame some hardship's that none of you were aware of. Perhaps you got a hind occasionaly but never the whole truth because a happy face was always put on. She/He made an imprint everywhere she went and it will be carried on always & forever.

Pat's reading for me, from my grandmother's ring

Pat's reading helped me get to know my grandmother, "Alkie," better, and what she said aligns with the bits and pieces I've heard from my mother. I thought my love for music came from my father, who played piano and organ, but I can see that a love of music could have come from my mother's side as well. As Pat's reading suggests, my grandmother was a skilled baker, and my mother must have inherited that; she could have won awards herself.

Of course, Alkie's generation lived through WWI, the Great Depression, WWII, and the Korean War, but those are not the hardships Pat refers to. My grandfather was injured in a coal mining accident, and a surgeon had to place a metal plate in his head. He died in 1931 when my mother was two. I don't know how their family was able to survive financially both before and after he passed.

What Pat quoted from *A Course in Miracles* was comforting to hear. A reading like that can bring forward a lot of memories, both painful and pleasant, and I know that at some point I can go within to reconnect myself to the stream of love within my family, and even more importantly, "abide" with God.

Pat struggled with self-doubt at one point in the reading—a part that could have affected the rest, but she stayed true to what she received by questioning and staying open to the message. Her ability to provide such a helpful reading didn't just occur because she is naturally gifted or has given several readings. Her confidence comes from not being afraid to allow a healthy degree of doubt.

Having confidence, however, can be double-edged. If we become overly self-assured, our ego takes over and causes us to miss information we need to share. Similarly, having too many doubts can be stifling. I can't help but think of the story about the monkey with his fist in a hollowed-out coconut. He wants the treat inside, but in order to release his hand from the trap and avoid getting caught, he has to let it go. Too much confidence can be like that—it's like a closed fist that won't allow anything else inside. Like Richard Rohr says, "Without a certain ability to let go, to trust, to allow, we won't get to any new place."[72] What we can learn from this is that

---

[72] Richard Rohr, "Faithful Resilience: Weekly Summary," Daily Meditations, Center for Action and Contemplation, January 27, 2024, https://cac.org/daily-meditations/faithful-resilience-weekly-summary.

when an experienced reader senses a doubt rising to the surface, it can be either part of the message or used as an opportunity for growth.

So how can we practice that? In the book, *Opening to Channel: How to Connect With Your Guide*, Sanaya Roman and Duane Packer say that doubts can be helpful because they "slow you down."[73] They explain that learning to channel (or, by extension, giving readings) brings more light into a person's life, and just as being in sunlight too long without adequate protection can cause a person to burn, channeling too much, too fast, prevents the body and/or the psyche from adapting. In other words, getting to know what our process is and whether—or how—to question what we're receiving is part of how we learn to improve.

Roman and Packer go on to say that we all have multi-faceted personalities that balance each other—a side of us that dreams and another side that's practical. The same is true for using our intuition or receiving messages; we have a receiving channel that opens us up to psychic dictation, so to speak, but we also have an inner critic that prompts us to question everything about that. "The difference between those who become excellent channels and those who don't," they say, "is that those who excel keep channeling and don't let their doubts stop them. . . . Those who ask, 'How can I be better?' use their doubts as positive forces, bringing through better and stronger connections to their guides."[74] One of their best suggestions for embracing that is giving our intuition a task to do— by asking it to only provide information that is useful.[75] As we continue to practice using our intuition, it's helpful to realize that doubt can be our friend. The goal is not to stop self-doubt but to grow from it, to let it serve as motivation, to ask our sixth sense to bring helpful information for ourselves and others, and then expect, in Elizabeth's words, to keep setting that bar "pretty high."

---

[73] Sanaya Roman and Duane Packer, *Opening to Channel: How to Connect With Your Guide*, (Tiburon, CA: H.J. Kramer, Inc., 1987), 177.

[74] Roman and Packer, *Opening*, 179-180.

[75] Roman and Packer, *Opening*, 179-180.

CHAPTER 19

Fourth Benefit: Opening Our Hearts

From feeling part of a like-minded community . . . to feeling the joy of helping others . . . to developing more confidence, each benefit of being in a psychometry group is interwoven with all of the others, which is particularly the case with this next one, experiencing the gift of an open heart. Although intuition is not completely separate from our mental awareness and sense of logic, the threads of our intuitive senses truly work best when they connect energetically to our hearts. Naparstek calls this "empathic attunement," or "keeping the heart open to the world around us—to people, places, ourselves, and the divine."[76] When this happens, she says, behavior "tends to become more patient, generous, and kind."[77]

Helen said that when she anticipated coming to the group for the first time, she felt nervous, but after reading the email I sent out, and feeling comfortable with Rita and me, she said, "I could see that this was a place without judgment, a place where I could practice opening myself up without fear of criticism." It's evident that having a connection was the first key to feeling more comfortable about coming, but the other necessary component is non-judgment, which, she says, allows her to open herself in a safe space. Both provide the necessary foundation for what often happens in the group: heart-centered conversation and personal growth.

Everyone's effort in the exchange of readings is naturally full of compassion and empathy. The comments and readings I'm including in this chapter reach even deeper to reveal vulnerability and openness.

---

[76] Naparstek, *Sixth Sense*, 49.

[77] Naparstek, *Sixth Sense*, 49.

Each example provides its own evidence of how heart-opening the group experience can be.

Phyllis's Precognitive Reading for Cathleen

Although I can receive part of a message a few minutes prior to picking up the object, some of the women in the group say that they sometimes receive messages days before we meet. This happened to Phyllis even though giving readings was a new experience for her. In light of what Penney Peirce says about compassion producing the highest, most efficient level of intuition,[78] I believe Phyllis's concern about her friend, Cathleen, opened her to receive the message she describes below.

> One of the first readings I gave was for my dear friend, Cathleen. As I sat heart-open to the messages I was to receive from this object I was holding, my vibration elevated. I just relaxed into this, trusting what was to come. I don't remember what was written, only that it was filled with pure love. The lyrics to a song came clearly to mind. "Carry on my wayward son. There'll be peace when you are done. Lay your weary head to rest. Don't you cry no more."
>
> I was impacted that Cathleen was the person to receive this message. For several weeks prior to our psychometry meeting, I'd been feeling that although my friend possessed deep compassion and wisdom and was sent here to share it, she was struggling to embrace who and what she was. So I thought the message of the lyrics was so perfect, and I think she felt the same way.

---

[78] Penney Peirce, *The Intuitive Way: A Guide to Living From Inner Wisdom* (Hillsboro OR: Beyond Words Publishing, Inc., 1997), 84.

Rita's "Sing to Me" Reading for Helen

Compassion and love are frequent themes from many of the readings within the group, and Rita has given a few readings that touched others so deeply that they cried. Several months ago, her reading for Helen confirmed the presence of love in her life. I asked Rita to describe how she felt as she wrote this particular message for Helen:

> First, I closed my eyes and held her object. Right now, I can't really remember the object, but it's the feeling I'm left with . . . the feeling that I had washed over me because I felt a great sense of love in her life and of her letting go . . . of light flowing through her. There was definitely a strong presence of love washing over her.

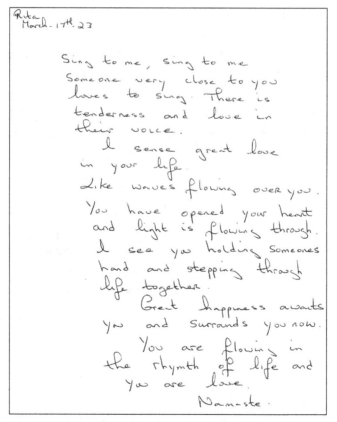

Rita
March - 17th. 23

Sing to me, sing to me
Some one very close to you
loves to sing. There is
tenderness and love in
their voice.
    I sense great love
in your life.
Like waves flowing over you.
You have opened your heart
and light is flowing through.
I see you holding someones
hand and stepping through
life together.
    Great happiness awaits
you and surrounds you now.
    You are flowing in
the rhymth of life and
you are love.
            Namaste.

Rita's Reading for Helen

The text of her reading is as follows:

> Sing to me sing to me. Someone very close to you loves to sing. There is tenderness and love in their voice. I sense great love in your life, like waves flowing over you. You have opened your heart, and light is flowing through. I see you holding someone's hand and stepping through life together. Great happiness awaits you and surrounds you now. You are flowing in the rhythm of life. And you are love. Namaste.

During our conversation about the reading—which occurred at least a week afterward—Rita held a copy of what she wrote and looked at me: "I'm left with—sitting here today—still that sense, that feeling of a heart opening and letting love into her life and of the waves of love washing over Helen and the other person as they step forward through life. I'm honored to have given her that reading."

The message mentions stepping through life holding someone's hand—which could be either romantic or familial. Either way, the reading resonated with Helen because after Rita originally gave her the reading, Helen laughed and stood up to hug Rita, saying, "Yes, yes. That's what my family and my boyfriend were doing recently—all of us singing to each other at the dining room table." The joy in her reaction was infectious. Helen is a single parent who loves and supports her two girls with every fiber of her being. They were singing as well, and Helen smiled broadly as she reflected on it for the group. As Helen finished responding to what Rita wrote and started focusing on the reading she would be giving next, I noticed a slight blush in her face at the mention of a new love in her life.

Readings that Inspire Healing Support

Two of the readings Lynda has given over the years shed light on what she referred to as "dark" challenges going on in two people's lives. One reading was for Pat which resulted in the group creating a healing circle around her (mentioned in an earlier chapter).

The other was given to Maritza. Lynda said, "I remember seeing a person trapped inside a shed, scared and alone . . . but there was a crack of light, and that small crack of light provided hope." After Lynda read this message aloud in the group, Maritza explained to all of us that her heart ached for her grandson who was going through a very difficult challenge at home with his father. This reading, just like the one Lynda gave Pat, opened our hearts. Several people hugged Maritza and spoke with her afterward, offering whatever support she might need. Immediately, we prayed for this situation to be resolved in the best possible way.

Lynda explains how a reading like this comes to her:

> The connection and supportive energetic exchange that occurred and continues to occur is an experience that is very deeply touching to my spirit. It is a complete surrender, dropping into my heart and being totally present in the moment. It is as if the veil drops, and I am able to see behind the curtain to receive the message that the receiver needs to hear.

When Lynda gives a reading, it comes from her heart. I sense that the "dark" readings she mentions came about due to others' need for healing, and this encouraged Maritza and others to feel safe while expressing such deep pain and sorrow.

A Reminder of Deep Love

It's not just readings that open people's hearts, however. When I asked Amy to share why she keeps coming to the psychometry group, she wrote the following description of each person's willingness to be vulnerable and receptive:

> After writing, participants shared their personalized readings with the object's owner. The vulnerability of the sharing connected the group. Each reader went beyond her comfort zone and spoke in phrases such as "I'm not sure this will mean anything to you ..." or "not sure

where this came from but ..." or "maybe you can make sense of this ..." The reception of the reading was just as gracious, with each receiver connecting its accuracy to her life experience and expressing gratitude for the gift of exchange.

Such vulnerability and courage, I thought, as I reflected. Such a gift each giver and receiver both offered and received in the experience! As the reader shared, she offered gifts of insight, attention, divine connection, and love; in return she received full acceptance, presence, affirmation, and gratitude. I was left with a sweet appreciation for each woman in the group, and for the heightened awareness of divine energy that is always present and available to each and every one of us.

The experience of that day changed me in a fundamental way. The connection within the room to the Divine translated as a reminder of deep love. I've continued participating in Kim's psychometry group for many years now and have improved my ability to connect to the seen and unseen.

Amy illustrates the presence of love within each exchange. It's not just felt but heard. Taking this reminder of love a step further, Eileen challenges us to let it permeate our thoughts as well, since "love is the driving force behind everything":

The biggest thing I must remind myself is that the only absolute is that love is the driving force behind everything even if (perhaps especially if) I can't see it right now. I can say, above all, "We are blessed, we are loving, we are loved." Knowing, not just intellectually, but also in my heart that the group is a safe, supportive, judgment-free space full of people who truly seek to uplift one another is one reason I keep coming back.

CHAPTER 20

Fifth Benefit: Self-Awareness and Trust

Developing Heart-Awareness

When I was young, Sunday school classes would often ask students to memorize scriptures, and I enjoyed that. Sometimes the scripture appeared below a picture, and I distinctly remember one beautiful image of Jesus standing at a wooden door, knocking. Of course, the scripture passage accompanying it was, "Behold, I stand at the door and knock; if anyone hears My voice and opens the door, I will come in to him and will dine with him, and he with Me."[79] The lesson that the teacher offered us from this was fairly simple: our hearts are like doors, and Jesus waits for permission to enter. Letting Jesus into our hearts was a common theme in the Baptist churches I attended, and I still carry this image in my mind, nearly sixty years later. But now the difference is that, to me, Jesus represents not only himself as a Divine being but an expansive state of higher consciousness.

Opening my heart to that level presents opportunities for continued spiritual and personal growth. It includes becoming more aware of my words and actions, staying open to my inner guidance, and setting higher standards regarding my character and well-being. Opening that "door" requires responsibility. Roman and Packer describe this as awakening to the Higher Self or Light Body. They say that while working with the fourth energy center, or heart chakra, "you may experience a stronger

---

[79] Revelation 3:20, New American Standard Version.

sense of personal power, ability to control your emotions, stay centered, release old blocks and stuck emotional energy, and respond with love and compassion."[80]

Contrary to thinking that an open heart can only make us vulnerable to personal attack, I believe that our heart can expand in such a way that it connects to and aligns all of our energy centers—from our base chakra to our crown. This alignment is the first step toward developing more inner awareness, trust, and strength. So while keeping our heart open, we become more conscious and aware, stronger yet more sensitive to our own and others' needs.

The following stories from the group illustrate how psychometry can support this kind of awareness.

Finding Her Voice, One Step at a Time

Previously, I mentioned that Claudia had closed herself off from her intuitive gifts. In a reading for her, Lynda mentioned that she saw a "looking glass through time" which showed "a way to see who we are." Lynda said that she felt no worries or fear in the message, only "glimpses of grace," and then encouraged Claudia to "let cool water soothe the ocean of her soul." Lynda also heard a song, too, and wrote down one of the lines, "Put one foot in front of the other, and soon you'll be walking out the door."

Working with our intuition is often like looking through time—sometimes mirroring the past, and sometimes gazing into the future—and we don't always know which is which. Whenever we receive a message for another person, it's important to express it and let it go because sometimes the messenger or recipient can get caught up in analysis, or even worse—rush to make major life changes without thinking. The emphasis in Claudia's reading is to "put one foot in front of the other"—to keep going, one step at a time. That is not only how we grow but how our lives change—through action as well as thoughtful, daily reflection.

---

[80] Sanaya Roman and Duane Packer, "Keys to Enlightenment: Awakening Your Light Body," Oren & DaBen, accessed January 29, 2024, https://www.orindaben.com/pages/light_body/abtlb111_6.

The reading mentioned a girl on a swing, and Claudia related it to finding her intuitive voice:

> That feeling of being "seen," a confirmation that the little girl she saw was my essence . . . not only an acknowledgment of my strengths and who I am at my core but also the fact that at that point in time I was happy and balanced.

After Lynda shared the reading, Claudia told us that it was important for her to know that she needed to slow down and take one step at a time. Later, she told me that she knows her "voice will come" so that, in time, she will be all she is "meant to be." Not long after that, Eileen's reading for her offered similar encouragement: "Create a sacred space inside you. You are a divine child of spirit, loved just as you are. The gifts you share are an added bonus for the rest of us."

Building Awareness: Elizabeth and Charlotte

Reflecting on their lives and personal growth, Elizabeth and Charlotte emphasize that the practice of psychometry has "opened" them up and helped them pay "closer attention" to whatever is happening in their lives. According to Elizabeth, psychometry continues to expand her self-awareness.

> Participating in SOFEA, group meditation, and psychometry are examples of ways that I continue to expand. Of the three things that we do (healing, meditation, psychometry) in our monthly sessions, psychometry has indeed given me the most growth. It has opened me up to consider other things that I have never thought of. It has caused me to pay closer attention to what is going on around me.

And Charlotte, who has been in a Psychometry Group for several decades, says that her "whole life" changed once she started attending:

> Going to those weekly psychometry meetings really changed my whole life because once I started going to

the group, I started becoming more aware of myself, my inner life. When you do psychometry, you really learn to open up your senses, and you really learn—not only that your senses are open—but I think you start to learn about yourself on different levels—spiritually, emotionally, mentally, physically. You learn to tune in to the message for the other person, and so you learn to tune in to yourself also. You learn to listen to yourself. You learn to sit and be quiet and try and figure out what's going on with yourself, and you know that's not always an easy thing for all of us to do. But the psychometry group totally changed my life, moved it in a different direction.

Over the years I have received and given thousands of readings. When we give readings, we try to give feedback to the person so that they know we tuned into the energy of the object they are reading. At this point I do not remember specific readings, but I do know that practicing psychometry changed my life. Every reading, given or received, has some part in it that is information to hear and learn from.

I have learned and/or am learning so much:

- To trust my intuition about everything,
- To have confidence,
- To trust my feelings and instincts.

Because of this, I am more able to love and to be understanding of everyone. I am also learning to be open to and to learn and change, to understand how energy moves and works for everyone. All this has helped enable me to give good advice and counseling, too.

Eileen: "What You Think About, You Bring About"

When group members review readings over the months and years to look for patterns, it's evident that they respect the guidance they have been receiving and are committed to spiritual and personal growth. As Eileen reviewed the readings she kept, she noted some patterns:

> Looking back over the readings I've saved, I don't find anything earth-shaking but there are several recurring themes.

1. *Letting go of fear and or worry.* Not so easy for someone who can play the "what if" game and has a 5th degree black belt in the art of worrying. This came up more frequently a few years ago than now. Once I began to accept the idea that "what you think about, you bring about," I've tried to be more aware of how I think. I still backslide, but instead of beating myself up for it, now I say "and next time I'll do better."

2. *Finding or being in a place of calm or at peace.* For me this is both very easy and quite difficult. It's easy when I'm out in nature, even walking around a lake here in town, or sitting on a shaded bench, or home with Elizabeth. It's most difficult at work. A lot of it has to do with my expectations and becoming agitated when they are not met. Even though I haven't yet made meditation a personal practice, I've gotten better at finding that quiet place within at will than I was before being part of Kim's group meditations.

3. *Surrendering to or being open to the light or guidance.* This is difficult for me. I used to perceive asking for help as weakness or lack of strength (which are similar but not the same). It took a long time, but eventually I did learn that knowing when to ask for help is actually a kind of strength in and of itself. Asking the universe for help or guidance is something I'm learning to do but I'm not entirely comfortable with as of yet. It does get easier as time goes on. I think I'm finally understanding that being open to something so positive has nothing to with weakness or the commonly accepted definition of surrender.

4. *Being aware of guides or elders.* Three different readings have made reference to my having guides or elders around me. Two of them mentioned Native American men specifically. I find this to be particularly intriguing because I had no idea that they were there.

I have an interest in Native American art and culture and have attended several powwows. I have always been drawn to their religion because it is earth and nature-based and has a lot to do with coexisting in your environment instead of conquering it. It's comforting to know that they are there even though I am not yet at a place where I can sense them myself.

Of the readings I've given, the recipient has always found at least one or two points that resonated, sometimes more. A lot of what comes through seems to be encouragement and validations. A message of love and encouragement is always welcome and even more special coming from the universe itself.

As Eileen looked back on her experiences in the group, she told me how much she appreciated "how we are learning to be open minded and not dichotomous thinkers . . . that we are emerging to accept the contraries and be comfortable with them without judgment." She continued, "that's something our nation needs, the world needs, like we can hold that tension, and it's okay."

A few years ago, Eileen provided a message of love and encouragement for me that supported my spiritual and personal growth. Part of her message said, "Everything we've created is perfect as it is. You needn't struggle to make it more perfect or worry that it's not perfect enough. Take joy in the perfection that is creation." I had been working on "perfecting" our new home, working on storage solutions, hanging pictures inside, and working on the plants on our outdoor patio. All during those weeks, I had been feeling that it was time for me to turn inward, and the rest of Eileen's reading confirmed that.

The message felt deep and valuable—far from the criticism, blame, or shame I felt with my religious upbringing. Rather than telling me what to do or asking me to stop doing something, the message inspired me to keep going—to open myself to love, learn, and grow.

Every time I look back at them, I feel a sense of awe from her inspiring words: "Your journey has turned inward to a space of learning, understanding, and growth. This is a wondrous thing for the more you open yourself to love and learning, the more you are able to learn and grow. There are no limits. The ability to keep learning is as infinite as the Universe itself." But the message doesn't end there; Eileen continues:

> Remember to keep part of your focus outward as well. Your next teachers are near at hand and may present themselves in unexpected ways. You, beloved, are a being of love, light, and power beyond imagination. Enjoy all that you are and all that you give.

It is quite humbling to take all of this in. As an only child, I have an inclination to be introspective, but the group allows me to explore that internal landscape from a different angle. I've learned to look at myself more positively and with more patience, knowing that I can find healthy ways to manage my critical mindset, perfectionism, and the maze of other internal barriers I've set for myself.

In the rest of her comments that follow, Eileen may be modest about her intuitive ability, but her uplifting words have always been wise and helpful for me and others in the group.

> Even though I feel myself to be a spiritual adolescent, especially in comparison to some of the other ladies in the group, I know I'm welcome and have something of value to contribute. It's one of the few things I have learned that you just have to let happen instead of do. Everyone has the universe inside them. I am more able than I knew and will continue to become more so.

Eileen mentions that we are not all at the same level, which is actually a wonderful mix; it keeps us from taking each other and our experiences for granted—not that we would. A great deal of active listening occurs in the group. Even from across the room, it's easy to see that each of us is listening with our entire being.

From my experience, because the act of doing a reading (like meditation) forces me to turn inward, my inner life becomes a little bit easier to access than it did before. As a result, I am more able to see things that I had become blind to. Once I see them, I can more readily explore what might be happening underneath the surface in my own reactions and choices. Perhaps that's a sign of spiritual or emotional maturity, but I believe that the readings speed up that process.

Eileen speaks of a similar experience with self-awareness as well, saying, "For me, it all comes down to choosing where my reactions come from: love or fear?" The importance here is the inner work of tracing our reactions and choices. This came through in another powerful message from Esther. What she shared with all of us felt universal—as if it were a message not just for our group but for everyone: "Remember that God is in you—you are perfect. We make a choice to think, 'I am perfect or not perfect.' We make a choice to see love or fear. Each of us makes a decision about which lens we use to see the world."

Her words still reverberate. As we become more aware, we can make choices like the ones she mentions, choices that affect our approach to work, home, relationships, what we absorb from the news, what we say, and especially how we think. But choosing to see love instead of fear can make us vulnerable, which is why a group like this, sharing together in such a safe and sacred space, can help us break through whatever blocks our sense of wholeness. Each person has the opportunity to heal within a supportive community rather than remain in isolation, where it's easier to circumvent whatever may be too painful to address. The writer of *A Course in Miracles* reminds us of this: "What is healing but the removal of all that stands in the way of knowledge? And how else can one dispel illusions except by looking at them directly, without protecting them?"[81]

A Lesson in Trust: The Psy-com-o-Tree Story

A few years ago, a neighbor and a tree provided a difficult but necessary lesson for the group concerning self-awareness and trust.

Rita and I had to be away from home during the normal weekend we had reserved for psychometry, so Cathleen and Angel volunteered to host. What follows is their account of an interesting reading that occurred that night and the events relating to it.

---

[81] *A Course in Miracles: Combined Volume*, 2nd ed., "The 'Dynamics' of the Ego," (Glen Ellen, CA: Foundation for Inner Peace, 1975), 202.

"As we prepared for the group," Cathleen recalled, "I parked my car and truck on the street in order to make more room for guests to park in our driveway. I found out later that Elizabeth and Eileen parked on the side of the street behind my truck, and as they got out of their car, the neighbor walked up to them, requesting that they move it. They didn't think anything of it, so they moved their car and went in. A few more people arrived, and as they pulled over along the street, the neighbor came out again, shouting this time and telling them not to park there. Now, no one had blocked his driveway, but he was adamant that nobody should park anywhere near his house."

"So all of the people who arrived ended up moving their cars, thinking, 'Okay, no problem.' As people entered, a few were curious about why the neighbor would ask them to move their cars. Hearing this, Angel and I looked outside and saw him standing in the street outside his driveway."

Angel interjected, "Then he started shouting, 'Don't park here. Don't park there either,' and so on."

During this retelling of the event, Cathleen leaned over to me and whispered under her breath, "At this point, I blew a gasket," making us laugh. She continued, "We walked over to discuss the parking situation with the neighbor, reminding him that this was a public street and that there is no HOA or rule regarding parking restrictions. As he heard this, he got extremely angry and confrontational. I looked right at him and said, 'Listen, you can't tell people not to park on a public street. This is a public street without any No Parking signs, and you have plenty of room to back your vehicles out of the driveway."

"After that," Angel added, "he raised his voice and screamed, 'It's my house and I can do whatever I want!' As he kept ranting, he corralled us both back across the street and into the yard. Cathleen stopped, turned around to him once more, and asked him, 'What if we called the police?'"

"If you call the police here, then I'll call them, too, and I'll tell them you started this."

"So, of course . . ." Cathleen said, raising her hands, "We called the police."

Angel described how the chaotic, disruptive, and late beginning made it difficult for the group to get into a deeply peaceful, meditative state. They took a break after the healing circle and waited for the police—which didn't take long.

"When the bell rang," Cathleen recalled, "Elizabeth, Suman, and I walked outside to talk to the officers. As we went over what happened, the officer escorted us across the street, near the neighbor's yard. A few moments later, a police car with two other officers arrived at the neighbor's house to take his statement."

"Needless to say, after such a dramatic start, Angel and I tried to dial down the frequency of all this and create a more tranquil atmosphere. Everyone else had accepted all of it without complaint, but it took us a bit longer to settle. Even after the meditation, we still felt shaken."

"So, when we were finally ready to pass around the psychometry bowl," Angel explained, "I picked an object and held it in my hand. As soon as I felt it, I was stunned. The object felt as if it had become the tree, and it started speaking to me immediately. It said, 'Don't be angry at your neighbor. Don't be angry at him because I'm using his anger to protect people and keep them out of my way.'"

Angel told me that she wondered even whether to write it down because it felt as if she was going crazy, "'This just can't be. This can't be!' But I calmed myself and wrote down the entire message. The most startling thing that happened, though, is the minute the tree started talking, my entire mood changed. It was like all of the anger I felt for the neighbor just left. It just drained out of my body right away because I was so humbled and in awe that this tree was talking. My eyes welled up with tears. I thought, 'This is so amazing' and it just was very humbling, and it immediately shifted my entire perspective, and my entire mood."

She continued, "Then when we went around to discuss our readings, I felt bad for the person who brought the object because I thought, 'Oh well, the message from the tree, however important it might be, has taken the place of this person's reading.' But when I looked at the circle and asked whose object it was, it turned out to be Cathleen's."

"Knowing that Cathleen had named this tree, I asked her, 'What is the nickname for that tree in your neighbor's yard?' Cathleen seemed puzzled but answered my question."

"Granfonda . . . I named it Granfonda."

"I said, 'Well, Granfonda has a message for you.' I saw Cathleen's eyes widen along with everyone else's. The message is, 'Don't be mad at the neighbor. The tree is just using the neighbor's anger to protect people.'

We weren't sure exactly what that meant, but it was just so beautiful and startling. Then Cathleen's mood quickly changed, too. Around the group, we were all stunned that the tree would be speaking through this neighbor."

"And then something even more interesting happened," Cathleen added with her eyebrows raised. "Two weeks later to the day, on a Friday, I heard this crunching noise outside the house, a bizarre sound, and I thought, 'What the heck?' It's very quiet that early in the morning, but what I heard was a creaking, crackling-type noise. And then I heard a big boom. Yes, the tree fell. Two trunks had actually fused together, but one side had completely split off."

"The tree was huge!" Angel blurted out, "And half of it came down exactly in the spot, that same area where the neighbor became belligerent, saying 'Don't park there and this and that.'"

"And the city had to come and put yellow tape around it because it was big. Police and city officials all had to inspect and rope off the area. My stepson used to park there because it was shady under the tree," Cathleen explained, "and others who come to visit would use that spot, too. It's also interesting how Elizabeth and Eileen automatically listened to him and moved their car. They didn't think anything of it and didn't argue with him about it."

"Yes, there were a lot of lessons that day, lessons about resisting the tendency to become defensive or angry because there could be something else going on. So even though the neighbor's mannerisms and tone of voice were intimidating, the thing is that underneath it all, the tree was just protecting people."

Trusting a Message From My Own Object

A few years ago during one of the group meetings, I picked an item out of the bowl as I passed it around. As I looked down at it, I discovered that I had picked my own object, a dendrite pendant. So, naturally assuming that this was not supposed to be the case, I covered the object with my hand and interrupted those who were passing the bowl to put it back, explaining what happened and that I would wait till the end. I placed the object back in, covered it up with the scarf, and handed the bowl back to its place in the circle as the group passed it around. At least ten other people still had to choose an object, so I thought I would surely have the opportunity to read for someone else.

While I waited during the silence, I heard a message already start to form. It came with drumming, and I saw an image of the American Indian Museum in Washington D.C. We had been there just two months prior, and I wondered what message this might be. As I let go of any mental processing, I heard, "You change an environment just by being there." I got the sense that the Native tribes had done this for America—added to the energy of the country, despite the sorrow and oppression they faced. It also seemed important to me that, for a while, I return to the form of meditation I learned in the beginning of my spiritual path, one that featured a Native American guide.

When the bowl finally came back around, sitting there for me to find once again was my own object—the dendrite pendant I had placed there from the start. Since I was already in a meditative state, as I picked up the object, I heard, "Have we got your attention?"

So, a bit surprised, I drew a line dividing what I had received prior to picking the object and what I would be receiving next, while holding it. Sinking back into an open-minded state, I waited for more of the message to unfold, and it did:

> Lots of ups and downs but will balance out. Are you aware of how you carry the Divine Source within? Do you tap into knowing and being aware of the greatness that surrounds us all? (We) humans with our limited ways of seeing and being are not using our gifts. We forget ourselves—forget that we are powerful. We are here to soften you, to calm your spirit regarding work and to help you let go. You forgot that you had authority. Apply this to more than just work—to being strong in who you are—to having authority over your body, your emotions, your environment. Count on the goodness within others and let that grow, too. You have much work ahead, but it will be a divine purpose, a delight given to you at the right time. No worries, everything in its own time.

Nov. 2016   you ∆ an environment just by being there

Drumming — An Index Move from D2   more of this world 2

My own object

(I started receiving messages beforehand) — 2x one object —

time we got you other?

~\/\/\/_____

Lots of ups + downs but will balance out

Are you aware of how you carry the Divine
Source within? Do you tap into knowing
+ being aware of the greatness that surrounds
us all?

(we) humans — ~~with~~ our limited ~~sight~~ ways of seeing
+ being are not using our gifts — we forget
ourselves — we powerful

    here
we are to soften you — to calm your spirit
regards work + let go —

you forgot that you had authority —
apply this to more than just work — to
be strong in who you are — to have authority
over your body, your emotions, your environment —
                        emotions

My Reading After Receiving My Own Object Twice
Note the line that has "ups and downs." I didn't realize that I
happened to be drawing an illustration of what I would be hearing.

First of all, I remember being amazed that I received my own object, twice, and even more surprised at hearing the question, "Have we got your attention?" Although, like always, I would have done my best to pay attention to whatever message came through from me for someone else (or vice versa), this unusual circumstance certainly startled me.

Occurring a few months before I retired from my full-time position as a college administrator, I welcomed the guidance about calming my spirit regarding work and "letting go," but this was an important message for me in other ways. I had been going through some challenges regarding my family too, and my spirit certainly needed softening. I had allowed myself to think, "Oh well, that's just the way it is" without realizing that I was not a victim.

I had been unsettled and reacting to events around me rather than responding with patience and love. Most importantly, I had also forgotten about "the greatness" that is at the heart of everyone in my family, everyone I had been worrying about. Becoming anxious about them fueled my fears; what I most needed to do was focus on calming myself and just trust. This message was an excellent admonition for me that being strong in who I am and having authority over my emotions and environment was the foundation for truly feeling peaceful and calm. I also learned to go deeper within myself in order to practice true forgiveness.

At a seminar I attended many years ago, I once heard Caroline Myss talk about forgiveness. She held up the eraser and said, "Forgiveness is like an eraser. It's just an object. You hold it, but there is no emotion around it. When you think about something that previously caused you pain and none of that previous energy exists anymore, it just becomes like this eraser—it's just a thing with no thought or emotion attached to it."

In terms of my reading, I felt humbled but took great comfort in the first sentence: "You change an environment just by being there." So, at that time, even though I still had to learn how to engage my own personal authority, it was comforting to think that the energy of a situation could improve just by being "present." Taking a slightly different—yet equally accurate—interpretation, we could say that "being there" is the act of living in the present moment, which requires us to think differently. We could read a thousand books on the subject or take classes from the wisest gurus, and it still wouldn't become any easier. But when we live in the present, moment by moment, we let go of the emotional sting of the past so that it no longer intrudes upon our lives.

It took me a while to learn this, and like the reading mentions, after "lots of ups and downs"—over the span of a couple years, in fact—everything did balance out. All the frustration and negative effects of what I experienced are now completely healed, leaving me feeling much gratitude for everyone in my life and for how I've been able to expand my awareness and keep my heart open.

CHAPTER 21

Sixth Benefit: Connecting to Divine Energy

One of the most important benefits of group psychometry is the opportunity to connect to Divine energy. Connecting to our inner voice and to an even larger sense of Divinity feels real—it's much different than a reflection or a new idea from our imagination. In the words of Episcopal Priest Carter Heyward, "Our senses, and the feelings that are generated by them become primary spiritual resources. In knowing one another through our senses, feelings, and intelligence—and intuition is a form of intelligence—we come to know God."[82]

Communication from this inner stillness appears through knowing, seeing, hearing, and feeling—so there's no denying it when it happens because whatever we experience through our senses certainly gets our attention.

Literally "Feeling" Divine Energy

What follows is Diana's account of how one reading opened her to feeling the presence of her angels and guides:

> Although all readings that we give and receive impact us in some way, one reading that I gave in April 2015

---

[82] Carter Heyward, *Wise Women: Over Two Thousand Years of Spiritual Writing by Women*, ed. Susan Cahill (New York: W.W. Norton, 1996), 316.

had quite an effect on me. In that reading, I gave a quite vivid "movie like" account of an event that had happened in Amy's life. What I experienced when this downloaded into my heart/spirit/mind was like nothing I had ever experienced before. At first, I doubted what was happening, until my Higher Self lovingly got in the driver's seat and opened the flow and wow did it flow! So that alone was an awakening/opening for me to receive more to give more.

Then, as I described a dream within the reading, I saw that Archangel Michael was present for Amy to protect her and comfort her. Since this time, both Archangel Michael and Raphael are with me almost 100% of the time. Like her, I literally "feel" their wings around me and the air moving from their presence—not always together, either. This kind of experience in a reading was new for me, and so wonderful. It felt so welcoming for me to look more into this unseen world we all live in but do not fully see. I am so grateful that I am starting to "see" more and more.

Diana is describing a metaphysical connection. Giving the reading, she says, opened her to receive more. We might relate this once again to the door of the heart. She opened the door to her soul from the inside while completely trusting what was on the other side.

Laura describes this feeling of connection as "limitless," filled with "power" and "responsibility"—as if "a whole new world" has opened for her as a result:

Being part of the group feels like a new world has opened for me. I got to a higher level in this ever-changing, multilevel, multidimensional game called life, in which I can be the player, the viewer, the game itself—or these three together. We are limitless once connected to the Higher Source, and with great power comes great responsibility!

A "Wake-up Call" for Me

The miracle of experiencing Divine energy is so wonderful, yet sometimes my not-so-Divine self creeps in during my daily activities, and I revert to living unconsciously. In those moments (which hopefully occur less and less frequently), I forget to tap in to the amazing, ever-present connection to Source that is available to all of us. In one of her readings for me, Pat lovingly but sternly reminded me of that:

> You love fairy tales—there are times when you get lost in them. I say, "stay grounded." There is so much within your grasp—you are oblivious to the reality of your potential. You truly are multi-talented; just listen to the still, small voice that speaks to you daily. Occasionally they get your attention, and you absolutely know that it is Spirit speaking to you, and the results are overwhelming. Your entire life could be like this on a daily basis—what are you afraid of? Go for it! Buddha said, "There are only two reasons why we fail: 1) not finishing and 2) not starting." Your magnificence stands alone.

In my heart of hearts, I knew for sure that my inner guidance was real. Her reading encouraged me to keep listening to this "still, small voice within"—messages I appreciated but had been putting aside, thinking and wondering if I had been imagining them or even worse, not paying enough attention to the guidance I had been receiving.

Divine Connections from the Other Side

Sometimes readings feature a unique message from a loved one who has passed—messages so unusual that they could not possibly be coincidental. In all cases, the message was unmistakable and healing for the recipient to hear. What an amazing way to experience divine energy! In Adrienne's case, it was comforting for her to feel supported and be reminded that she is not alone:

The second time I attended the group, I received a reading that family members in spirit were sitting in a circle sending me healing and love. That they have been there all along through this tremendous life change. They wanted the message to bring hope and for me to know there is new life now and a rebirth. These family members in spirit were surrounding me in a circle of love and said that they would continue to hold this for me. What a good feeling to know I wasn't alone.

In one of the first meetings of our psychometry group, Elizabeth recalls a reading she gave to a woman who attended for the first time:

Unbeknownst to me, Celeste's mother had passed away within the last year, and she was still going through a great deal of loss and sadness. Little did I know that what I held in my hand was her mother's class ring. In my reading I told Celeste that I saw a garden gate with the trellis over top with flowers and it had a white picket fence across the front. The gate was partially opened, it wasn't closed, and it asked her to walk through it. It was a message of "Don't worry be happy, it's okay, I love you. Don't be sad."

As I was telling Celeste her reading, she began to weep. I didn't know what was going on. Her partner at the time, Jill, explained to me—in between her sobbing while I was giving the reading—that the ring had belonged to Celeste's mother.

After I finished the reading, they told me that the vision I gave them was actually the artwork that was used on the outside cover of her funeral service worship aide. Celeste said that it was time, and that it was what she needed to hear and validation even though she was still grieving terribly. I was shocked. I wrote to Celeste what was in my head and put it down on paper. You never really know when a message comes what it means for the other person, or how real it may be, or if they will understand, or if it will be good news.

After the meeting with Celeste, I knew at a soul level that I could do this and that there would be a lot of value for me and for anyone else that I could share my new gift with. That was validation for me.

Each of us has the ability to access an inner voice, and when we practice that connection, we can become more aware of specific messages that Divinity, our angels and guides, and departed loved ones have for us. In a message I received from Lynda, she wrote:

I feel loss, the loss of a loved one. That loved one is happy, settled, and preparing for the next journey. She wants you to know how excited she is for the next step.

There is so much to learn about the unknown. Simply by slowing everything down to take the time to be in stillness will allow you to begin to see and experience what it is she is seeing and experiencing. Don't waste this precious time. There is so much life to live. You are vibrant and alive. Find your joy and happiness.

Lynda's mother had just passed within the year, and after sharing what she had written with the group, she said, "I have waited for my mother's spirit to talk with me, but as much as I have wanted it to, it hasn't happened yet. My sister has more traditional religious beliefs than I do, yet she has had several visitations from her." While listening, I couldn't help but feel that Lynda's mother was actually speaking through the page she had just handed me. It felt like a Universal message that included the voice of my loved ones, too. Also, this powerful message included something significant for both of us to hear—about there being "so much to learn about the unknown" and to "slow down," to take time to "be in the stillness."

I believe that no matter what religion we profess to be or what our background is, it's possible for anyone to settle back into their heart and quiet their mind through meditation, prayer, or contemplation. Through practice, this can build a pathway for connecting to our loved ones as well as to an even greater sense of Divinity than any departed family members or friends could convey. The timing for those connections, however, may not always align with our expectations, so we must trust that their wisdom and encouragement will bubble up in our consciousness at the best possible time.

Messages from departed family members, especially grandmothers or mothers, occur in the group every once in a while—certainly not every meeting—but in a several cases, the identity of each "sender" has been shockingly definitive. Suman gave a reading for Kate a few years ago that mentioned pink roses blooming. Suman said that she didn't understand why she kept hearing and seeing, "pink roses, pink roses," but evidently it was a special sign from Kate's grandmother. When Suman read the message aloud, Kate raised her eyebrows and confirmed that her grandmother had once said, "If you ever try to connect with my spirit after I pass, you'll know it's me when you hear 'pink roses, pink roses.'"

In another memorable reading, Kate, who was a first-time attendee at the time, held the item she picked, an heirloom bracelet, up in the air. Shirley said, "I brought that," and Kate started reading aloud from her notes. As she did, just like Suman heard "pink roses, pink roses," Kate had repeated the word "biscuit" over and over. She said, "I don't understand the meaning, but it seemed as if I had to keep writing down 'biscuit' without much context."

When Shirley heard the word "biscuit" repeated so much, she had tears in her eyes because she knew it was a message from her previous partner's grandmother, whom she shared a special connection with and loved. "Biscuit was one of her favorite terms of endearment for her grandchildren." Shirley loved her and called her "Meemaw" with the rest of the family.

Who would have known that words like "pink roses" or "biscuit" could be so meaningful? We never know if a unique phrase or word is important when we do readings, but the point I'm making through these examples is that we have a connection to Source beyond what we see, hear, and feel with our "normal" selves. This reading impacted Kate so much that a few years later, when I spoke with her about examples for this book, she said that her reading for Shirley was one of her most memorable experiences with the group, as the word "biscuit" came up really strong.

Another example of a powerful image appeared in Claudia's reading from Suman. In this case, the reading featured a dragon. Suman wrote down the message, just as she had received it, without interpreting it. None of us would have guessed what this description meant to Claudia, but she told me that it was one of the most impactful readings she had ever received:

> At one point of her reading, the dragon stopped circling and stood behind me, transforming into a woman dressed in white. I don't remember the rest of it, but I do remember that it sent chills down my spine because my mom had recently passed away and the way Suman described the woman standing with her hands on my back, I was certain it was my mother. She was dressed in white because she was an avid Tai Chi practitioner, and the dragon is a very powerful being in Chinese culture, which she was absolutely connected to. I just remember being overcome with emotion and there was no doubt in my mind that my mother was there with me. I felt elated, grateful, overwhelmingly happy.

The gentle prodding of our female ancestors is not usually so dramatic. They tend to send messages about taking care of ourselves and remembering their love for us. Once in a while during a meeting, Suman will joke and share the highlights of her extra-sensory conversations with her mother's spirit. Recently, she told us that she had not been sleeping due to an abundance of energy. After work, Suman said that she had been rearranging things in the house, starting creative projects, and planning ahead—putting her entire self into busy activities at home, long after her normal bedtime.

On the day before we were all supposed to meet for psychometry, Suman said that the spirit of her mother spoke, persisting in telling her over and over again that she needs to go to bed and get some rest. Suman imitated how she talked to her mother's spirit this time and said, out loud, "This is just my imagination. I am not hearing this from my mother!" But immediately after, she told us that she heard her mother's voice pipe back, "Oh yes, it's me, and I'll show you."

No one else knew until later that this "conversation" had happened or even that Suman had been overly energetic and sleep deprived.

The night of the group, Suman reached under the scarf to pick an object from the psychometry bowl. The group followed the usual procedure, and Elizabeth volunteered to go first. She held up a pendant which turned out to be Suman's object. The reading began with, "It's a beautiful day. Let your creative juices flow" . . . and then in the next part of the message, Elizabeth raised her voice, looked directly at Suman with sternness, and said, "Sleep, sleep, sleep. You need rest!" Suman laughed out loud, explaining that she had been full of energy lately but had not been able to settle down enough to sleep longer than three hours a night. She joked that her mother's spirit said the same thing the day before, chiding her about getting rest.

But as if her mother's message through Elizabeth's reading had not accentuated the message strongly enough, Suman ended up with Elizabeth's object, a pearl bracelet—something she had not placed in the bowl before. When it was time for the reading, Suman, held up the pearls and immediately said, "Oh my God, my mother! She loved pearls. She wore them everywhere. She had so many different kinds and sizes." Two of us in the group had worn pearl earrings, too, a bit unusual for a casual summer night in Florida where most of us wear shorts. All of us got a great kick out of this, of course, but we were amazed, too. Suman's mother certainly proved her point.

In a reading that Amy gave Phyllis one evening, Phyllis's mother came through with an added emphasis. Amy was in the middle of sharing the reading for Phyllis aloud to the group, and said, "Your Mom says 'Hello' and that she loves you (dearly)." In the middle of Amy's reading, she paused to turn the page and opened her mouth to continue. At that point—while Amy was in mid-sentence, my phone began ringing with the chorus from Etta James' "Tell Mamma" (which is the ringtone I use for my daughter's calls).

Prior to this, after a decade and more of hosting these meetings where a phone could ring and interrupt a meditation, I had always placed my phone on vibrate. The ringtone certainly got everyone's attention, and we all enjoyed a hearty and meaningful laugh.

To continue Phyllis's "Hello" message from her mother, Amy read, "She fears that you have forgotten this love and is here to remind you." Then Amy followed that with the words, "Big loving energy" to emphasize what Phyllis's mother wanted to convey.

The next part of Amy's message mentions ancestry and then a triangle. We all knew that Phyllis had been a caregiver for her 90-year-old father, and I had considered that this might be one point of this triangle. Caregiving, of course, requires commitment as well as a great deal of time and attention.

Phyllis told me, "When I received the reading, yes, I thought the triangle was between me, my dad, and my wife, and that I was being pulled in all directions. I also believe(d) wholeheartedly that Mom was definitely talking about dad's influence. However, I wouldn't call it 'influence.' I'd call it something stronger, but I can't think of the word right now. I think there was something about not forgetting I'm loved."

Below is the text of Amy's reading for Phyllis as well as an image of it:

You are being provided a clean slate—Tabula Rasa— on which to write. What will you fill your board with? Choose intentionally, for your creation is to remain for many years. Do you fill your board with hearts and bubbles? Or lines and squiggles? Either, you choose . . .

Life beyond you is a circus. For now, you may play on the tricycle of life . . . as a young one oblivious to the sounds of the chaos. Do not pay attention to the turmoil—but instead to your present moment, content with where you are.

You are a master architect, building your life from the inside out. Keep going to those places you were unsure of—the rooms you did not know existed that have gems for you to handle and hold.

We wish for you to keep gazing, looking for the passageways you have not traveled, for the treasures are deep and the rewards great. We are with you.

Your mom says hello. And that she loves you (dearly). She fears you have forgotten this love and is here to remind you. (Big loving energy)

There is a castle that awaits your arrival. In it you will find yourself in awe of your ancestry and the spirit of hope. You will know the place once you enter.

Are you in a triangle? Take a closer look to create that better outcome. What will you add to your white board *(Amy says this refers to the Tabula Rasa)*.

You are surrounded by so much love and admiration by those around you. You can have <u>all</u> that your heart desires. Continue forward, lighting the world with your presence—as we see you happy, healthy, and beyond this realm of knowing. Stay centered in the loves that you are encircled by. You are so blessed. We love you. Namaste and big, big love.

P.S. You can see the vision now, yes? *In the corner, Amy added a note about Aretha Franklin, "Tell Mama" (really by Etta James).*

5/27/2022

    You are being provided a clean slate — Tabula rasa —
on which to write. What will you fill your board
with? Choose intentionally — for your creation is to
remain for many years. Do you fill your board
with hearts & bubbles? Or lines & squiggles?
Either you choose ...

    Life beyond you is a circus. For now, you may
play on the tricycle of life ... as a young one
oblivious to the sounds of the chaos. Do not
pay attention to the turmoil — but instead to your
present moment, content with where you are.

    You are a master architects, building your
life from the inside out. Keep going to those places
you were unsure of — The rooms you did not know
existed That have gems for you to handle & hold.
We wish for you to keep gazing, looking for the
passageways you have not traveled, for the treasures are
deep & the rewards great. We are with you.

    Your mom says hello. And that she loves you
                               (dearly)

She fears you have forgotten this love & is here to remind you. (Big loving energy)

There is a castle that awaits your arrival. In it you will find yourself in awe of your ancestry & the spirits of hope. You will know the place once you enter.

Are you in a triangle? Take a close look to create that better outcome. What will you add to your white house?

You are surrounded by so much love & admiration by those around you. You can have all that your heart desires. Continue forward, lighting the world with your presence—as we see you happy, healthy, and beyond this realm of knowing. Stay centered in the love that you are encircled by. You are so blessed. We love you. Namaste & big ol' big love.

P.s. You can see the vision now, yes?

Amy E.

Amy's "Your Mother Says 'Hello'" Reading for Phyllis

Creating "a better outcome" for the triangle challenge is certainly much harder to do than it is to imagine, yet this reading is a reminder that not only Phyllis but all of us can envision a better way and focus on manifesting something different. Isn't that what our mothers—present and past—have always wanted for us?

CHAPTER 22

Seventh Benefit: Experiencing Wonder and Joy

"Psychometry never ceases to amaze me—how everyone's vibration and the individual's own world they live in is open to the Universe, and we can get a glimpse of it."
— Pat, Psychometry Group Member

Wonder is an expansive state that captures moments so inspiring or amazing that we cannot find words to describe them. Perhaps, in the introduction to this book, that's what Lynda meant when she said she didn't have words to describe what her first time with the group felt like. Group psychometry always instills me with awe, and from what I've witnessed in each meeting, it inspires a similar sense of wonder and joy in others as well.

Over the years, I've seen many readings in the group that are awe-inspiring, but it's not just individual readings that leave me feeling that way; sometimes several messages during a meeting share a certain synchronicity that seems more than just coincidental or, at the very least, display a pattern that captures everyone's attention.

Group Energy

Even though we are quite unique, being together each month over the last decade or so has created a familiar "group energy" that, for me and others, feels comforting. Amy describes our psychometry group as "an avenue for returning 'home' to our essential nature of spirit and to love."

Such group energy can help us in far more ways than we realize. For me, providing a reading from within a group is more enjoyable and more powerful than doing one on my own, but that's only part of it.

Communication is complex and involves more than just what we can see and hear. For example, when we feel at ease around another person (or when others feel more at ease around us), we are experiencing the effects of an alignment whether we are conscious of it or not. The same could true for times when we feel misaligned, when we're talking to someone and, out of the blue, we start feeling anxious, tired, or cranky.

According to research by Moran Cerf, a neuroscientist at Northwestern University, "when two people are in each other's company, their brain waves will begin to look nearly identical. . . . This means the people you hang out with actually have an impact on your engagement with reality beyond what you can explain. And one of the effects is you become alike."[83]

Naparstek writes about this as well, discussing it in terms of an expansive energy field:

> The direct, energetic influence of someone with a strong field and more fully developed capabilities—a teacher, healer, friend, or relative—gives us some extra juice, and just from hanging around such people we can hitch a ride on their energy frequencies and accelerate our progress. This is because consciousness is contagious, and there is a powerful energetic aspect to the mechanics of psychic opening. Along with the alterations in our biochemistry and the shifts in brainwave activity during psi, an even more basic change occurs, a change in the way that energy oscillates all around and through us.[84]

---

[83] Chris Weller, "A neuroscientist who studies decision-making reveals the most important choice you can make," *Business Insider*, July 28, 2017, http://www.businessinsider.com/neuroscientist-most-important-choice-in-life-2017-7.

[84] Naparstek, *Sixth Sense*, 43.

What she describes is not just being swept into a swirl of emotions or group expectations. It's a biochemical, electromagnetic process. The healing circle and meditation prepare the groundwork for each person to expand their awareness in order to receive helpful, intuitive information through psychometry. It's cleansing, but it also guides us in focusing our energy on sending love and blessings to others who are hurting or in need of support.

After this, the meditation further opens our hearts. The HeartMath Institute has measured the breadth of the heart's energetic field to an area extending up to three feet from the body in all directions.[85] According to research by Naparstek and others, the powerful energy of an open heart can dissolve physical and psychological boundaries: "The I-Thou distinctions, the line between self and not-self, disappears. It is no longer a matter of just you and me, but, rather, I become you and you become me. My energetic field opens, expands, and intersects with yours, and all our realities merge. Or, if I carry it further, I merge with my family, my country, my species, with all of creation, with the entire universe."[86]

In addition to sharing similar attitudes and camaraderie, we also provide support through helpful readings that often inspire synchronicity and healing. So it's not surprising that people who attend the group tend to exhibit similar emotional qualities and, even more importantly, reinforce them in each other, including gratitude, kindness, non-judgment, and respect.

Synchronicities Within the Same Meeting

It's quite often that a particular meditation or group theme strikes a chord with most or all of the group. One night Eileen placed the key fob from her first car, a Saturn, in the bowl for someone to choose. Even though the reading she received wasn't about a car, the automobile theme continued. Rita received a very clear, spontaneous image of a red car, an older one that she had liked a lot, and when Esther received the reading

---

[85] "Science of the Heart," Heartmath Institute, accessed February 12, 2024, https://www.heartmath.org/research/science-of-the-heart/energetic-communication.
[86] Naparstek, *Sixth Sense*, 72.

from Rita, she joked, "Is this message for this week or tonight?" She explained that driving over she had observed her car's odometer reaching 100,000 miles and wondered if she would have to buy another car.

The same night, in Elizabeth's reading for Suman, she mentioned the urgency of dealing with an issue regarding a car. Suman said that it was already done. She had difficulties with her car a week ago and had it fixed. But, she said, something curious happened while she was driving this week. While at a stop sign, she saw an older woman standing outside a house, smiling at her. Suman asked her son about it since he was sitting in the passenger seat, but he didn't see the woman: "There's nothing there," he said, continuing to look. Suman could see the woman anyway and heard her say, "My son and I were very happy in this house." She seemed to be welcoming us there, but people were living in the house, and it wasn't for sale. Suman said the woman was a spirit, and later she realized it was an older version of herself. So even though what she shared with us wasn't about a car, the confirmation of having her car repaired and the message she received while driving that week were both significant.

Suman's reading carried forward a second theme that evening, that of home and family. Diana's reading described a house with fields all around. She didn't mention who the reading was for at first, and as everyone listened, Derek, who had only attended a couple times, said the description felt like it was the house where he grew up. Although the reading was for Eileen, the feeling carried through for more than one person, which is natural—a house with a field around it carries a universal sense of home for most people. But the idea of home, and especially family, reverberated so strongly that it appeared in two other powerful messages that night.

It seemed fitting that the theme featured fathers on one of the rare times when a male attended the group. Derek had brought an old toy that he had found hidden at his grandfather's home prior to his father's death. It was a small, metal fireman, which most likely belonged to Derek's father when he was a child. At the time, Derek asked his grandfather about it, and he said, "throw that away." He didn't even want to look at it.

Sabrina's reading for Derek was positive, saying that he is a wonderful person and that there was a lot of love in his heart; it was healing for Derek to hear. Then, in our conversation about his reading, Derek told us that his dad had recently passed.

As others continued, an even deeper truth came forward regarding healing home and family traumas regarding two fathers. Derek said he was treated severely as a child and was subjected to physical, mental, and sexual abuse. Routinely, toys he loved most were taken away as punishment. Derek told us that for many months, he had done a lot of meditation while holding the toy, clearing himself of past pain. He was brave to bring the object, not knowing what would come up in the reading. Afterward, Derek said that he felt as if he could picture his dad as healed, too, because his dad had also suffered from a cycle of abuse.

One of the women on the other side of the room wanted to see the little fireman that had survived two generations, so Derek allowed everyone to see. As we passed it around, Suman touched it and said that it felt as if the little boy inside him could reach out now . . . to be held and welcomed. She felt "innocence." That night tears welled up for Derek and many of us because the healing process appeared so powerfully for him and others in the group who had experienced family trauma.

We've witnessed several of our own go through various processes of healing from loss, abuse, and other kinds of suffering. The process is never easy, yet sometimes a reading comes through that evidences how much someone has grown. For example, that same evening, Esther had brought an object that her grandmother gave her. Rita, who had picked it up from the bowl, shared how it contained a message about Esther's deceased father and his effect on her life. After the reading, in her feedback, Esther talked about her father's former life concerning his problem with anger and drinking. She said, "This object actually carries my father's energy." As she said this, though, her countenance did not waver and remained peaceful and smiling. "He is gone, and all of that negative, conflicting, and harsh energy is in the past. His former self doesn't affect me anymore. That's all clear now. I talk to his spirit every day and feel his love."

All of this occurred during one meeting—starting with seemingly idiosyncratic thoughts of cars and ending with healing words that soothed deep familial wounds.

Every month it seems that something wondrous happens that affirms how a Divine energy—whether we call it Source, the Universe, or God— is always guiding us toward continued healing and wholeness. Further evidence of this is when something so unique happens that it seems to be more than just coincidental, as if we are receiving an affirmation from the Universe that the group is on the right track. For example, during one night, two different people, without coordinating beforehand, brought cufflinks. Our group consists of women (except for a couple meetings over the dozen years), so it's even more unlikely that two different women would bring—on the same night—something few people even use anymore.

On another night, we had two separate messages from two people mentioning a thunderbird and two others mentioning caves. On a different occasion, three separate readings mentioned cleansing. Another three mentioned forests. In a meeting in May 2021, five people mentioned boats in their readings.

An even more impressive example of this occurred with a common theme across several messages within the group. At least five emphasized a bright feeling of happiness—with messages for two different people repeating the words, "happy, happy, happy," others saying "happier times are ahead," "enjoy your happy place," and "let go of seriousness …" These are examples I remember; many, many more have happened over the last several years.

These repeated phrases in different messages across the same meeting are in line with Cerf's theory of group alignment and also with Naparstek's research on dynamic energy fields. It's also likely that the unity within the group creates a place of oneness that encourages synchronicity (or at least connects to one). After the words "happy, happy, happy" were repeated in readings to such an extent that it we could not call it coincidental, we discussed it in the group. Suman said that she sees it as evidence of "how connected the group is." The rest agreed. It's not only the bond we have with each other but our connection to whatever we might call that mystical yet palpable energy of Divine guidance, higher consciousness, or the Universe.

The Universe Often Speaks "Economically"

When I attended one of Laura Day's workshops, she told us that the Universe is not only insightful but very "economical." Quite often, she said, when a person provides a reading for another, the same information applies to both the reader and receiver. This may be true across an entire message or with parts of it. Of course, it's possible that something in a reading is very specifically meant for a particular person and not meant for us. Or even more likely, perhaps it doesn't apply in our current mindset, but as we reflect, or as time passes, quite often the details meant for us will surface.

From all of what I've shown in this book, it's clear to me that those attending the psychometry group meetings amplify each other's energy fields. Amping up these positive qualities in each other is far more valuable than merely observing synchronicities across readings. Even so, it's important to understand that many of the statements in readings apply on both sides, and no doubt there are multiple examples of this principle in much of what our group has shared with each other over the years. In some cases, a message generically applies to the reader and receiver because it's a bit more general and uplifting, but even so, we can catch specific references as we look back and analyze parts of it. For example, in a reading that Angel gave Pat, she mentions that Pat is a "truth teller" and a "bringer of light" whose "being-ness" activates a positive vibration to everyone around her. Although Angel may blush to be told this, those words she used to describe Pat are an apt description of herself, too. The end of the reading applies also because like Pat, Angel is dearly loved by many and is a true treasure as well.

To be more specific, I'd like to delve into two other readings that provide excellent examples of this principle of "economy." Interestingly, both involve Amy, once as a reader and then as a receiver.

In a previous section, "Divine Connections from the Other Side," Amy gave Phyllis a reading that said, "Your mom says 'Hello' and that she loves you (dearly)." In terms of this specific reading, Amy said that she is not sure whether that communication was from her own mother, but she told me that several other parts of the reading resonated with her, particularly this one: "Do not pay attention to the turmoil, but instead to your present moment, content with where you are." Reflecting on that, she said,

> My life has been chaotic these past few years, and I've had to stay centered at my core. The triangle in Phyllis's reading was likely reminding me that I was not to overshare or that I was in triangles that I shouldn't have been as well as other people triangulating with me.

Most of Amy's friends are aware, too, that she is a successful manifestor of what she needs. She is always growing with intention and seeks to live an active, meaningful, purposeful life. The words in the reading reiterate this: "look," "pay attention," "keep going," and "continue forward." Even such small details and seemingly insignificant phrases can carry important meanings within a message.

The second example of the principle of economy appears in a reading that I gave to Amy, who provides her own reflection of it, as follows:

> My many years of psychometry readings are kept in a binder. Between sessions, I often reread to gain greater perspective on life's happenings. Kim McCauley provided me a reading in April 2023 which continues to remind me that I am on my right path.
>
> Life changes can be difficult for me. Before significant life shifts take place, I typically experience high energy— usually in the form of an "intolerance" for present circumstances. As if a butterfly breaking from its chrysalis, I may struggle before the change occurs and transforms into relief and freedom.
>
> The reading I received in April 2023 reminds me to keep pushing in the direction of impending change.
>
> Through purge and release (and sometimes a good rant), I feel something greater is being born. I am in the middle of my next great rebirth—and will continue to use Kim's reading to remind and propel me through.
>
> New friends. New ideas. A reset. Yes!

Below is the text followed by an image of the reading I gave her:

> Guidance in healing my relationship with my daughter. "Circle of Excellence" from Insight Timer app.

If you are feeling heaviness in your chest and heart—something weighing heavy on you, I sense that you need to "get it out"—Blehhh—upchuck and let it go. Perhaps a word dump—journal or a good healthy talk with someone who needs to hear what you have to say. Relief—Freedom—Release is almost instantaneous after that. Your body, your life will vibrate anew—like being reborn . . . a new vibration! *(I drew little notes and wrote "Good Vibrations" to draw attention to the uplifting lyrics of the song.)*

What are you starting anew? Like a clean slate? Are you thinking of "eating clean?" I think it's a good idea. Try it and see? Only you can decide that of course. You may not have been seeking to turn over a new leaf, but somehow the leaf found you—Be Leaf it or not :) *You are lighter now*—Your light shines brighter after the reset (Eclipses are reset buttons, by the way).

What's going on with a car? What have you found lately? New ideas? New friends?

You are being given a great opportunity to start fresh. How are you going to restart? What would you do differently this time?

Blessings and Love to you on this new and wonderful journey. Go for it!

P.S. (And tell me how it's going)

Guidance in healing my relationship up my daughter.
"Circle of Excellence" from Insight Timer app.

If you are feeling heaviness in your chest & heart —
Something weighing heavy on you, I sense that
you need to "get it out" — Blehhh —
upchuck & let it go. Perhaps a word
dump — journal or a good healthy talk
with someone who need to hear what you
have to say. Relief — Freedom — Release
is almost instantaneous after that.
Your body, your life will vibrate anew —
like being reborn. a new vibration! 🔔
GOOD VIBRATIONS!

What are you starting anew? Like a clean
slate? Are you thinking of "eating clean"?
I think it's a good idea. Try it & see.)
Only you can decide that of course — But You
may not have been seeking to turn over a new
leaf, but somehow the leaf found you — Be -
Leaf it or not ☺ YOU ARE LIGHTER
NOW — Your light shines brighter after
the reset (Eclipses are reset buttons BTW)
What's going on w/ a car?
What have you found lately?
New ideas? new friends? Kim 4/24/23

you are being given a great opportunity to start fresh. How are you going to restart? What would you do differently this time?

Blessings + love to you on this new + wonderful journey. Go for it!
P.S. (+ tell me how it's going)

Kim's Reading for Amy, April 21, 2023

The statements here also applied to my circumstances at the time. I was going through a rough period as well. I tried something new in the group that month, asking each person to write down something they wanted the receiver to hold in the light for them. In my own note at the top, before the readings started, I wrote that I was seeking guidance that would help heal my relationship with my daughter. I also made note of the meditation we used that night, which happened to be "Circle of Excellence" by Fr. Carel-Piet van Eden. In this meditation, the speaker asks the listeners to create a circle of excellence for themselves, and in their minds, step inside it. I thought that the meditation would help us all focus on the positive, something I felt I needed to do for myself and also for Rita because in the previous few months we had both experienced outward turmoil in our lives and had each lost loved ones.

In the week before I gave the reading for Amy, I had felt a huge sense of heaviness because of challenges my daughter and I were facing, primarily the difficulties she faced with her health, the stresses of life, and of living so far away. I didn't know how to resolve any of it. The words brought forward my heaviness and the feeling that I needed to talk to someone and "get it out" even though I wasn't conscious of it at the time. A week later, I had a counseling session that allowed me to say everything I needed to say. It was so validating, so healing, and indeed provided "relief, freedom, and release."

In reference to "eating clean," a question about a car, new friends and new ideas—all applied. Rita and I recently decided to eat "clean," which to us means focusing more on gluten-free, organic plant-based meals. We also needed to make a tough decision about whether to replace the transmission in one of our cars. And although I'm not sure I've officially made new friends, I attended a workshop a month later that allowed me to connect with peers and learn something new.

Almost a year later, yet another miraculous "coincidence" occurred that was specifically related to this message. Eight months after I gave that reading to Amy, my daughter ended up moving closer to us. She had been diagnosed with P.O.T.S. (Postural Orthostatic Tachycardia Syndrome) and was having difficulty walking due to full-body tremors. Right before she moved, she consulted a new physician for help. He spoke with her via Zoom and emphasized the importance of eating whole foods (which I interpret as "eating clean") as well as eliminating gluten and dairy from her diet. Coincidence #1: it didn't take long for her new diet to give her a huge boost in well-being. By minimizing stress, feeling a sense of hope, and applying her new diet, my daughter—who arrived at the airport in a walker—dramatically improved so much that a few months later, she was well enough to drive. Our relationship has improved, as well—she lives closer, we communicate more often, and we both continually try to focus on the present and let go of the past.

Coincidence #2: When my daughter borrowed one of our cars (the same one mentioned in the reading), she noticed that the side of one of the tires had a gash and needed replacing.

Within a day or two before or after this, Rita had been reading an article in *National Geographic* about ultra-processed foods being harmful to the body and brain, so we discussed it and made decisions about how we can take time to read food lables and decrease the amount of ultra-processed foods we were buying[87]—coincidence #3.

It seems miraculous that nearly a year later, my daughter's healing, diet, and the same car all re-appear, yet the same message applied for both time periods, calling everything to our attention in a big way. In addition to this, I know, absolutely, that Amy (as well as others in the group) had been praying for my daughter and for me. I feel such gratitude for all of this healing and for these obvious confirmations that caught my attention.

Because circumstances can apply across time and space, a reading can be so much more expansive than we think. As we grow individually and as a group, the spiritual practice of psychometry helps us learn to process intuitive information, view it from multiple perspectives, and continue to reflect on the guidance we've received.

When we're open, we receive the support we need at the right time, in the right way, and from the right person—including ourselves. Of course, everything doesn't always fit reader and receiver so thoroughly, but when we take time to reflect, we find that—in the words of The Rolling Stones—"You can't always get what you want, but if you try sometimes, well, you just might find . . . you get what you need."

---

[87] Janis Jibrin, "How Ultra-processed Food Harms the Body and Brain," *National Geographic*, February 29, 2024, https://www.nationalgeographic.com/premium/article/ultra-processed-foods-damage-brain-depression-anxiety-cognitive-decline.

"How Did I Know to Write All This?"

As I mentioned before, newcomers can be among the best readers because they have fewer preconceived ideas about what psychometry is. They also have no basis for comparison, so early on, they develop a beginner's questioning mind. One woman, Jaye, who attended a few times said that she came because she was invited by a woman she had been dating. She said that she was a little nervous because she had never heard of psychometry and was worried about making "a fool" of herself to the group and also her friend. But her feelings turned around:

> The minute I walked in, I was made to feel like I had been part of the group for years. Then once I held the item that I picked from the basket, I was so concerned that I would feel nothing, but that feeling only lasted a second. I found myself writing continuously. Things started coming to my mind, and I would write them down. I wrote what seemed like two pages, and I was wondering, "Where was this all coming from? How did I know to write all this?"
>
> When I finished reading aloud what I had written to the person whose item I picked, she cried. She said I was right on the money about everything I said. I was amazed.
>
> I left that night counting the days until I could attend another session. I feel so blessed to have had this awesome experience.

Like many first-timers, Jaye found herself in a moment of awe: "Where was all this coming from," and "How did I know to write all this?" Her amazement in what it felt like is not unusual because it's not like anything a person typically does. It's like observing yourself playing like a virtuoso without having practiced the instrument. We all have the gift of intuition, yet most of us have forgotten that this is a natural and wise part of who we truly are.

Laughter Is Good for the Soul

Previously, Lynda mentioned that she gave a couple of "dark" readings, but they were purposeful, and both women experienced healing as a result of the message. These "dark" or heavy readings happen rarely. More often, we share a sense of silliness and belly laughs from the quirky sense of humor that pops up in the readings, as was the case with the "Tell Mama" ringtone and Suman's mother's determined way of getting her message across.

All of us belly laughed one night when Lynda acted out her reading for Cathleen. After Lynda received the message, she said that Spirit told her to "lie down, curl up, and 'lay in the bog.'" When it was time to read what she wrote, that is certainly what she did. She curled up on the floor in the middle of our living room!

The reading also shared a beautiful image: "While you are lying down," she said, still reading from her paper, "roll over and experience the beam of light directed toward you. It's twinkling with stardust. Rise . . . Rise . . . Rise."

As Lynda rose from her position on the floor, she persisted in telling Cathleen that it was a must for her to visit the archeological site where that is, somewhere on the East coast of Florida, near Venice.

After Cathleen soaked in this information, she looked around the room and joked, "Well, Lynda, you've taken psychometry to a whole new level now!"

On two other occasions, another group member, Laura, brightened the evening by sharing her sense of humor. Because she attends regularly, Laura has given lots of readings through the years. In one of them, she looked at the entire group and said, "I sensed royalty as I held this item" and asked, "Can a queen share her wisdom without speaking? Are you the queen?"

Because Charlotte responded that the item Laura had chosen was hers, most of us chuckled when Laura smiled and read, "Are you the queen?" Everyone familiar with Charlotte knows that she loves crystals so much that it has empowered her to claim that she had been the Queen of Atlantis in a previous life. After the lightheartedness and laughter settled, Laura ended the reading with seriousness: "Your wisdom and knowledge needs to be shared." Laura's intuition connected to the unique person that Charlotte is in order to emphasize that important message.

During another meeting, Laura wrote what she received but when it was time to read it, she had to squint because she had forgotten her glasses. She borrowed someone else's and began to speak, explaining that the feeling she had in the reading seemed as if a baby had matured to adulthood: "Through eyes I now see clearly ..." Before she could finish the sentence, she started laughing, and everyone else joined her because of the hilarious context (squinting and then putting on glasses).

After the laughter settled, Laura continued, "Eyes now see past judgment, from innocence to wisdom. Through love I see you. A new journey with clearer vision full of love. Meditation is actually connecting to your inner guidance. Instead of allowing external occurrences to influence you, go within."

Eileen, who had brought the object, confirmed what Laura said as she reflected on the reading, noting that during the last few years she had been working on being less judgmental and more accepting. Eileen had also been meditating more often over the last few months.

Despite the hilarity that occurs time to time, the information we need to hear is not clouded or diminished by it. Laughter can disperse the heaviness we sometimes feel in life and helps us remember the importance of taking time for joy as we grow.

Psychometry Makes Us Better

In an earlier chapter, I quoted Belleruth Naparstek's statement about how practicing intuition could make us even better human beings. After reading about the seven benefits of group psychometry with several examples in each, how could anyone disagree?

Pat makes a similar point, yet her words feel prophetic, as if she were speaking to those who would be reading about it in the future:

> I think there are times in everyone's life that we do things
> that are against the rules that society sets forth for us.
> We can always justify these actions by various ways of
> erroneous thinking. I think perhaps psychometry makes

us better, more spiritual people. It shows us that there is another world out there. We can overcome our erroneous thinking and become better people by listening to God when He speaks to us.

Pat's words could not be more aligned with the goals I held in my heart when I began the group—to create a sacred space for growing spiritually, learning how to help ourselves and others by listening to our inner guidance, and connecting, collectively, with Divine energy.

One evening, a message started coming to Laura while she drove to attend a psychometry meeting. She said the message was unusually clear and kept going and going, as if she could pull the car over and write down ten pages. That night, she received Angel's object, and the words came to her again, with even more strength and energy. Laura wrote down whatever came through, and as she shared it, Angel lowered her head in thought. Angel asked Laura to repeat a few of the phrases, and after she did, the room was still and quiet as Angel processed all of the information.

Then, as if lightning had struck in Angel's mind, she widened her eyes, sat up in her chair and said, "This reading has absolutely changed my life. I was talking with Suman about something we were both worried about earlier today, and this reading just . . . well, it just takes all that worry away." After Laura handed her what she had written, Angel looked at it again, repeating some of the phrases to us and explaining the nuances. The concern she had felt in the last week had been very deep, and even though she kept the details private, the look of relief on her face lifted the room. Angel smiled at Laura and said, "Laura, I know that sometimes you doubt your abilities, but there's never, ever a need for you to do that because this reading was absolutely so helpful and amazing. Like I said, it changed my life. Thank you." Angel's example is just one of many life-changing moments that have occurred during our psychometry/meditation group meetings through the years.

In the nineteenth century, Joseph Buchanan's dreams of using psychometry to revolutionize science, medicine, and history may, even today, still be reaching too far. But the practice of group psychometry could, in the not-too-distant future, transform conventional approaches to spirituality, counseling, healing, and more. What I've shown in this book about the power of psychometry brings to mind a famous statement attributed to Margaret Mead: "Never doubt that a small group of thoughtful committed citizens can change the world. Indeed, it is the only thing that ever has." Maybe it's just me, but I think group psychometry has more potential than just to make us better people . . . it gives us an opportunity to create a better world.

PART 5

Creating a Psychometry Group

"Let ordinary people meet by the millions across the borders.
Let them create a universal network of love and friendship."[88]
– Hagen Hasselbalch

[88] *Earth Prayers: 365 Prayers, Poems, and Invocations from Around the World*, eds. Elizabeth Roberts and Elias Amidon (New York: Harper One, 1991), 111.

CHAPTER 23

Deciding to Form a Psychometry Group

If you're interested in starting a psychometry/meditation group of your own, the following chapters may help set you up for success.

Perhaps it sounds easy enough to pick a day and time and get going, but I've learned a lot from making mistakes; I've also benefitted from talking with others and seeking answers from my own inner guidance. Starting a group is challenging, but it's also exciting and rewarding.

Although I'm a positive person, as I begin something, my first thought is wondering about all of the possible challenges, and my next thought is what can I do to prevent them? Some of the lists and details I provide may seem overwhelming at first glance because my goal is not only to help you analyze the pros and cons but also to help you avoid any mishaps. I hope you will see past my obsession with lists and see them as suggestions rather than absolutes.

For starters, my biggest suggestion is to see what's out there—explore what groups already exist. After that, the next two decisions are the most important: who will lead, and where your group will meet.

Timeline for Creating Your Own Psychometry/Meditation Group

The list here is just a quick reference for those who are thinking about creating their own group. In Eileen's words, the structure of our meetings is like a "recipe" for getting us in the right head- and heart-space. Below is a brief timeline—an overview—followed by chapters that detail all of the steps.

At Least a Month Ahead of Time

1. Look for similar groups in your area and attend a few.
2. Choose your "tribe"—this could be friends, like-minded people you already know, or you could choose to advertise on social media.
3. Decide on a leader, location, and day/time.
4. Prepare and send your invitation.
5. Explore different meditations that would be appropriate for your group (see Chapter 28, "More About Group Meditation").

During the Week Prior

1. Decide on what bowl you'll use for the objects along with a cover or scarf. (Note: a metal bowl could create too much noise.)
2. Make sure you choose your own object for the bowl, something that carries your unique energy.
3. Check to see if you have needed supplies (a specific list is in the upcoming chapter, "Planning at Least a Week in Advance").
4. Plan and prepare what snacks you'll have available. (I hope you don't choose to skip this part because chatting over food is a wonderful way to ease anxieties and create stronger bonds between people.)
5. Estimate how many chairs you'll need depending on who will be coming.

The Day/Evening Prior to Your Meeting

1. Place the chairs in a circle or conversation grouping.
2. Put out the utensils, snacks, semi-thick magazines, paper, pens, the psychometry bowl, and a scarf for its cover.
3. Clear your space, say a prayer, make sure that you are ready, too—by meditating and taking a few calming breaths. Try to be relaxed yet also upbeat.
4. Right before guests arrive, play soft, light music if you wish.
5. As everyone arrives, be as welcoming as possible and look them in the eyes as you do. Direct them to the snack area and chat. Show guests where to place their item in the bowl. Make sure to add your own item, too.

After Everyone Arrives

1. Wait about 10-15 minutes, then announce that the meeting is about to start. You can ring a Tibetan bowl, a bell, or just ask them to gather, sitting in a circle.
2. Begin with affirmations (for example, "I am Kim, and I am grateful").
3. Ask everyone to stand for the healing circle, using the guidelines from the following section, "More About Affirmations and the Healing Circle."
4. Begin the meditation.
5. As the meditation closes, pick up the bowl and pass it to your right so that each person can select an item. I typically wait until it comes back to me before picking an object.
6. Give everyone adequate time to focus within and write down their readings. You will be able to tell when people stop writing.
7. Someone might volunteer to go first, and after they finish, the person who received that reading goes next.

Closing the Group

1. After everyone has given and received a reading, the leader can ask all to stand, and then close the group. Typically, I close the group energetically by asking everyone to stand, hold hands, and send gratitude to their left, but you could ask people what they'd like to share about their experience if it's their first time and then end with a prayer. Someone's excitement might generate more interest in the next meeting.
2. Take time again for snacks and chatting.

CHAPTER 24

Specific Planning - at Least a Month in Advance

Find Your Tribe

All over the world, a variety of spiritual circles meet regularly. If you are truly interested in connecting with your inner guidance and using it to help yourself and others, it's incredibly important to "find your tribe." In order to do that, you will need to be a spiritual adventurer by discovering what groups work for you and making new connections. At the very least, all of this will help you decide whether or not a psychometry/meditation group is needed in your local area.

A few types of groups that focus on intuition and/or healing require some prior training; others don't. I'll list the "no training required" groups first.

Meetups

After a few years of going under the name "Psychometry Group," on Meetup, the group that used to meet at the Cosmic Bookstore in Tampa realized that not very many people on the "Meetup" app knew what the term, "psychometry" meant. After they changed their name to "Connect with Your Spirit Guides through Psychometry and Meditation," like-minded people started coming, and attendance started ranging between six and twenty-two attendees.

Finding a local meeting online will be a whole lot easier than moving to Tampa, though. Why not look online for a similar "Meetup" group and see?

Laura Day's Healing Circle

I was first introduced to Laura Day's work when I wrote my dissertation and read her book, *Practical Intuition*. I loved her approach and said to myself, "I have to meet this woman." Not long after I noticed that she was giving a workshop in Miami as part of a Hay House "I Can Do It" Conference, so I went. When I walked up to her after the workshop to say "hello," she was kind but also gracious by giving me her email address and inviting me to attend her retreat at Esalen in California. That was nearly 20 years ago, and since then I've been to two of her "bootcamp" training retreats at Esalen and look forward to going back sometime in the future.

What Day does is rare because of her unique, direct, no-nonsense style of teaching. There is no "woo-woo" involved. To her, intuition is natural and evidential. Reading Day's books, *Practical Intuition*, *The Circle*, and *How to Rule the World from Your Couch* all helped me hone my intuition, which at first was quite unfocused and undisciplined. The core of what she teaches is from her book, *The Circle*. Day asks us to write down a life-changing affirmation of our own, a statement in present tense that describes what we choose as our dynamic "new reality." I mentioned this as the jumping off point in the chapter on how to give a psychometry reading.

She sometimes offers healing circles in New York City free of charge and may still be doing those from time to time even though she moved to London. Day does not ask to be paid for her healing work—only her intuitive training classes. Far beyond the course, she generously mentors students as often as she can. I truly admire her work and all that she has given to help others.

If you're interested in learning more, Day offers healing circles online via Instagram and in-person workshops in New York, California, and London. I have to say that Day is one of the toughest and best teachers I've ever met. Her workshops absolutely changed my life—or, I should say, put me on the path to changing *my own* life.

Women's Groups

When I lived in Tampa, Charlotte hosted a women's group that focused on metaphysical topics. Each month, a different woman in the group would take the lead, so they had a different subject every month. Charlotte explains that the women in her group were acquaintances of hers who were comfortable with each other:

> I think hosting people you already know is a different thing than going somewhere new where you don't know anybody, and in that new environment, learning how to give a reading. I think it's very intimidating. In the women's group we did everything—colors, iridology, aromatherapy, sound healing, Reiki, psychometry, etc. We got together every month, and everyone looked forward to it.

Bookstore or Spiritualist Groups

Every large city seems to have a metaphysical bookstore or at least one eclectic enough to advertise something metaphysical. However, psychometry groups are a bit hard to find.

Shifting Souls, a metaphysical bookstore in Orlando, offers psychometry meetings twice a month (http://shiftingsouls.net). In Cassadega, Florida, the Southern Cassadaga Spiritualist Meeting Association also offers psychometry meetings occasionally. A few different ministers lead those groups, but they are not always advertised on the association's website: http://cassadaga.org.

Sometimes a local metaphysical publication can be helpful in finding a group. Practitioners advertise their services, but local happenings might include a variety of things—sound healing sessions, intuition workshops, or other opportunities for spiritual development and meeting like-minded people.

Local Church Groups

Most local churches, especially those that focus on prayer and contemplation, also offer workshops and retreats. Silent retreats—which are offered by many different denominations—can be very restorative. Other topics can focus on meditation, healing, and/or prayer.

Richard Rohr's teachings have opened my mind to a more expansive approach to Christianity than I ever had before. A few years ago, Rita and I attended a couple conferences and workshops offered by the Center of Action and Contemplation, founded by Rohr, and we met people there from many different faiths.

Five or six years ago, I taught a workshop on intuition for a Unity congregation at a retreat center. Although a church retreat may be an unusual place to learn about intuition, it's entirely possible to feel "spiritually comfortable" when our hearts and minds are open.

The following groups require some initial training, but they're worth it if you want to learn more:

Akashic Record Reading Groups

I first learned how to read the Akashic Records from a friend, Gabrielle Orr, who still teaches these classes (See GabrielleOrr.com). She offered group reading sessions for all of us to practice, and those were always helpful, fun, and thought-provoking. Once as I was learning to read the records, I thought I saw something happening to her father and told her about it. I was inexperienced and didn't know how to frame a reading just yet. I got caught up in worry and transferred that worry onto her. Akashic Records are not typically used to read the future, so what I thought I saw or felt was most likely something I misinterpreted. I will always regret causing her such worry, but I think it was an important lesson for me.

Gabrielle has published a few books on how to read the Akashic Records that I hope you check out, but there are others on the subject, too. The most well-known of these is by Linda Howe.

Once you've taken a class, I'm sure you'll be able to participate in a local group.

Reiki Share Groups

Usually a Reiki share group requires that only practitioners attend because it gives them a chance to discuss their practice with each other and provide group sessions. Having participated in many of these, I can say that there's no feeling like having 4 or 5 Reiki practitioners standing around the table "running energy" with you—whether it's your turn to receive as the "client" or not, it's truly an amazing experience.

Every city seems to have several teachers offering classes in Reiki 1, 2, or 3 and at least one Reiki share advertised online. Local metaphysical bookstores or churches may also offer Reiki shares periodically.

Choosing a Leader (or Deciding to Be One)

Whether you plan to begin a group in your home, bookstore, or elsewhere, you will need to have a leader, at least in the beginning. It's natural for the host to be the leader of the group, but if you don't feel comfortable with that, ask a close friend or find someone local whose personality blends well with yours. Let's discuss how those alternatives might play out.

Asking a Friend to Host

Asking a friend may be a good choice if both of you are flexible, balanced, well-organized, and positive. The benefits seem obvious: you have a sounding board whom you trust, you both have close-knit support as you grow together, and you both can share responsibilities so that the weight is not just on one person's shoulders. You can even switch hosting at each other's homes or occasionally take turns leading a meeting.

The group management might become easy, so easy, in fact, that a friend might feel so close to you that he or she could make assumptions without checking in first. You both may not always agree, for instance, on the size of the group, who does the inviting, who is invited, whether the format is flexible or routine, and who answers the inevitable questions about what the group is, how to do a reading, and how the group proceeds when one or the other person is ill or on vacation. In this case, your good friend would need to double-check with you about those significant issues and avoid making any relatively important decisions independently.

I believe that a good friendship is more important than the decisions you'll be making about the group, and when you have dear friends who know you so well that they can fill in the rest of your sentences, the decisions could become more difficult when you disagree—that is, unless you make problem-solving less of a burden by intentionally playing devil's advocate for each other.

So given all this, it's possible that of all three options, asking a friend may be the toughest unless your friendship is rock solid. And even when you've successfully chosen which one of your social circle will be leading the group, other like-minded friends who have similar talents might feel overlooked. Leading the group solo avoids most of that drama.

However, hosting with a friend could be a lot less stressful than my worrywart self is saying here. If you really want to host with a friend, I strongly suggest that both of you try to imagine worse case scenarios and write a list of options for each. Going over the list together and having fun with the scenarios would certainly get you both laughing and get your creative juices flowing as well.

Asking an Acquaintance to Host

If you decide to ask an acquaintance, it's likely that you believe this person would be a good leader, perhaps someone who has experience with meditation, readings, and teaching or group management. If he or she has a following, then you would need to make decisions about who would invite the prospective attendees. If you leave that to the acquaintance, you can expect people you don't know to be attending. This is important to decide up front, especially if you will be hosting in your own home.

Because challenges can sometimes intervene, consider what you'll do if the leader you've picked can only attend occasionally. What if he or she becomes unreliable or overbearing? Either of those two extremes can hinder your group's success. The same is true if you've chosen a friend to lead.

Other decisions become easier once you decide upon the ground rules concerning how you will be inviting people, how you both will make final decisions on format, how often to meet and where, etc. My advice here is the same as leading with a friend: go over worst-case scenarios together and see what comes up. Chances are that you can prevent challenges before they start.

Hosting on Your Own

It's much easier to make scheduling decisions on your own because you alone decide when and where your group will meet, who you will invite, and what the format will be. The only downside, if anything, is doing all of the preparation by yourself, including emailing or texting everyone, using a social platform, and preparing the meeting room.

If you're hosting at home, it's easier to decide whether to have snacks and how you want to set the atmosphere.

- Will it be quiet and undisturbed?
- Will you have enough chairs or cushions, plates and napkins, coffee, water, and tea?
- Will participants be bringing snacks to share?
- Will you light candles or just dim the lighting a bit when it's time for the readings?
- Would using some soft, wordless music during the first part of the meeting help your guests to relax and feel welcome?

Identifying Possible Participants

It's not unusual for a group to have a sprinkling of regular as well as sporadic attendees. For some, psychometry provides the specific support they need at certain periods in their lives. Then they move on, attending a different group or becoming busy with work or new relationships. Also, each month, the group's attendees might differ slightly if someone can't attend due to family commitments, busy work schedules, or vacations.

The group may consist of people with varied ages and races. The energy can be palpable and symbiotic. As the group "gels," the bond becomes unmistakable, and, somehow, that is divinely protected. As Pat explains, "The people there, you know there's no limit to what they would do for you if you really need it . . . and you feel the love and companionship, the warmth of your home." She goes on to explain that "occasionally someone comes in who disrupts the group, but they don't stay." Also, sometimes an individual wants to dominate the conversation or lead us in a different direction, but the group is too cohesive in its group sensibility for any one person to stand out.

Part of your future group's identity will come from a higher level of alignment or purpose. Everyone who enters the door contributes their own stories, their own experiences, their energy of giving and receiving, all of which are important. But it's the energy of listening, caring, and providing loving support that blends and binds everyone together. If we are overly focused on our own internal issues and spiritual progress and overlooking others' experiences, then there would be no purpose in forming a group.

The Importance of Who (and Who Doesn't) Attend

The first thing you must consider as you begin thinking about starting your own group is being conscious of who you invite. Does their personality and inner spirit blend well with other group members?

In the "Group Energy" section, I mentioned the work of neuroscientist, Moran Cerf. Individual mannerisms, the noise level and even the smell of a room, according to Cerf, "aligns our brain" with those around us.[89] I am mentioning this research again in order to emphasize the importance of sustaining a positive, welcoming, and compassionate atmosphere within the psychometry/meditation group. The loving and uplifting nature of each meeting depends on the consciousness of every person who attends, so perhaps it should go without saying that, as much as possible, avoid drama and gossip.

Group alignment takes time to create, so, at first, don't worry if you make a mistake with an invitation or two and someone ends up coming to the group who doesn't seem to really belong. Friends and acquaintances who can no longer maintain the same level energetic alignment will tend to lose interest while, at the same time, those who start growing spiritually and aligning with their own higher goals in life start spending time with those who share the same "vibe." Remember that as you treat everything as a learning experience and seek positive outcomes for every situation, the group will inevitably mirror your own development and benefit from all of the ways you grow and mature.

Secondly, I can't emphasize too much that basing your invitation on whether or not someone is "good enough" for the group is not the point. Someone can be totally unfamiliar with the process of psychometry or

---

[89] Weller, "Most Important Choice," July 28, 2017.

giving readings or even meditation yet could be a wonderful addition to your circle. At times, experienced "readers" can become so focused on the quality of their own performance that they forget about the importance of spontaneity, vulnerability, and listening to what others have to say. Everyone needs to know that judging the quality of each reading can be harmful to group solidarity because it sets up an unnecessary hierarchy that impedes communal sharing and loving support.

It's also helpful if each member understands that in order to receive a reading, they must give one. Our group tends to put more effort into the giving part than the receiving part. If someone is just wanting a new experience or is just being curious, they're usually not invested in spiritual growth (for themselves or others). Curiosity or receiving helpful guidance are not reasons to attend—or at least, not reasons for continuing.

As a way of preventing this from happening, I have an agreement with the angels and guides who protect the group, asking them to guard us from guests who would disrupt the open and supportive community we share. So if anyone joins us for the sole purpose of receiving a reading and puts almost no energy into the giving, we've found that the Universe consistently diverts the "takers" to find many other things to do during the time of our monthly meetings. If anyone attends whose energy doesn't match, then I ask for life to present them with a better opportunity to grow, something that doesn't interfere with the sacred, loving atmosphere we create together. The result is that this person's desire to attend usually fades after the first couple of visits.

Protecting the Sacredness of Group Connections

In the early days, someone would occasionally invite a friend without letting me know in advance. I understand that it's natural for people to be excited about the group and want to share that excitement with friends and loved ones, but just because a friend is interested doesn't mean their "energy" will blend well with the rest of us.

I've had to be very firm about protecting the sacredness of the group's connections. This means having to be tough and not let other people's feelings interfere. If I accepted everyone who wanted to attend and used their friendliness or sociability as a gauge, our home would be over capacity every month and the close connections in the group would be at risk.

In ten years, though, I've only had to say "no" twice when an attendee asked if they could bring someone else. In the first case, I knew that this person was more interested in receiving readings than in giving them. A few times I had witnessed this person asking several people in our group to give her readings on the spot or calling them on the phone asking for intuitive advice. In this case, the decision was easy.

In the other case, I knew that the partner of a guest someone asked me to invite had a bold personality; she was an amazing woman, for sure—both women were. However, since the partner had been colleagues with someone who was already in the group, I checked in with the colleague first before accepting the request. This colleague, I'll call her "Ann," told me what I already suspected, that even though one person in the couple would be a wonderful addition to the group, if she brought her partner later, some members would feel uncomfortable sharing pieces of their personal lives. I couldn't tell a new person to attend by herself, without her partner, so I had to play gatekeeper. It was a relief for me to avoid the personal complexities of the situation by relying on the fact that our group had grown to a comfortable number, with no room to expand, even for two more. That felt just as true without causing harm, so that's the response I used.

Coming along with a spouse or girlfriend or joining just because psychometry is interesting might be okay reasons to join in once or twice. However, the best reason for attending, I believe, is a person's desire to grow and be part of a supportive community. I am proud to say that each member of our group truly cares about their own and others' spiritual development. They put their whole being into giving the best possible reading for someone else and are genuinely interested in the readings others receive. We often celebrate each other's messages or well up with tears when we hear another person's reading. Our sense of community is the primary focus. The reason for this is that we are interested in maturing together and growing spiritually rather than just learning more ways to be "psychic."

Over the years, I've learned from my early mistakes regarding who is invited or not—especially since the group has grown to be so loving and fulfilling. The author of *The Art of Gathering*, Priya Parker, reiterates that a communal intention for a group is important, especially since "the purpose of a gathering can remain somewhat vague and abstract until it is clarified by drawing the boundary between who is in and out."[90] In determining the list of who to invite and who to exclude, Parker prompts group organizers to ask themselves questions such as "Who not only fits but also helps fulfill the gathering's purpose?" "Who threatens the purpose?" "Who, despite being irrelevant to the purpose, do you feel obliged to invite?"[91]

The most difficult decisions regarding the attendee list, she says, relate to "politeness and habit."[92] How do gathering organizers keep from filling the group with those whom they feel obligated to invite yet do not contribute to fulfilling the group's purpose? Parker labels the typical irrelevant attendee as "Bob." "Every gathering has its Bobs . . . Bob your friend's girlfriends' brother. Bob your visiting aunt. Bob is perfectly pleasant and doesn't actively sabotage your gathering."[93] Yet, she urges, "The crux of excluding thoughtfully and intentionally is mustering the courage to keep away your Bobs."[94] This is particularly important in small groups where everyone's contribution is important. Even one person who is not on track with the rest creates an imbalance that can affect the entire meeting—and not just for a single afternoon or evening meeting, but for future ones as well.

Once a welcoming invitation is extended, it's nearly impossible to retract. Since the kind of psychometry and meditation group you will be organizing requires being sensitive to individual and group energy, I strongly suggest that you not only pray up but suit up: gird your loins, recharge your intuition batteries, and put on your thinking cap. Do this in addition to placing a shield of protective light around your meeting space before you extend any invitations.

Remember that when you are strong and restrict invitations only to those whose energy supports the purpose of your group, your loyal attendees will feel safe and free to express themselves. Although each person may not know how you are protecting them or be able to voice the empowering way that this safety affects the group, they place their

---

[90] Priya Parker, *The Art of Gathering: How We Meet and Why it Matters* (New York: Riverhead Books, 2018), 41.

[91] Parker, *Gathering*, 42.

[92] Parker, *Gathering*, 43.

[93] Parker, *Gathering*, 43.

[94] Parker, *Gathering*, 43.

unspoken trust in you, completely and without question. It's up to you to ensure that meetings they've grown to love can continue to provide trusted opportunities for growth and empowerment.

Special Cases

Should children attend?

At what age would it be appropriate for a child to either sit in with the group or become part of it? That would depend entirely on the maturity of the child. Psychometry meetings can last between ninety minutes to two and a half hours. Could a child sit that long without whining, talking at inappropriate times, or wanting to go elsewhere? Would other members be patient with a child's innocent interruptions?

Perhaps a teenager or two could attend, depending on their interest. Or, alternatively, a teen could go in another room during the meeting as long as she or he could work on a fair amount of homework or could use a device with headphones. Even this, though, for over two hours might be too much.

Maybe this sounds overly harsh, but I have had a decade or more experience as gatekeeper and even more experience being the mother of a (now grown up) well-behaved only child. I've also come to believe, though, that anything is possible. Children who are old enough to understand and apply the process of meditation and psychometry could benefit from it. The dynamic of the group would certainly change, so decisions about whether to welcome children in the group would, hopefully, be a communal decision decided well beforehand.

Also, these decisions could relate to adults with conditions that have limited their cognitive abilities. Charlotte told me that one of the women who attends their Tampa psychometry group brings her daughter who has Down Syndrome. This daughter has given readings, sometimes written with just a few words, but often, she says more. That's the extent of what most newcomers write, anyway. Charlotte described the girl as "so sweet— just pure love," so the Tampa group has been very supportive and loving in return. Who is to say that this girl should be prevented from attending and connecting with her inner guidance and helping others in the process?

Perhaps in the future some amazing person will create and lead a children's psychometry group. Courses on well-being in some elementary schools have started to include meditation, which was certainly far from the public school mindset when I grew up in the sixties and seventies.

The truth is, I've never had to be concerned about a parent bringing a child to our meetings. The only case I remember occurred once when a woman needed to bring along her thirteen-year-old son. He only came once, and when he did, he was perfectly quiet and happy to be alone so that he could play video games until the meeting was over. In fact, he was so quiet, we forgot he was in the other room!

It's always been self-evident that we offer a calming space for adults, one without distractions or disturbances. When each person focuses on the object they picked and thinks about what to write for the reading, the concentration in the room is so heavy with intent that any distracting sound could potentially be a bit jarring. Usually animals are calm during this time, but in the last ten years or so, even our sweet dog has barked a few times at the wrong moment (defending us from some imperceptible noise outside). Just as unexpectedly, another member of your household could walk into the kitchen for a snack, or the sound could carry from someone turning on the television in a nearby room. As a potential host, you'll need to know whether other members of your household will be home the night of your group and whether your quiet time could possibly be interrupted. All this is important to keep in mind, especially if you have toddlers or children in elementary school.

Couples in the Group

Knowing that the divorce rate in America is between forty and fifty percent, it's likely that some members of your group may split with their significant other at some point while they are attending. If husbands and wives or partners come to the group separately at first, then bring their spouse later, they may not always feel comfortable if their previous partner keeps attending. I've had a couple situations surrounding this issue, and I wish I could share some perfectly wise advice so that you can prevent these challenges, but all I can do is tell you how the Universe worked things out in these cases.

First, I have to mention that I was single when I started my own group, but I had set the firm intention beforehand that my future partner would not only have to be aligned with attending but would join me in continuing the monthly group for as long as we were able to host. This was so important to me that as part of my online dating profile, I listed hosting a monthly group as one of the most important parts of my life. Needless to say, all that worked out extremely well, and my wife looks forward to the group as much as I do.

As the psychometry group grew over the years, yes, a few couples split. In one case, the breakup was so tough between two female partners that neither would feel comfortable if the other attended the same night. I'll use pseudonyms for each. "Stella" had been coming solo for a couple years, and then she invited her girlfriend "Holly" after their relationship blossomed.

Early after their break-up, Stella expressed that in order to heal, she needed to be separate from Holly. Both women wanted to continue coming to the psychometry group, yet Stella did not feel comfortable attending since her ex-girlfriend planned to keep going, regardless. Stella called me and expressed disappointment that by continuing to attend the group, Holly would not be providing her the space she needed. As a temporary compromise, they agreed to attend on alternate months. This worked for a while, but eventually, Stella said that psychometry had always been like a sacred lifeline for her and after coming consistently for two years prior, the discontinuity of going every-other-month became disruptive.

Since Stella had initially invited Holly, I encouraged Stella to reach out once more to her ex-partner with another direct request—by asking her not to attend and reminding her that Stella was one of the original members of the group.

Maybe that wasn't the best approach because Stella reported back saying that Holly refused her request.

At this point, I planned to talk with Holly myself and ask her to stop attending—not easy for me to do because both had been coming together for a year. Yet I felt protective of Stella and was disappointed that Holly assumed that the sole decision of continuing to attend "my group" was hers alone. This was difficult because no matter what I decided to do, someone would be hurt.

As it turned out, we had to cancel the next psychometry group because my wife broke her ankle and had a concussion. During that two-month period between groups, Holly changed her mind about continuing to attend psychometry because, as she shared, she started feeling distant from the group. I know that I missed an opportunity to have an open conversation with Holly, but I was nonetheless grateful for her decision to move on to other spiritual opportunities.

What I learned from this experience with Stella and Holly is that in the very beginning, I failed to clarify my role as "group gatekeeper." Since the group meets in my home and is under my direction, I must make final decisions concerning who may or may not attend. Yet, even as I say this, I'm aware that I'm not "really" in charge. In this case, and in every case, the Universe steps up and takes over. Rather than confronting Holly myself, the result ended up causing less pain thanks to divine timing and grace.

Another breakup occurred with a different couple, yet they handled their breakup so well that it seemed to be a role model for how to end a long-term relationship. After each attended every other week for a few months, their friendship for each other never failed. I'm sure they had their own separate heartaches, and it must have been extremely difficult for them, especially when both eventually attended a meeting at the same time. They continued parenting but handled their separation in such a way that never, at any time, did either of them speak of the other in a way that was anything other than positive or supportive. That's so rare, that I don't think I've ever encountered that before with any of the other couples I've known who have gone their separate ways. Both women in this role-model couple still attend, and all of us look to them as the best possible example of a couple that can continue to be loving despite no longer being in love.

So, given some of my mistakes regarding who to include or not in our psychometry meetings, my guides and angels had to step in. I am still learning, and I still have to pray up and stand up, but I continue to be grateful that everything works out for the best when I focus on community and purpose as the two most important ingredients.

Choosing a Meeting Space and Time

Instead of occurring in the evening, the meeting time could be morning or afternoon, depending on what works best for you and your guests.

Where Will You Meet?

Which is best for you and the group, a public or private space?

If your meetings are advertised to the public, you'll need a few key members to ground the group with a solid sense of collegiality and familiarity. It's best if these people are familiar with each other and like-minded. If by chance a couple visitors attend on a particular night when their energy seems off-putting, the presence of your key members alone can offset that, making the whole tone of the psychometry meeting much lighter.

You can rent a room in a library, bookstore, or community center, either weekly or monthly, and it's important to decide whether your meeting times will coincide with the store's open hours. If you'll meet after it's closed, who will be responsible for unlocking the room? Will noise in the store or community center become a problem during the meditation and reading process? Will you be able to offer snacks to share, and if so, will you have time to clean up?

If you set up in a bookstore, local center, or church, remember that establishing a sense of community will require your attention. It takes time to develop group cohesion, and even more time when the meeting occurs in a public setting, so allow some leeway for that. As Charlotte explains, "That sense of compassion and generosity and sense of openness to 'what can I do to help you' is part of why a group can succeed. When strangers come to a bookstore, they don't necessarily have that sense of 'I want to help you . . . I love you, etc.' You do that to friends, in your own life's soul group."

Also, it would be important to be aware that if meeting in a public place, you probably won't be able to have food or use candles. If you are allowed to have snacks, you'll need to bring them (which means that the list of napkins, water, cups, serveware, etc., could grow quite long). Using music would be easy with a portable bluetooth speaker, but if it's connected to your phone, it's possible that potential attendees could be calling you for help with directions, parking, or texting at the last minute.

Overall, you'll need a quiet area, "psychometry" supplies (see below), and the ability to set a strong intent for having a successful meeting. I suggest reading ahead in this book so that you are prepared for the healing circle and meditation portions of the meeting.

If you decide to make your group private or, in other words, establish it via word-of-mouth, it's just as important as it is when going public to begin with a core group of people who will attend fairly often. Hopefully, the names of the people you can invite for that will come easily to you. If not, then try attending a few meditations or metaphysical "meetup" groups on your own. You could also find a local Unity congregation or open-minded church.

The key is creating a connection with others who share similar beliefs about energy healing, meditation, and intuitive messages. Once that important component sets the foundation, everything else comes easily.

Creating the Invitations

The group generally lasts between two to two and a half hours, and hosting a group of nine is ideal. If you have more than a dozen people, you might need to reduce the time everyone spends chatting. Hosting more than 15 people in one meeting might make it difficult to focus the group energy and have adequate time for all of the readings.

Sending an Invitation by Email

From a week to a few days prior to each meeting, I send a reminder email to everyone who signed up. It took a few tries to get the wording just right because I realized that some were forwarding the email to others who may not understand what we typically do in a meeting. For example, some who were unfamiliar with our routine expected to receive a reading without giving one, and when they came to the group, it seemed clear that they were fidgety and less receptive to the readings that the other women gave to each other. After that, I modified the email, emphasizing that each attendee must give as well as receive a reading and that each person needed to check with me before inviting someone else. Below is the typical email format I use for the monthly meeting announcement:

Hello to our psychometry "family" and friends!

On Friday evening (insert date), we're hosting our monthly psychometry/meditation group at 7:00 PM (our address is at the bottom). We are so honored to welcome this amazing group of people, all of whom lift the energy of our lives and our planet.

Next month, plan ahead to meet at our house on

_____

This psychometry/meditation group is very special. If you are receiving this invitation for the first time, please read the info below. I'll will have the following snacks available:_____ *(NOTE: This varies. It could be fresh fruit, veggies and dip, cheese, gluten-free crackers and hummus, etc.).* Regular attendees, if you'd like to bring something to share, please do.

Our love and appreciation for this group grows and grows. We see such wonderful results when every person wants to give a reading that helps someone else. Each month something special happens with the shared readings to uplift everyone. We learn so much from each of you, and the opportunity this group provides for all of us to expand our awareness is just amazing. Because this is an invitation-only group, I am grateful to you for protecting the sacredness of our meetings, checking with me before inviting anyone else, and also for supporting each other so well.

What we do and advice about giving a psychometry reading:

As you know, please bring a small object that you can hold in your hand and put in our psychometry bowl. Come with an open mind and heart, and please remember that our goal is to practice connecting to own inner guidance for the purpose of helping each other. That's actually the key to why this group has been so special to us—reaching out to each other in friendship and love.

We start with affirmations, then create a healing circle to send light to those who need it, and after that, start a meditation. Once the meditation closes, I pass the bowl around and ask you to pick out an object that is not your own. Then we take time to apply our intuitive insights, write down thoughts, impressions, etc., and share what we "received" with the group. After that, we give the written reading to the one who brought the object.

Giving a reading is so easy—it's the letting go of judgment about saying the right thing that's so hard. Just be open to what you see, hear, imagine, and feel the lightness of giving a reading. Breathe deep a few times. Allow the message to unfold. Wait for it to come to you rather than grasp for information, and you'll see what I mean. It's my hope that we can all say something useful and productive in our messages to each other, but even if something doesn't seem to make sense at first, no one judges each other's readings. If you only receive a few words or a phrase or two, that's totally ok. Expect to hear something helpful and be willing to receive.

Also, it helps us to know if you're coming. No need to reply if you can't attend the group this time.

Sending blessings and love to all!

My name
Address
Email
Cell phone number

Note that I included a potential date for a current and future meeting, a reminder about bringing an object, and a note about whether to bring a snack. If you are paying a fee for your rental space, decide how much money you will charge for your event. Also remember to include information about parking and the promptness of your group start-time. If you're going to chat for a while first, that serves as a buffer, but once the healing circle starts, lateness can become disruptive.

It's been over a dozen years since that first email invitation, and it seems that over the last two years, some of the attendees who attend once or twice a year lose track of the email announcement. Due to having so much spam or relying on text message communications, I could potentially use a Facebook group in addition to email, but most of the regular attendees know when the meetings are and spread the news to each other. Because the group isn't so big that anyone has to sit on the floor, and also because it meets in my home, I prefer to stay clear of any public social media announcements.

Start Small and Watch it Grow

As you begin to plan, I suggest scheduling three to six meetings to give yourself and/or your co-host time to dive in, learn from some minor mistakes, and allow group members to feel comfortable with the process. In the introduction, I mentioned that Lynda needed to give and receive three readings before it began to feel natural. Give your group some time for those types of adjustments.

As you continue your advance preparation, you can refer to the brief timeline I mentioned earlier. It's straightforward and, hopefully, easy to follow.

The next couple chapters, though, take an even deeper dive into how we begin an actual meeting, specifically in terms of how to start the affirmations, direct the healing circle, and lead the mediation.

CHAPTER 25

More About Affirmations and the Healing Circle

Prior to standing for the healing circle, we begin the group sometimes with a ring from a Tibetan bowl or just with a welcome. One evening Lissette brought a rattle that she bought from Mexico. She circled the group and cleared the energy for each of us. Sometimes Lynda plays a flute, which unifies and clears energy as well.

After that, we start with the person on my right who begins the affirmations. We say our names (when we have newcomers) and then state something like, "I am Kim, and I am peaceful." If Charlotte attends, she usually extends her affirmation, which always makes us smile: "I am Charlotte, and I am grateful for my family, all of my friends, my health, my home, and for my many blessings," Or, "I am Charlotte, and I am always in the right place at the right time." My point in saying this is that we don't have to stop at just one word. It's important to express positive affirmations, especially when our emotions can back them up. They express part of the wonderful person we truly are at that time and also add good "juju" to the group.

Like the rattle and the music, affirmations are important for a practical reason; they focus everyone's attention away from distractions, away from unfinished conversations, and into the group centering process.

Placed just after going around the circle with affirmations, the healing circle is next. It serves the multiple purpose of opening our hearts, grounding, clearing the space in preparation for the meditation, and supporting ourselves and each other through a prayer that we back up with a big blast of vibrational healing light. Elizabeth describes the healing circle as something she looks forward to every time we have a session.

> When we do the healing and the healing circle, and we get the energy going, it is incredible for me. I can feel it very intensely moving through my arms and out my palms from one side and down the other into the next person. I was able to experience that very early on in the very first sessions.

> At first, when we start the healing circle, the energy is a little sluggish, and then the more we start to move through it, and when we start to pump up the energy, it starts to clear more and more, and the more it moves, the more intense it is. Actually, it's like we are amping up the energy that is forcing the blocks out of everybody else in the circle, and we are strategically placed exactly where we need to be with whomever is around us. That's why the energy is so powerful—it's that we are healing each other. That energy field puts us in the mindset to give the best psychometry reading that we can possibly give.

> And without a doubt, I know that the energy that gets generated in that circle for all those loved ones whose names that are spoken and unspoken must feel some of what we are generating, they have to. It is so intense!

> And because generating that energy was effortless for me, it gave me validation that I was in the right place doing the right thing.

From Sabrina: "I was amazed at the energy I felt within that room and within that circle. The room seemed to spin with energy and flowed with light—even though the room was dimmed."

From Eileen: "The healing circle connects our hearts."

From Adrienne: "Having worked as a healer, I can tell you that when we did the healing part of the circle, it was powerful. You could really feel the energy flow, and I believe the reason for that is because we were all in accord with each other."

Although I describe what occurs in our healing circle in the chapter, "Example of a 'Typical' Group Meeting," I am listing the steps below to reinforce its importance and also make the sequence easier to follow. Of course, I might vary what I say here occasionally, but this is basically the gist of it:

1. Stand and close your eyes.
2. Breathe slowly a few times and focus your energy on your heart. You will begin to feel warmth there as your energy expands.
3. Let's let go of any stress or whatever isn't our highest and best by sending it to the Earth to be recycled and cleansed. As we feel the refreshed energy rising through our feet, it travels up through our legs, torso, arms and head and then back down again, into the Earth, balancing our energies and encircling us with light.
4. Next, hold out both hands, left palm up and right palm down. As you hover over each other's hands without touching, you might be able to feel the energetic waves. Direct their flow to the right, counterclockwise, from person to person, to open the energy of our circle. As you do this, consciously send love to the person standing on your right.
5. Now, while still hovering over each other's hands, say the names of those who need healing, including yourselves, either silently or aloud.
6. As we finish, move just your right hand only in a flat, counterclockwise circle above the other person's hand to your right. As we pump up the energy and it starts to build and grow stronger, we imagine rainbows of healing light reaching each person and situation in need of support, wherever and however they need it most.
7. From this powerful feeling of intention, let's hold hands and repeat our healing affirmation: "Healing rays . . . from the Divine Source of all power . . . are penetrating my body . . . making me perfectly whole."

Charlotte has led the healing circle in Tampa thousands of times. She has often told me that "sending healing in the energy circle is like prayer . . . it *is* prayer, actually."

Eileen visualizes the energy of the healing circle and can also sense the heat from it:

> Going from the healing circle straight to the meditation makes sense now that I think about it. We are all calm, open, and in the present so the amount of energy we generate gets fairly intense.
>
> I picture this energy as a sort of inverted whirlpool that we generate, contain, and focus. Each name we declare, verbally or not, enters the base of this whirlpool, spirals around it gathering energy, and then shoots out the top seeking the person it has been sent to. I have heard others express seeing the energy as light or feeling it like a hum or buzz or even electricity. I sense it as a flowing heat or warmth. Because of that, in the beginning, I mistook feeling the energy for a hot flash until I realized that the heat I feel flows, pulses, and can change direction.

The power of this part of the evening is something we can never take for granted. We may not always hear about each other's experiences, but we know, just as Elizabeth said, "The ones whose names that are spoken and unspoken must feel some of what we are generating, they have to."

After we finish this part of the evening, I ask everyone to sit and get comfortable as I begin the meditation.

The next chapter explains this part of the "psychometry group recipe," and provides some recommendations.

CHAPTER 26

More About Group Meditation

"One meditates, then, not in order to produce a successful meditation but in order to be transformed into an ever more compassionate person."[95]
—Professor and Episcopal Priest, Vincent Pizzuto

If you are interested in hosting a group, my assumption is that you've had some experience meditating on your own as well as with others. The more experience you have with it, the better, because all too often people think that spending time in quiet reflection is the same as meditation, but it's not. Reflection is usually a strictly mental activity; the kind of meditation I'm recommending here is more connected to heart-energy. Sometimes getting into a meditative space requires us to relax, which is the first step. But going beyond that to a deeper heart-space is the goal. That space can be so expansive that our physical presence seems to be without boundaries, yet, at the same time, connected to a wholeness of being that is content and indescribably peaceful.

The quality of the group meditation is key on several levels:

1. it draws our attention to the present;
2. it fosters each person's connection to a deeper sense of the Divine within;

---

[95] Vincent Pizzuto, *Contemplating Christ: The Gospels and the Interior Life.* (Collegeville, MN: Liturgical Press, 2018), quoted in Center for Action and Contemplation, "Fruit of Our Labor," December 10, 2020, https://cac.org/daily-meditations/fruit-of-our-labor-2020-12-10/.

3. it raises the frequency of energy in the room from the mental and physical level to the heart/soul level, and

4. because of all this, it serves as the cornerstone for the rest of the evening because it creates a private, sacred space for each person.

"The benefits of meditation alone are fabulous," Charlotte says, "but psychometry takes it to a whole, higher level." Elizabeth expands this point to say, "The meditation gives everybody an opportunity to shake off the day, to settle down, focus, get in the now, and I think that's the reason why the readings themselves are so valuable. I think if it was done in the reverse, if the meditation occurred afterward, it would not be quite the same." She also explained that the kinds of meditations we do in the group were much different from the meditation practice that she had been used to before:

> I had done a little meditation previously and found it to be a positive and relaxing experience. So I was open to that. I have never experienced meditation in the ways that it has been done in the monthly sessions. Sometimes it is like taking a small vacation, sometimes it is being tuned in through reminders of chakras and clearing and meanings and purpose. Sometimes it is a recording with a very soothing voice that takes you on a journey and then brings you back again. All of them were excellent and gave me peaceful and uplifting energy.

Eileen says that at the time she started attending, she thought meditation "had to be solitary to be effective." But experiencing group meditation changed her mind:

> I have since found that, at least for me, it's easier to put aside the concerns of the day and find that calm stillness when surrounded by others seeking that same place. Could it be that, subconsciously, we help each other find that still place within? I don't know for sure, but it feels that way to me. I find that meditations offer the same feeling I get when I'm out in nature. Whether the meditation is

structured or more free form, I am able to find that place of peace and calm, that place of openness and acceptance, that place to just be. It is a place of safety, connectedness, and boundless love.

The order of placing the meditation prior to psychometry is very important because guided imagery opens the heart and expands our intuitive range. Each section below provides some advice on how to use different kinds of meditations in a group setting. There are many kinds of guided journeys and many ways of listening to them. Consequently, there are so many belief systems and creative approaches that it's hard to discern which might be best. Whatever meditation we use, setting a clear, compassionate intention for yourself and the group is most important. In this section, I hope I am able to narrow the field a bit while also providing hosts the space to find the best fit for themselves and their group.

When the meditation goes well, the whole room fills with positive, powerful vibrations. One evening, I had finished a meditation on the chakras, including the colors. As we opened our eyes, we saw a beautiful rainbow shining on the lake outside our sliding glass doors. Experiences like these in meditations and in the healing circle have helped our psychometry group expand spiritually by highlighting the larger purposes of our lives and enhancing our abilities to let go of the everyday dramas that tend to clog our energy fields.

Attending the group in Tampa every week helped me grow, reminding me that when I experienced frustration, it usually got stuck somewhere in my body. Sitting in meditation with the group helped me clear that energy both physically and emotionally so that I truly felt lighter afterward.

Live Meditations

Almost always, I prefer a "live" meditation rather than a recording. It's best to keep them short enough to allow time for the reading exchanges later on (so not over 15 minutes) and yet long enough for everyone to fall into that wispy and blissful semi-trance state and stay there a bit (not less than ten minutes for the whole meditation). The words or the flow of the imagery doesn't matter as much as the energy of your intention—of your heart.

Although it's important that everyone can hear you, the individuals sitting before you can *feel* the energy no matter what words you say or whether your grammar is perfect or whether you take them on a journey to a beach, sit on a cloud, put themselves in a bubble of light, or ride a magic carpet.

During a live meditation, each of us remains open to a guided journey that takes us through a new and unexpected experience. In the Tampa group, one of us would volunteer to lead, and even if the same person offered to provide a meditation for a few weeks in a row, each one always felt new because it introduced us to a range of journeys that could include waterfalls, serene beaches, or deep forests—all inhabited by angelic beings; joyful, fairly-like guides; or ancient, wise masters. The meditations alone were enough to keep me coming back every week, so giving and receiving insightful readings was an added bonus.

Giving voice to a live meditation yourself or recruiting a volunteer will have benefits far beyond what you can imagine right now. With everyone sitting around you, the words just come. Trust me. It's as if you are activating what you see or feel in your own trance-like meditative state. Remember, your intuition flows faster than your imagination. Allow it to rise naturally from your heart, and once you've established a sense of trust with the group, everyone will follow your lead without having to think about it.

Using Recorded Meditations

Audio meditations can be wonderful, but I strongly encourage you to test several prior to using one for the group. When I attended Ruth's Thot-watchers at the Cosmic Bookstore in Tampa, sometimes we used a recorded meditation, depending on the group's needs and interests. I remember one from Ted Andrews called "The Middle Pillar," which combined Kabbalistic and Christian terminology. Andrews has a powerful voice, and this, along with the music, gave me chills. I could sense the energy of the words traveling through my body, which is an experience that helped me understand that meditation was not just going on an imaginative journey but, instead truly experiencing it on multiple levels—through my mind, heart, body, and soul.

Many spiritual writers and speakers today have recordings available that would be appropriate for group meditation. As you listen to them, make sure the words, message, tone of voice, and music (if any) all work together to support the group environment you wish to create. I have a few meditations of my own posted on Insight Timer, but as I mentioned, there are thousands of others available, too. In the past, I've used audio meditations from Ted Andrews, Sonia Choquette, Diana Cooper, Laura Day, Esther and Jerry Hicks, and many others.

Longer Meditations – Some Do's and Don'ts

Once the group is well-established, you could offer longer meditations at a different time or day than the regularly scheduled meetings. This is important because readings can often call attention to an area of someone's life that needs unpacking or healing. To some degree, the energy people share together helps with that, yet from time to time it's beneficial to offer more intensive, longer meditations as a separate event which provides an opportunity for a deeper level of spiritual awakening than what the typical group evening can provide.

One evening I invited a small group of friends to hear the "Crystal Cave Meditation" by Josie Ravenwing, which is about 40 minutes long. In the meditation, she takes her listeners through a ritual in which they can receive messages for themselves as well as the opportunity to offer or accept healing through maternal and fraternal family lines. It's quite powerful and profound, requiring quite a bit of meditative focus and emotional processing. Although we shared some food afterward, conversations were muted and quiet rather than chatty and vibrant. The whole tone of the event was much different, but also much needed once in a while.

So whether a meditation is 40 minutes or just 20, if it involves healing work, grieving, forgiveness, and letting go, it can be all-consuming and deeply intimate. After such inward intensity, it would be difficult to switch gears and provide another person with a helpful reading.

Silent Meditations

A minute or two of silence after a group meditation is essential; however, I would not recommend using silence as the entire meditation. I have been meditating for over 30 years, but it's only been in the last decade that I would feel focused enough in a group setting to slip into Zen mode and stay in the silence for 10-15 minutes. It's taken me years to filter mental and physical distractions, so I wouldn't expect a group of people who have varying levels of experience to be able to do that.

Some people can arrive at a deep meditative state through focusing repeatedly on their breath. Although this kind of silence is comforting, its purpose is not the same as with a guided journey. Cleansing the mind, soul, body, and emotions as preparation for receiving guidance creates a place of expectancy and openness. Clearing this pathway through breath, in my opinion, seems more like entering a void or emptying the wastebasket of your mind. Entirely useful, but why stop at the first stage? Guided meditations usually take listeners further as they aim for expansivness—toward a state of awareness rather than emptiness.

Short Meditations

Shorter meditations truncate the time people need in order to calm themselves and unwind into stillness. A prayer put to music might be okay, depending on the group, but usually a song lasts only a few minutes—not long enough for people to really relax into a deeper state of consciousness. Beginning with a song and then following it with a ten-minute period of soft music for deeper contemplation could work as an alternative, especially if you're seeking variety or still need time to practice giving a live meditation.

For one meeting, by recommendation, I used the song, "Deer's Cry." The rising swell of the music and lyrics carry the essence of Celtic spirituality—a mixture of Christ-consciousness and nature. Because the song is short, I followed it with a 10-minute playlist using wordless, soft music. Since everyone in our group is mature enough to welcome spiritual points of view that are a bit different from their own, a song with the words, "Christ with me, Christ before me, Christ behind me, Christ in me ..." translated well enough to each person's experience.

Speaking for myself, I would not enjoy offering the same audio meditation every month or every week, so offering something new each time is important to me. If you can only provide a short, live meditation, try playing some wordless, non-sectarian music underneath your spoken voice. For instance, Solfeggio Frequency tones or Binaural Beats might work well. Typically notes from an extremely high-pitched, loud flute or bird squawks from nature tracks can be jarring, so just like my advice for audio meditations, try out a few different ones first.

As an especially important side note, if you choose to use meditation music from an app such as YouTube, Spotify, or Pandora, make sure that advertisements don't pop up unexpectedly and ruin the tranquility you've worked so hard to create.

Using Written Meditations as Guideposts

Reading a written meditation to help the group tune into their intuition would be acceptable, but I would only use one as a last resort for two reasons. First, the person reading the script misses out on the opportunity of experiencing a deeper connection with his or her inner guidance. Second, the emotion in a prepped reading is less active than for a live one. Live readings are more engaging because they sound and feel real. Both can carry a sense of wonder for what happens next, but it's difficult to read from a piece of paper or a book and convey the same sense of "aliveness."

Of course, there can be exceptions to this since we all need to turn to resources to spark our imagination when we feel our typical meditation time might be growing stale. So, in such cases, allow me to offer several suggestions. Remember that these are just guides. My best advice is to practice a few of these until you can narrate them without needing to read anything word for word.

Written meditations appear in a variety of publications. If you're new to leading meditations, try using a written one that is clear, with steps that are easy to remember. In my own practice, I've discovered a few that fit into this category, in no particular order:

- Belleruth Naparstek's book, *Your Sixth Sense*, has several guided meditations that can be read or recorded and played for the group. Try her meditation titled, "Imagery to Dissolve into Universal Wisdom," and the one following that, "Imagery for Receiving an Answer as a Gift," pages 125-133. I highly recommend reading her book and using several of her meditations on your own so that you can present them comfortably when introducing them to the group.

- Paul Selig's book, *I Am the Word,* includes a meditation featuring a ladder that rises into the clouds (see pages 81-83).[96]
- Rebecca Rosen's book, *Awaken the Spirit Within,* provides several short meditations asking readers to focus their breathing and then imagine themselves as a huge, "magnificent tree." See page 94 for one example. Her "Enlighten Up" meditations are extremely useful and powerful as well.[97]
- For more information on ways to connect with spirit guides, Edwin Steinbrecher's *The Inner Guide Meditation: A Spiritual Technology for the 21ˢᵗ Century* includes some very specific instructions (see "How to Contact the Inner Guide" on page 53 in the second edition).[98]
- Many years ago, I discovered a card deck called *Angel Journey Cards* by Terry Lynn Taylor and Mary Beth Crain.[99] Each of the 27 cards includes the script of a different guided meditation with wide-ranging topics such as "water, ether, moon, music, fire, silence, freedom, St. Francis, abundance, adversity, vision, transformation, artful dreaming, humor, feminine wisdom," etc. Any one of these would be wonderful.
- You may also find that you can write your own or compile a meditation using a selection of translated phrases from "The Lord's Prayer" in Neil Douglas-Klotz's book, *Prayers of the Cosmos: Reflections on the Original Meaning of Jesus's Words.*[100] Keep in mind that prayer—with time for contemplation and reflection—is a kind of journey, too, because it focuses everyone's hearts and minds toward the energy of wholeness and healing.

---

[96] Paul Selig, *I Am the Word* (New York: Jeremy P. Tarcher, 2010).

[97] Rebecca Rosen, *Awaken the Spirit Within: Ten Steps to Ignite Your Life and Fulfill Your Divine Purpose* (New York: Harmony, 2013).

[98] Edwin C. Steinbrecher, *The Inner Guide Meditation: A Spiritual Technology for the 21ˢᵗ Century* (York Beach, ME: Samuel Weiser, Inc., second printing, 1989).

[99] Terry Lynn Taylor and Mary Beth Crain, *Angel Journey Cards: 55 Cards and Companion Guidebook,* (New York: HarperSanFrancisco, 1996).

[100] Neil Douglas-Klotz, *Prayers of the Cosmos: Reflections on the Original Meaning of Jesus's Words,* (New York: Harper One, 1990).

An entire world of meditation resources awaits your discovery—from spoken audio to music to the written word, and I hope you enjoy exploring them as much as I have.

In the next section, you'll see a written version of one of my own meditations, called "The Gift of Giving," which is available as a free recording on Insight Timer. I am also providing the text of a couple more that are basic enough to memorize, vary, and extend. I am not including these in an effort to promote my work above others'; instead, I want them to serve as a preview for those who might be unfamiliar with the variety of what I'm calling "guided meditations."

If you use the text of these for your group, in each case, provide enough pause time for everyone to imagine and process the steps.

My Own Meditations

Sample #1 – "The Gift of Giving"[101]

As you relax, sense the edges of your body from the top of your head to the tip of your toes. Your energy field begins here, and as we go through this meditation, you will actually feel it connecting with the more expansive parts of you.

So close your eyes, breathe deeply and slowly. While we meditate, place your thoughts and plans to the side. We'll plant them in the Earth as seeds that will germinate into the best possible outcomes.

Now focus again on your body, with each breath, you can feel your inner awareness unfolding.

Your spirit rises within and around you.

Focus on feeling your heart. If you wish, you can put your hand there for a while. Notice how it grows warmer and warmer.

Imagine a candle flame there, glowing bright and warm, flickering with the energy of peace. This warmth spreads to the outer realms of your conscious mind, extending into the landscape around you.

As you relax and go deeper, you feel yourself expand and grow lighter.

---

[101] A recording of this meditation is available on the app, Insight Timer, under my name, Kim McCauley.

This warmth spreads beyond your heart into a sacred circle around you, and an angel comes forward. Archangel Raphael, who cultivates healing and abundance, glows with a velvety green aura.

As he draws closer, you feel bathed in vibrational waves that are both cleansing and empowering. Within these waves, your energy centers realign, promoting a sense of wellbeing and peace.

If you have areas of your physical body that need healing, you can ask Archangel Raphael to join with your intention and send energy there. Both of you are creating a space for healing that regenerates from the inside out.

You can even place your own hands there as he can foster healing through them . . . . For in these moments, anything is possible.

As this process continues, he showers you with glowing green light that fills your cells and revives you physically, mentally, emotionally, and spiritually . . . fine-tuning you for today and the days ahead.

Now as your field opens beyond the edges of your body, your third eye projects a vision of Raphael as he stands before you.

"This is a time" Raphael says, "for us to visualize unlimited abundance for everyone."

He holds an empty, silver tray and invites you to create a wish for someone and place it here.

You might offer them the gift of whatever it is they seek or might need, whether you know what that is or not. Perhaps your wish is that they get back on their feet, enjoy a wonderful career, experience total wellness, receive some specific help they need, or feel such love and happiness that their whole face lights up.

You can send these gifts to whomever comes to mind, whether it's just one person or a few.

No matter what positive wish you send, the energy ultimately helps them open to a new sense of guidance and purpose, broadening their understanding of their own and others' lives.

Place all of these wishes on the silver tray Archangel Raphael holds before you. As you join him in showering these gifts with love and blessing, the silver tray becomes surrounded with twinkling golden light.

Raphael smiles, certain that your gifts are already manifesting wonderful outcomes.

Now as Archangel Raphael fades from your view, turn your attention to how your spirit has expanded.

Notice how the edges of your field reach farther than before.

In this expansiveness, the energy of giving blooms and grows.

The gifts you've imagined sparkle continuously from one person to another, bringing joy and blessing. As we witness hope and healing flourishing across the globe, it feels as if we could wrap the entire Earth in a blanket of love and bring it home to our hearts.

The soft, glimmering flow of light envelops us with peace. Let this settle into your body and into every cell.

Because we are all connected, each of us is uplifted by the joy of giving. Blessings we share always return with love, and what we give from our hearts opens us to recognize the gift in all that we have and all that we receive.

As this meditation comes to a close, draw your attention back to your breath . . . back into that warmth of the candle flame in your heart, the warmth you carry with you every day.

And so it is.

Thank you for sharing your light. Thank you for being here.

Sample #2 – Meditation Spreading Light to the World

It's time to sit, get comfortable, and close your eyes. As you open your inner landscape, dwell within it for a moment. Exhale softly, allowing anything other than your highest and best to fall away. Take a few, slow and easy breaths. The heavy energy you may be carrying continues to leave your body and flow down to be cleansed within the energy of the Earth.

As you begin to feel lighter, place your attention on your heart. Imagine that as you breathe in and out, you can sense it getting warmer and warmer there, opening into a larger, comforting field of energy that fills with light. As it expands, and grows, this field begins to cover your whole body, from the tips of your toes to the top of your head.

This beautiful energy fills every cell of your body and then starts to form a column of light, stretching below your feet and above your head. Gradually, it begins to form a connection, a ray of light between the Earth, below your feet, and the heavens, above your head. Breathe in this healing light. We can label this whatever we want—the Holy Spirit, Your Higher Self, God, but no matter what, this light aligns our energy toward the highest good, like a divine template of whatever is best, in this moment, for our physical, emotional, mental, and spiritual well-being. At this point, healing *is* happening—in your body, mind, and soul. The love you can feel within this light supports you and will continue to support you.

Such love cannot be contained just in your own column of light. It spills over to the friends and family that you also love so much. As thoughts of them come before you, allow them to shower you with their love just as you shower them with yours. As this love-filled light continues to expand, imagine them showering their friends with love and then their friend's families with love. This goes on and on through acquaintances . . . through workplaces . . . to schools and cities, governments and nations.

This spark of love and healing cannot be contained within our own circle but billows outward—to the rest of the Earth—its animals and trees, to the oceans and everything in them . . . and then spreading even farther . . . beyond the Earth . . . to the stars.

We are all one now as you feel this glorious expensiveness. In the softness behind your eyes, infinite paths of light surround you—above and below, side to side, forward to back.

One step at a time we are beginning to heal not only our own life and others' lives . . . but our connection to the planet and to Divine order as it surrounds us and supports our growth.

Stay in this expansive space for a few more moments . . . .

Now focus again on the energy of your heart.

Remind yourselves that we are always surrounded and uplifted by love . . . .not just for this day or this week . . . . It exists within every cell of our bodies and transforms the way that we think . . . and speak . . . and act.

As we gradually come back, become aware again of your breathing. Take a few moments to resurface. Notice the edges of your body now and your presence in the room.

When you're ready, open your eyes.

Thank you for being here.

Sample #3 – Group meditation "Fire-Circle"

Take some slow, deep breaths . . . Let your inward breath peak, and then release the air gently and easily, letting your breathing come to rest before inhaling again.

The next time you exhale, imagine letting go of any heaviness that rests on your shoulders. Feel it roll down your body and into the Earth to be cleansed and recycled. Do this a couple times as you let go of anything that holds you back from being your best possible self.

While letting go, you can imagine the strands of this energy swirling into a purifying fire created just for us by the angels. The extra energy you've been holding as it relates to other people, places, or things falls away . . . watch it go . . . and as it does, it is absorbed and transformed within a bowl of flames . . . cleansing us, purifying our energies and everything around us.

As we continue, our breathing no longer needs our attention or control. Our energy feels lighter, and we begin to sense the edges of our bodies disappearing into an expansive and boundless sense of peace while, at the same time, feeling invisibly supported and surrounded by love.

This is you in your wholeness, as you exist in the purest sense. The fire begins to turn to embers now, calming us and getting us ready to go deeper.

In your own expansive state, you receive the energy you need as well as power and direction from your own inner compass. We can rely on this. Absorb this energy into your body and mind, allowing it to uplift and balance you at this point in your life. Let this energy settle into every part of you. And as you do, it feels almost magical—like glimmering pixie dust.

We can use this energy for healing and prayer, sending love and blessing to ourselves and others. The sparkling light goes where it needs to go. We can rely on this, too.

As you embrace this uplifting feeling of wonder for a few moments, notice a sense of gratitude welling up inside yourself. We are grateful for this moment, for each other, and for life itself as it exists all around us.

The angels now move toward the sacred bowl containing the cooling embers. They lift the bowl and place it in a safe place for the energy to be transformed for healing. As they return, each of them begins to surround us here, standing one by one, connecting to our hearts, and welcoming our gratitude.

You can take time now to sit in the bliss surrounding us, talk to one of the angels, or invite a guide if you wish. We will allow a couple minutes of silence for that.

All these enlightened beings send blessings of grace that fill the room and extend to each of us. Breathe this in.

Once again, focus your energy and warmth of your heart.

As we gradually come back, become aware again of your breathing. Take a few moments to resurface. Notice the edges of your body and your presence in the room.

When you're ready, open your eyes. Thank you for being here.

PART 6

Meet Our Psychometry Group Family

"Alone we can do so little; together we can do so much."[102]

— *Helen Keller*

[102] Helen Keller, "Script for Helen Keller and Anne Sullivan's vaudeville appearances," (26 May, 2015). American Foundation for the Blind, Helen Keller Archive, Box 95: Television-Vaudville, Folder 9, Item 30. https:/afb.org/about-afb/history/helen-keller/helen-keller-quotes/helen-keller-quotes-progress.

Now that you've vicariously attended one of our meetings, learned about psychometry, and read messages from most of the group, it's time to meet these amazing individuals one-by-one.

Not everyone who comes to the group was able to provide a profile or an example reading to include in this section, and some have written longer profiles than others. However, I've tried to honor each person's words just as they related them to me, either from an interview, over email, or in conversation at one of our meetings. At the beginning of each profile, I provide a brief introduction of my own to illustrate the many ways people found their way to the group.

Listed below in alphabetical order by first name, all of these attendees are real people; only a few have chosen to use pseudonyms. Each person is wonderful and unique, and I'm grateful for all of them.

Adrienne

Adrienne came to the group as a result of meeting several psychometry attendees at other events—for example in a "Yes" group, started by Mary Hayes[103] and Rita Ray.[104] I asked Adrienne to tell us a little about herself

---

[103] Mary Hayes is a spiritually-inspired intuitive counselor and medium who lives locally and works internationally, https://www.maryhayes.org. She is also the author of her own book about using intuition, *Express Your Yes!: A Simple Guide to Inspired Living*, published by Progressive Communications in Lake Mary, Florida, 2014.

[104] Rita Ray (who shares the same first name as my wife, Rita) came to me to ask if she could attend a psychometry group in order to use it as a template for her own.

and to describe her experiences with the psychometry group, and this is what she wrote:

> I was born in Brooklyn, New York and moved with my family to Miami at age five. I have since lived in several areas in Florida.
>
> Even though I grew up within a practicing Catholic Family, as children, my brothers and I were sent to a Baptist Bible school and then to a non-denominational church. As a teen I was introduced to Spiritualism. My mother became ordained, opened her own church, and I began working as a healer there. As I matured, I continued working with healing and traveled to several churches in the area along with leading small classes and giving lectures.
>
> During this time, I traveled to England and attended the Arthur Findlay College where I studied healing and mediumship. I have certificates in Theta Healing and Reiki Level 2. More recently, I started classes to study Medical Intuitive Training and have put together workshops to help people understand how their body speaks to them through dreams and through the Chakras. I have always had a deep and abiding love of nature similar to Pagan thought and have learned much on my own.
>
> I feel very blessed and divinely guided to have found this group. What a beautiful gift they all are to me.

Allie

Discovering us through mutual friends, Allie came to our group for the first time several months after her partner had passed. She doesn't attend very often, but when she does, we all sense the gentleness of her spirit. On Allie's first visit, she shared how difficult her grieving process had been, and the object she brought had been her mother's. The readings she gave as well as received helped her through the healing process. In the following passage, Allie says a bit more about her other impressions regarding the first group meeting she attended:

> Going to psychometry my first time, I was a bit anxious because I had not participated in anything like this before. Thankfully, the people in the group were especially warm and welcoming. Kim and Rita were very generous hosts offering tasty treats, coffee, and warm hugs.

Amy

Amy has been attending our psychometry/meditation group nearly every month since its first year. She is part of the SOFEA group and is friends with several other like-minded women who are part of both.

I first met Amy at a SOFEA meeting and was struck by her calm demeanor; her words were quiet and compassionate, and the wisdom she shared seemed beyond what one would expect from a person a decade or so younger than the rest of us. She teaches manifestation principles, and she and her wife, Lynda, offer sound healing and other spiritually-themed events in their home.

This is her story:

> I was born into a middle-class family in Boca Raton, Florida. Both of my parents were college-educated, my father a successful businessman and my mother the first director of nurses at a local Hospital. Two years before I was born, my two-year-old brother drowned in our family pool, so upon entering the world and for many years to follow, my family was heart-broken and struggled. My mother turned to alcohol and drugs after the death of her only son, and the inevitable loss of her job soon followed. When I was age 13, my parents divorced and at 17, my mother died of cirrhosis of the liver.

As one might imagine, I absorbed my family's struggles at a young age. As I moved through my early years, my focus was not clear, and the unpredictability of my home-life kept me ungrounded. Fortunately, I liked to dream, and I shared life with two older sisters (9 and 10 years my senior) who helped me lift my thoughts from the chaos.

Coming from a long line of Catholics, my mother attempted to raise her family Catholic. Both of my sisters attended Catholic school while I, coming along years later, attended public, then private, then public school (after a few administrative reprimands prompted by "at-risk" behaviors). I received less religious attention than my sisters, but occasionally attended church with my middle sister Lisa, who grasped Catholic creeds and rituals for emotional anchoring; she taught me to do the same.

I can't recall when I first recognized I had "spiritual" beliefs, but the divine companions who I often turned to in moments of uncertainty kept me grounded. My spiritual foundation was strong—not because of how I was taught, but because of something I cannot completely explain; from my earliest recollection, I knew deeply of God, of my ability to call upon Spirit for support, and of a spiritual realm beyond the physical that I could describe to others in clearest detail.

Julie, my oldest sister, found a path to her own alcoholic recovery while I was in college in my early 20s. During this time, she taught me recovery principles and I became more deeply involved in new age thought, self-help, and metaphysics.

My path eventually led me out of organized religion and into a more psycho-spiritual approach. I attended retreats, new-age conferences, psychotherapy, and studied the works of authors such as Marianne Williamson, Gary Zukav, Brian Weiss, Wayne Dyer, and Debbie Ford. Due to a void and a craving for a deeper community connection, I found a way back to church through a spiritual (vs. religious) -based church in my mid-thirties.

My dedication to higher self-recovery continues in finding new avenues back to divine realms. Meditation and forgiveness have become conscious rituals. Today, I look for the magic in life and feel honored to receive the gifts found in the present moment. Spirit continues to be my source on life's journey.

Angel

Angel started attending the psychometry group a few months after it began. She heard Jaye rave about it, which piqued her interest, and the following month, she and her partner came to one of the meetings. Angel is devoted, kind-hearted, and humble. One of the first things I remember learning about Angel is that each morning she walks around in her backyard barefoot as a way of connecting with the Earth and beginning her day with a spiritual focus. She attends the group regularly, and in those moments when it's time for her to share a reading or provide feedback, she states her words with conscious intention. In those moments, all of us can sense her grounded energy and depth.

The following is her own description of her spiritual journey.

I grew up in a suburb of Chicago and come from an Italian Catholic background. I was raised as most Catholics are, believing that God, Jesus and Mary are beings outside ourselves and require constant devotion and supplication in order to help us through our life.

I spent many years as an adult attending daily mass in order to feel close to God. Then one day a friend handed me a book of metaphysical teaching. I felt like I was given a great treasure and soaked up every word and it struck me as "truth." I finally had a path I could pursue to feel God and spirit directly in my life.

Although I will always honor my Catholic experience as part of my journey, I feel that it was just the beginning to set me on a lifelong path of discovering deeper truth. The best part for me is that I'm still able to learn from Jesus but in a more multi-dimensional way than before. I'm now open to learning from all religions but from a spiritual perspective and not a religious point of view. I feel more connected to God now than at any other time in my life.

Cathleen

After I moved from Tampa, I started attending a local Metropolitan Community Church (MCC), and one of the reverends there, told me, "Since you are interested in meditation and read metaphysical books, you need to meet Cathleen. She is the most metaphysical person you could ever meet!"

Not long after, I connected with Cathleen and several other like-minded women during one of the bi-annual SOFEA camping weekends. I remember getting to know several of the women there by doing individual card readings at a nearby picnic table. Cathleen and I really hit it off, as we talked about books we'd read and some of what we'd experienced on our own spiritual paths.

Cathleen has been attending since the beginning and brings her own special energy to the psychometry group. One moment, while she is deep into the details of a topic, she can be quiet and serious, and then the next moment, she can break out into a giggle. She is generous and wise and as thoughtful as she is spunky.

A few times over the years when Rita and I have been out of town, Cathleen hosted the psychometry group. Earlier in this book, I included two different experiences that occurred at Cathleen's home while the group met. One occasion is detailed in a section called "A Lesson in Trust: The Psy-com-o-Tree Story," and another featured Pat's group healing experience (mentioned in the section titled, Impactful Messages Occurring at the Perfect Time).

Here's Cathleen:

I was born and raised in the city of Chicago. My father's side of the family were Italian Catholics; my mother's side of the family were German Catholics and Russian Jews. Perhaps a nontraditional mix even in this modern day and age.

Due to religious laws during the time when my maternal grandparents planned to marry, the Catholic priest (who would not marry them in a church), required they both vow their children would be raised Gentile. And so they agreed.

I was baptized Catholic and attended catechism. Neither side of my family ever really seemed overly religious, yet "going through the motions" undoubtedly provided a foundation that I was later able to work with, in my own way, as I journeyed through this experience called life.

In many religious belief systems, it's taught that God is this big powerful individual sitting on a throne, judging every thought, decision and emotion passing through our fragile human minds. As a result of my young psyche being hijacked by Catholic/religious beliefs, my thoughts and emotions were imprisoning my life. I don't recall ever feeling a sense of mercy or reprieve. I was certain I was destined to a life of purgatory and that my eternal existence would be trapped in the unforgiving realms of the so-called underworld. These feelings of judgment and condemnation remained with me for many years.

In my late thirties, a personal crisis showed up in my life, and I was completely unaware of the extraordinary gift this life shattering event would ultimately unfold. It wasn't until years later that I was able to *recognize* that this was a very important crossroad, and I was being prepped for a radical awakening.

As I slowly began to wake up and experience many new and energizing levels of consciousness, I somehow felt deep within my being that these rejuvenating patterns of thought were not only going to bring balance into my life but offer me a sense of peace and self-love I never imagined possible. Since that time, I continue to absorb myself in a myriad of metaphysical books, seminars, classes, and anything relating to our existence that helps us stretch our minds beyond current levels of awareness and understanding.

Today, I can say that I am no longer content with my littleness, and I faithfully work toward embracing my magnitude—learning to release patterns of thought that no longer serve me has been a tremendous gift in my life. I believe our human experience, our pilgrimage through time and space is to help, teach, and remind us how magnificent we truly are!

Even though it's been said that human beings are of divine origin, but not yet of divine dignity, I believe without doubt, we have been endowed with the capacity to recognize our ability to untether our minds from the bondage, limitations, and chaotic world we live in.

Today, I have not the words to express my gratitude for having the courage and willingness to wake up from the sleep of forgetfulness. I feel fortunate to have *allowed* myself the space to surrender and to trust in the rightness of timing . . . to heal, to live, and to experience what happiness, contentment and peace can truly feel like in our life. And so it is. Amen.

Charlotte

I met Charlotte at Ruth's psychometry group in Tampa—the group I loved so much that it inspired me to create one of my own after I moved. Charlotte loves life, laughs a lot, and is a gifted intuitive and healer. For nearly 50 years, she has honed her psychometry skills weekly with this like-minded group in Tampa. I asked her to tell me about her life, and this is what she said:

> I was born and raised in Fort Wayne, Indiana. From the time I can remember, maybe five, I knew things. I also knew not to tell anyone that I knew things. I knew about things before they would happen, and I also knew when people would lie about things.

> My parents only went to church on the big holidays. I was sent to Vacation Bible School a couple of times, and when I was 13, I was sent to classes at church. I think it was a regular congregational church, Methodist perhaps. I remember thinking that when the minister spoke, he was lying.

When I asked Charlotte, "What brought you to psychometry?" she said, "In 1976, a friend was going to the Cosmic Book Center, and since Ruth, the owner, had astrology classes, I initially went for those. Within a couple months, my friend started going to psychometry meetings, and I eventually started going to those, too."

> I so loved Ruth and all the classes. My soul was so happy. I started going to the Tuesday night Thot-watcher group which did meditation and psychometry. Some years later, we added affirmations and a healing circle. A lot of people attended then, averaging about 15 per week. There were so many, it seemed as if the circle of chairs were really crammed into the bookstore.

> Ruth's group survived in the Cosmic Bookstore for a long time. Every Tuesday, after the meeting, we walked through the door from the bookstore into her home for sharing and snacks.

It's very different starting a group somewhere else. At the beginning, it was very strange for Patricc and me because I've been going to Ruth's every week for 40 years and Patricc for 30. After all those years of going every Tuesday night, with the occasional exception of illness or vacation, it was almost like cutting off an arm and a leg when Ruth needed to stop having it.

Charlotte took the lead to continue the group's public meetings since, after Ruth's passing, they could no longer meet at the Cosmic Bookstore. Over the last decade, the Thotwatchers met regularly at local metaphysical bookstores—first Earth Angels and then Mystikal Scents, but both stores are now closed. When I last spoke to Charlotte, the group had recently found a new venue and are meeting in the fellowship hall of a local church.[105]

According to Charlotte, the group has changed a bit and now includes mediumship once per month. When they practice this, they ask everyone to either bring an object from a loved one, a piece of paper with the loved one's name written on it, or a picture of him or her. "It's a fine line between psychometry and mediumship," she says.

Because of that, we ask that they know this person a little bit. We give them ideas of questions to ask so that they have some sort of validation. For example, knowing for themselves, the person's name, age, how they passed, whether they owned pets, if they had children, hobbies, and so on. Then the group tunes in on the picture, piece of paper, or object without knowing any of those answers in advance. We write down what came through and share it with the person who was seeking information. We've had pretty good success with it.

Throughout the years, Charlotte and I became close friends. We've traveled together, practiced Reiki together, and taken several other energy healing classes together. She is one of the most gifted, determined, and positive people I've ever met.

---

[105] The church has indicated that they appreciate but don't necessarily endorse the group.

Claudia

Raised in Guatemala, Claudia told me that she received messages as a child and had always felt empathic, but she closed this part of herself because she was not allowed to speak about it. She shared that being part of the psychometry group allowed her to use her gifts once again and also to feel "connected, seen, and understood."

When she discussed the details of some of the readings she received, she said, "All my readings have left me with little nuggets, small pearls of wisdom that I have cherished." One, in particular, she told me, made her very happy. It was a message from Suman who described a dragon transforming into a woman dressed in white. Claudia felt certain that the image represented her mother, who had recently passed away.

I also think that the image of transformation applies to Claudia herself, and we can witness that through her own words:

> Being a part of the group influenced the trajectory of my spiritual journey. I am convinced that the energy that is created in that sacred space allows me to connect with my intuition in an even more powerful way. When I first joined, I doubted my ability to connect with my Knowing, I felt alone and isolated. After partaking in the powerful sessions I felt more connected, not only to the other women, but to myself and to my intuition. I am so grateful for every single reading, every single meditation, every single moment I share with this circle of wise women. I truly believe the Universe speaks through us; our collective energy elicits all the ancestral wisdom of the unconscious, and as a united circle we become conduits to those messages that impact and transform our lives.

Dee

Dee has been attending the psychometry group over the last six years, but her evening work schedule often prevents her from coming regularly. She is a Licensed Mental Health Counselor and Clinical Psychotherapist holding master's degrees in counseling and divinity. As a ministerial student in the Unity Worldwide Spiritual Institute, she has a passion for the community experience and tells me that she "looks forward to Pastor-Teaching." Her areas of interest are diverse and include leadership; congregational care; relationship development and renewal; death, dying and bereavement; pastoral psychology; growth and development of persons and congregations; and spirituality in recovery. The following description of herself is in her own words:

> I was born in West Palm Beach, Florida, and my family attended the United Methodist Church (UMC). When I was between the ages five and eleven years old, my mother experimented in nondenominational/charismatic churches, Pentecostal churches, the Kingdom Hall, and we both participated in Jehovah's Witnesses Bible study groups. I was grateful when we returned to the UMC.

> I love what the mainstream would consider "unconventional" ways of being open to Spirit. I believe Spirit speaks in many, many ways. Delving inward and creating safety within a trusted spiritual circle is my jam.

> I have reread messages that I have received many times over the years. At different points of struggle in my life, or, if I just need to be reminded of what is true for me, I pull out my binder where the messages are all stored, and I review them. I think about the intonation of the messenger and reflect on the quality of potency at that time, and I revisit the message's significance then and now. One of my most meaningful messages was from Lynda. She assured me that this circle of life is what it is, that I've done it before and will do it again, and that in this life, I will come to know that my path has truly led me to what is mine to do and that I will be very fulfilled in it.

Diana

Even though it's been a while since Diana attended, we still consider her to be part of our group's "extended family." This is her story:

First, I am of the belief that everything . . . everything . . . that happens in our lives has brought us to where we are today—by our choices, beliefs, and decisions based on those beliefs and more. And I am choosing to be a beneficiary, not a victim, of my life's happenings . . . with a knowing.

I grew up in a "broken home" with my older sister and mother. My mother was an alcoholic and chain smoker who only got worse over time. She died at age 63, having been practically bed-ridden for about ten years prior due to illness, cancer, and emphysema. She did her best to love us, the best way she knew how, dealing with her own pain, never seeking help, just numbing herself to her emotional pain. In addition to this, there were many episodes of attempted suicide, of which, unfortunately, I would find her lying in a tub of water "out of it" with partially slit wrists. I look back on this time and have a clearer understanding as to the possible reasons I grew up feeling so unworthy and unimportant. I became aware I needed to heal my own memories and forgive my mother. After she passed, within a few years, she came to me through a conversation with a Medium. She expressed her sorrow and grief about the life she gave me. I was able to forgive her, and we reunited.

I came to an understanding of God in my life at a very early age—sort of a presence I felt was with me, when I was alone, which was often with my mother either being gone or drinking when not working.

Later, when I was 17, I experienced a real physical healing, a time when God healed me. I had never fully started my periods by this time and was not feeling well at all. I was taken to the doctor only to find out there was some mass in my abdomen that would need to be removed along with a complete hysterectomy. I was horrified and my mother was completely freaked out. When we got home from the doctor that day, she went directly in the kitchen for the bottle, and I stood beside our piano, and said this to God, "Okay, We have a problem here, and the way I see it, there are only two ways this can be worked out. Either you heal me completely or, with the doctor's help, I am healed completely but will have all my organs in place, because I want to have one child in my lifetime—One. So, God it is in Your hands."

Keep in mind that at this time I was attending a spirit-filled Baptist Church in Macon, Georgia. I had seen God heal others and had even laid hands on others to assist in healing them. Now, my pastor, Brother Don, and my doctor, Doctor Cox, both went heavily in prayer believing that this healing would happen. Well, I was healed completely by God's hands and now have one wonderful daughter and two gorgeous grandchildren. I am blessed beyond measure.

As further confirmation of the love, grace, and power of the God I know and love, two other wonderful events occurred due to this. Brother Don and Dr. Cox fell in love and got married. In addition, my sister—who had come home from college to help both my mother and me—went shopping and met the man she has now been married to for over 40 years. Some real good came out of all of this, not just for me, but for many. God is good.

Now, as my life's journey continued, although I was quite aware there was a God, I still lived quite unconsciously. I still did not love myself or feel worthy of much, and at this stage had attracted an abusive marriage (that brought me the one child I wanted). This marriage ended in my late twenties when I found women, alcohol, and drugs. For the next three years, I went down a path of self-destruction, leaving both my now ex-husband and child by partying and such until I was thirty. It is a miracle in itself that I am here today, given the drugs and alcohol that I consumed during this time. I truly did not want to live and felt that God had forsaken me due to my gay lifestyle. However, it was I who had done the forsaking at that time.

Another miracle is that my daughter and I are on a healing journey. She came to live with me to go to college and has since gotten married but stayed living in the same area as me. She and her husband have two wonderful children that I love dearly. I love having my kids and grandkids so close.

Moving fast forward from age thirty through age sixty, I had one long term relationship of eight years with a gal that truly tried to save me from myself. For a while, that worked for me until my deep-seated anger and wounds from my childhood could be contained no more. Our relationship ended, and I started getting help with talk therapy and more.

I dated many women during this time—many women— seeking for love in all the wrong places, none of which lasted for any length of time. Some were even abusive, especially in the latter years, so I have spent the last few years of my life staying out of romantic relationships. I am working instead on my relationship with God by continuing to nurture and care for my inner child, my shadow, my ego, and my higher self.

I am blessed to be a part of the conscious spiritual souls in the Unity church, where I have found the teachings, love, and connection I needed to learn to love and accept all of me, totally. I now do, and I am looking at life so differently, loving who I am and what I must give and want to freely give of myself as Spirit guides me. I am also blessed to be a part of this conscious community of wonderful women with the psychometry group. I hope to continue being broken open to the path of being a healer in my life.

I have been away from the group since 2015. In this time frame, I have found other ways to fulfill my spiritual walk and have made some interesting choices that have led me to where I am today—free from corporate America, following my dream and passion of truly being able to help "heal" business owners with proper loans/lending and have the freedom to grow. I am also free from toxic intimate relationships, focusing on continuing my own inner healing. I will be coming back to the group to reconnect with its amazing people, to the safe, spiritual place for growth and intuitive insight.

Eileen

For over a decade, Eileen, along with her partner, Elizabeth, has attended nearly every one of our monthly psychometry meetings. Like Cathleen and a few others, both women heard about our meetings from mutual friends in the SOFEA women's group.

Eileen's words are measured and wise, and her demeanor reflects that. She refers to her friends in the group as "Sis," which makes each woman smile, knowing that the connection between all of us is indeed like family. This is Eileen's story:

I grew up in Chicago, Illinois. Throughout my childhood, we lived in the same two-flat that my father and his brothers grew up in and went to the same grammar school that they did as well. My mom was raised Lutheran but has never been what I would consider to be religious. Looking back, I wonder if the fact that my grandmother was raised Catholic but had to convert to Lutheranism because my grandfather refused to allow his children to be raised as Catholics had anything to do with our lack of connection to church. When I was little, we would go to church every Sunday, and I remember being in Sunday school classes while my mom and grandmother attended service. By the time my brothers came along, all three of us would attend service with them. I don't remember feeling anything special about church. Usually, I was trying to keep my brothers quiet and waiting for coffee hour to start. My father, a Vietnam veteran, always said he was Methodist but only went with us to church on Christmas and some Easters.

The older I became, the less often we went to church. Except for high holidays, we'd stopped going to church by the time I was twelve. I've always had a rather strong desire for things to be fair. The apparent hypocrisy of most organized religions turned me completely away from even the idea of "church." A God of fear, punishment, and hatred has never made sense to me. I did try to attend a church in the town where I went to college, but the pastor was a fire and brimstone person. To me, God is about love, without exceptions or exclusions. God will always be bigger than any box that we try to squeeze Him/Her/It into. Not surprisingly, my connection to God/Universe is strongest when in nature. By nature, I mean everything from noticing (and bring grateful for) the clouds in the sky, from the birds and flowers we see on our way in to work to being immersed in nature and appreciating it.

I was introduced to Joy MCC Church in 1997. It was a nice surprise to find a place where everyone is welcome just as they are, but I still only went at Christmas. I would say that my greatest growth spurt spiritually began in 2008 when Elizabeth and I got together. Because church has always been a big part of her life, we began attending Joy regularly. We were offered the opportunity to take a course called Creating a Life that Matters (CLM). We also began attending SOFEA meetings and functions. SOFEA introduced us to ideas we hadn't really considered before and created soul-deep friendships with a diverse group of amazing women who are bound by acceptance, compassion, a desire to learn/grow, to find what speaks to us spiritually, and (most of all) love. It was through this group that we met Kim, and she introduced us to the healing circle and psychometry. Everything is connected.

As for where I'm at now, I would say . . . still learning. Over the years, the group has given me more faith in the validity of my own intuition. It has also introduced me to concepts beyond my experience initially—from meditation to spirit guides to healing circles.

Elizabeth

Like her partner Eileen, Elizabeth heard about the psychometry group through friends at SOFEA meetings. Both have been coming regularly since it started in early 2012.

Elizabeth is one of the most organized and responsible women on the planet, and this stability shows in her demeanor. Her kindness is often reflected through her gifts as an active listener and loving friend. When we begin the reading portion of the group meeting, Elizabeth almost always volunteers to share her reading first, which, she admits, helps her to develop more courage and put aside any fear related to public speaking. When I asked her to talk about her life and her experiences with the psychometry group, this is what she said:

Where am I from? I am from everywhere. My father was in the United States Air Force for twenty years. By the time I was seventeen years old I had lived in six states. I was born in Fairbanks, Alaska and my father retired in Panama City, Florida. My childhood was spent living on military bases. This can be a very closed environment as you can imagine. I was born Catholic, baptized when I was only a few weeks old. My mother came from a family of very devout Catholics and is still one to this day. My father married her in the Catholic Church and tolerated Catholicism, only attending church a handful of times during my childhood. When I was a preschooler, my mother and I went to church every day that she wasn't working. I attended Catholic school until fifth grade when we moved to Missouri and there was no Catholic school near the military base. Because I didn't know anything else but Catholic school, I very much felt like a misfit in public school. Growing up Catholic meant attending Sunday Mass and Holy Days of Obligation and saying prayers before every meal and at bedtime. I prayed the rosary almost daily with my mother in the kitchen while she was cooking supper. We went to confession every Saturday so that we could attend mass and receive Communion on Sunday, all forgiven.

Looking back on it now, I can see that I didn't fully engage in services. I chose to join the choir as a little kid and continued singing through my adulthood. It was acceptable, and for me it made "going to church" have another meaning. It was a way that I could actively participate and engage in the liturgy instead of passively sitting in the pew. I was very active locally in the Catholic Church until 2008. I was a member of the Adult Choir for fourteen years, and it was a crutch, the "go to," the place of comfort and predictability. Also, because the Catholic Church frowns on homosexuality, being in the choir made it less obvious as my partner sat in the pew.

In 2007 my life was in flux, my thirteen-year partnership terminated, my daughter graduated from high school and moved to California, and I hit a pedestrian on South Orange Blossom Trail. The Catholic Church connected me to a spiritual director during this time and this was the first turning point for me. My spiritual director was a retired Episcopalian Bishop who I absolutely adored, and he sat behind me in the choir. He encouraged me to talk to God and to be quiet and listen. After a while, I grew increasingly dissatisfied with the Catholic Church. I was tired of not being able to practice my religion as my authentic self.

Around this time, I met Eileen and she introduced me to Joy Metropolitan Community Church. She was not a member but had attended a few times and thought maybe I would be more comfortable there. Also, during this time my daughter bought me Neale Donald Walsch's book, *Conversations with God,* and my spirituality has not been the same since then, the second turning point. The God that is described in the book is now the God that I choose. My spirituality has expanded more in the last nine years than it did in the 48 years previously.

Metropolitan Community Church is not a complete fit for me. I have come to understand that Jesus is one of many prophets. I have come to know God as Universe, and I have a different understanding now. I choose to find the goodness, focus on the positive, and try to live my life in gratitude. I do get tired of the "Jesus factor" at Joy; however, there are so many other things that I enjoy about the church and community there—not to mention I can worship with my partner by my side and be my authentic self. I appreciate the intermingle of God with the Jesus at Joy, but it's not enough. So, I looked to other things to fill in the gaps and continue to nurture my spirituality.

To think I had never heard of the word psychometry before I started attending, and so much has happened since then.

Esther

Although Esther has not been able to attend the group for several years now, we still miss her always-smiling good nature and unique presence.

She heard about the group through her connection to mutual friends, Rita Ray and Mary Hayes, and participated with us for over a year. Whenever it was time for Esther to share what she received, she would typically close her eyes and talk in a waterfall of words similar to stream-of-consciousness. This is her impression of the group:

> As we proceeded with the readings, and one of the women said that she was thinking of opening up to talk to people more, I was thinking, "there are the ones who speak, teach with words and the ones who hold the love silently, the ones who express acceptance and the ones who live it. Some interact with the world, some unite through meditations or healing." I am mesmerized that our group has it all and that we are nurturing incredible compassion, joy for ourselves and for the world.

In her description of the group, she talks about the group consisting of mesmerizing people, but she was even more so. It felt as if her readings, when spoken that way, came from deep within her heart as well as from a place beyond space and time.

Helen

Readings within the group are usually serious and light at the same time. The information that ends up on the page shines through the filter of the person giving the reading, which often shows through with little extras from our personalities—facial expressions, leaning in, laughter, and compassion. When Helen gives a reading, she leans forward within the circle and looks intently toward the person whose object she has. She asks questions as she speaks, sometimes cracking a joke to break the seriousness, connecting the dots, or helping the person who is receiving her reading to feel supported and respected.

Helen is full of life, reflected by her ability to share it with others through laughter, elbow-ribbing rapport, active listening, generosity, and compassion. She is an active member of our group and attends whenever she can.

When she joined the group, I was only aware that she had been married before and had a family. I sent her an email to ask if she would talk about herself for the book. When she replied with her answer, I admit to being unprepared, not expecting to hear about the horrible circumstances of her early life:

> I grew up in the UK. I was ritually abused as a child in church from age five to age fourteen. It's not appropriate to go into details, but I experienced extreme sexual, physical, emotional, and spiritual damage. The reverend from the church told me, "God won't love you if you tell anyone." So, by age six I believed that I was completely unlovable. For years this kept me in a state of separation from any kind of divine love because I was bad (shame) and God/spirit etc. meant abuse (fear/pain).

> When I was twenty-one, I got clean and sober and began slowly over many years to open up to spirituality. When I began to finally feel safe to connect to a divine consciousness (many years of therapy later), my intuitive abilities opened. Even then, throughout the years, I would shut down, eat to repress my intuition, or use other avoiding tactics because I'd start to feel unsafe. With our group I was able to step into my true intuitive self, using the safety of the group until I was able to consistently feel safe internally. I am *so* grateful!

Jaye

Jaye participated with the group a few times, and whenever she did, expressed her gratitude. She was invited to attend through a woman she had been dating and was so excited about the group that she invited others, including Suman and Angel. This is her story:

I was born in Ocala, raised in Ocala and never left there for more than a week and never moved away from there until love moved me closer to where I was introduced to your wonderful group.

I have been involved with animal rescue my entire life. Even as a young child I was bringing home injured birds and mice and anything else that I could put in my pocket and take home with me. I have dedicated my entire life to taking care of animals and I know that Spirit put me on this earth for that reason.

I was a deputy sheriff for 32 years and head of the animal cruelty department. I had to retire in 1999 when I lost part of my right leg saving a dog's life. I would do that again in a New York minute to save an animal.

I believe in Spirit. I am not so much religious as I am spiritual. I'm Native American, so I practice a lot of the beliefs of my heritage . . . and Spirit is very very important to me.

I thank Spirit everyday for giving me the opportunity to love and share my life with the animals.

I am very blessed.

Laura

I first met Laura at a Reiki share hosted by the local Unity church. She was highly respected as a Reiki Master and massage therapist, and although she kept very busy with work and family, she took time to volunteer at church and help others whenever she could. In addition to all this, she is an excellent cook and frequently takes meals to someone who is sick or in need of a boost.

A version of her story appears earlier in the book, but what she says here provides further background about how she grew up:

I was born in Milan, Italy, in 1969. My parents were born in the south of Italy and moved up north, separately, in their twenties for business purposes. They had to adjust to a very different culture from the one they were born into. It was very difficult, especially for my mom, as she was humiliated many times because of her accent at work.

From the southern perspective, how things appeared on the outside and also a family's social and financial status were and are very important. So "judging a book by its cover" served as the main focus. Strangely enough, this made people (relatives included) feel comfortable, even if that meant not being true to oneself.

Laura is one of the most generous and loving people I know, and her laughter is infectious. Like her parents, she has made many sacrifices for her family—including raising two boys and caring for her father after her mother passed. Despite the difficulties she has faced in life, she carries on, always thinking of what she can give to others.

Lindsey

Lindsey started attending the group during a time of transition, and it didn't take long for her to create a sense of belonging by becoming an active part of the psychometry group and the Unity church. This is her story:

I grew up in the Northeast in a large Irish Catholic family. Religion was complicated . . . it was harsh, judgmental, and shameful. I was not taught how to connect with a God. Instead, I was told I was a sinner, which I internalized to mean that I was bad.

I spent most of my early childhood with feelings of deep loneliness, and to my surprise, I looked to the rosary as a comfort. I guess my intention was working. This carried me far and opened a door to begin my first transformative process, twelve-step recovery. I felt at home for the first time; I felt like I belonged.

I grew up in all ways—emotionally, mentally, and spiritually. I began attending Unity Church, studying the Course in Miracles, attending twelve-step meetings regularly, and working closely with mentors.

I no longer felt like I was going it alone. I found a new and improved God, and my life took on extraordinary meaning and purpose. I blossomed beyond my wildest expectations.

Along the way, I have sought many avenues of growth. One of these avenues was being included in a psychometry group. I felt curious, excited, nervous, and open to see what God had in store for me. The format of the group was so loving and inviting; I found the group of people to be warm and accepting. Nothing seemed weird or far out.

When she received her first reading, she said it "coincided with a recent move from living by the ocean to living inland." She describes it, here, in her own words:

A kind, gentle, old woman with a smile in her eyes, arms out, puts a stone into your hands. She really wants you to have this beautiful stone (sound of waves). It has energy on it (waves), vibrations of joy. It was a part of something, a fond memory . . . a beach . . . comes to mind. This piece is magical. It's very warm and represents a sacred space to be in. It's full of memories and joy, uplifting. This is a piece of something, a memory for you to have and feel warm about, a piece of magic for your life, for you to feel warmth. (The reader drew a heart at the bottom.)

I found great comfort from the message. The move kicked up a tremendous amount of grief and loss, having sold my home of ten years and leaving my community of seventeen years. The object that was read was a stone from the beach I had lived on. The message validated everything I was feeling and allowed me to shift my grief to joy, knowing that the beach was always with me, a very real part of me.

I felt right at home and totally loved my experience. I dropped into my heart and felt a clear channel to my own knowing. It has truly changed how I see and show up in world.

I am still thriving and growing deeper in effectiveness and understanding of God's will for me every moment. Today, I have a loving relationship with God and myself, and I experience deep joy and peace more than suffering, one of many shifts. This group served me spiritually for a couple of years, and it gave me the confidence to open bigger and wider doors. A true blessing.

Lissette

Lissette heard about the psychometry group through like-minded friends from the SOFEA camping event. She lives over an hour away, and doesn't always have the chance to attend, but when she does, her joy is contagious. Like Pat, she speaks her mind and although she can be serious when talking about her spiritual experiences, most of the time she grins from ear to ear and uplifts us all.

I am from Puerto Rico, grew up in Catholic family, and went to a Catholic school. I would say that my current belief system is non-traditional in the sense that I believe all religions provide a route to the oneness that is God or universal energy. We are here to learn and experience. There is no Hell.

I decided to attend because I like to experience different ways that connect me to others and the higher power. My experience is always great. Even though I live far away, I work on coming as much as possible. I feel grateful afterwards because of the amazing people and great insights.

Lynda

Lynda and I first met when she joined several people I knew for an evening out at a local Comedy Lab. It wasn't long after that, that she and Amy started dating, and of course, since psychometry had been so important to Amy, Lynda eventually joined her.

Lynda loves nature, art, and music, and is a creative artist, using the natural elements that "call" to be nurtured and included in a particular piece. Even though she works as a property manager full-time, over the last couple of years, in her free time, she has expanded her artistic repertoire by introducing us to sound healing either before or after the meditations. She does this by bringing and playing indigenous, handmade flutes and always seems to know what will put us in a blissful, receptive state.

When I asked Lynda to share her story with us, this is what she said:

> I grew up in a small town in upstate New York. I was raised in the Catholic church. My mother converted to Catholicism when she married my father. However, she remained a Congregationalist at heart. She did not subscribe to many of the thoughts of the Catholic church, and the message that she gave me was that the church provides a foundation when you have nothing else to believe in. She always supported us in whatever spiritual path we followed.
>
> Many areas in Upstate New York were spiritualist due to the influence of Native Americans and the women's rights movement. This has been a great influence in my life. I no longer consider myself a Christian. I believe in Source energy and co-creating with Source but not from a Christian perspective. I remember while in religious instruction being told having sexual thoughts was a sin and certainly being gay was a sin. I felt this was not true because I knew I was a good person, and my God would not judge me for that. I have had several "close encounters" where Source/Spirit has divinely led me, and I know the art I create is all divine downloads with messages intended for the receiver.

Maritza

Maritza became one of my Reiki 2 students in 2010. She continued practicing Reiki and eventually studied with me to become a Reiki Master. Around that time, I invited her to attend the psychometry/meditation group so that she could meet other like-minded women in the area. She's been attending monthly for over ten years now.

Maritza was born in Cali, Colombia and came to the U.S. in 1980. She grew up Catholic and still observes that but respects the beliefs of others and incorporates some indigenous native spirituality in her life as well.

I asked Maritza to talk about some of the readings that had an impact on her.

> Lately, the one that impacted me the most is a reading I received from Suman. She mentioned "prickly" energy, saying "life can be prickly, but it's important to release the judgments." She picked up on how I was handling something in my life, and that moved me, really moved me.

In that meeting, Suman further clarified what she meant by non-judgment: "This is not about tolerating or putting up with something; instead, the message here is for you to consider saying, 'No, that doesn't work for me' and then not holding judgment about it."

Maritza took all of this to heart. Several months after Suman's reading, the evening when the word "happy" was repeated in several readings, Maritza looked at all of us and said, "I'm in a good place, and I can honestly say that I'm happy, really happy. I've learned to let go and also say 'no' when I need to. It feels good."

Pat

In addition to being the eldest of the group, Pat has quite a bit of experience with mediumship and clairvoyance, having studied professionally through the Arthur Findlay College in England. Earlier in her life, she worked as a psychic reader with a group that traveled the world. Pat's energy is strong but not overpowering. She always expresses how grateful she is for everything, and all around our circle, we can feel her love. The evening is never quite the same without her. She laughs often, has a big heart, and always, no matter how open or blunt it might seem, speaks her mind, which quite often makes us laugh out loud.

Pat wrote about herself and some of her experiences with the group for me to include in the book:

> I was born in Alton, Illinois, a small town on the Mississippi right across from St. Louis, Missouri. Shortly after my birth, my parents divorced, and I was sent to live with my grandparents along with my brother who was three years older and was my protector for the rest of his life.
>
> My mother finally got her life together, which is really a misnomer, because she never did. She didn't work after that, and we lived on welfare which was rarely spent on us or for food. I went to bed hungry and woke up hungry, which accounts for the typically "overstocked" kitchen I've maintained in my adulthood.
>
> We survived through those early years and my mother spent most of her time in taverns and drank daily. She died an alcoholic's death at an early age.
>
> My brother and I were teenagers by then and had to go to Chicago to live with our father and stepmother. My father had never told her he had any children. That was quite an adjustment for all of us. I managed to graduate high school and vowed that I would never be a product of my environment.
>
> I met my husband Al, and we lived in Chicago Ridge. We had two boys, and we adopted a baby girl. We all moved to New Port Richey to open an automotive business with Al's brother. I never wanted to move to Florida. I loved Chicago. For many years I wallowed in self-pity for myself, mad at my mother for dying and leaving me at such a young age and her unloving treatment throughout my youth.

After several years of discontent someone told me about a psychic artist that would draw your "guides" and was going to be a guest at a local Spiritualist church. This spiked my interest, so I went to church for the first time in many years. I had no previous knowledge of who God was, but when I walked into that church, I knew He had never given up on me. My life changed forever that day.

After several months of inner work, I totally forgave my mother. My appreciation for my family became more loving, and we financially prospered. We moved to a big old house on the river. The sunsets were indescribably beautiful.

Time went on and my oldest son went off to college and then to medical school. My younger son received a full scholarship in football at Eastern Kentucky University and graduated in four years. I am totally proud of them and do not take any credit for what they made of their lives.

In the Spiritualist church, I developed as a psychic and loved helping other people with messages. The church struggled financially, and we eventually closed. My yoga teacher introduced me to Unity after that. I loved Unity and their teachings.

We sold our property in Florida and moved to Murphy, North Carolina. After Murphy, we moved to several states. This is the second time we have lived in Florida. My husband died a few years ago, and each day is a new adventure. My life is full of wonderful spiritual friends and family. We are all bonded and continue our path to spiritual freedom and knowledge.

I first heard about Kim's psychometry group from Cathleen. She and I attended a Course in Miracles group at church for quite a while and became friends. One night we were talking afterward about a paper I had given her on automatic writing. Cathleen's partner passed on the article to Sabrina, a woman who worked with her and who had been rediscovering her own intuitive gift of mediumship. Cathleen said that she was going to a meeting in which she held something of someone's and gave them a message from the vibrations. She couldn't remember what it was called, and I told her that it was called "psychometry," and that was one of my strong gifts. She said she would ask Kim if I could come, and this started my connection with the group.

Kim, you had a class at the Yoga center in Apopka in which Rita Ray and Wendy attended. After that class, you invited a few of us to come to your house for lunch and to give Rita and Wendy a demonstration on how you conduct your psychometry group. As we did the readings, I wrote this "prayer":

My Dearest God to Thee, I humble myself to Thee
I am your grateful servant. I dedicate my life to you.
I haven't always known you or you have not been part of my life,
But from this day on, I shall honor you, with my heart, mind, and soul.
My entire body will be dedicated to your work and your
son's life, who walked this earth to show us the way.
My light will be your light.
My words will be your words.
My heart will be your heart.

Phyllis

Phyllis and I met when I first attended an informal gathering of friends from Unity, SOFEA, and others at her home. She is loving, supportive, and has a very special gift of connecting people together, so many of us refer to her as "the Hub"—the unassuming center of the wheel that keeps all the spokes together. She has an infectious laugh and is inquisitive about life—always asking questions, always learning and growing, but primarily for the purpose of helping others. In fact, over the last few years, she and her wife assisted with the caretaking of Phyllis's father before he passed, something she accepted with wisdom and grace, despite its many challenges.

This is how she describes herself, her approach to spirituality, and her experience with the psychometry group:

> I am from a large, patriarchal, and loving Italian family. Suffice it to say that all four of my grandparents and several uncles/aunts on both sides emigrated from Italy to Ellis Island in NYC. I was born in and have remained in Florida all my life. Not unexpectedly, we were raised Catholic, and I attended Catholic school to fifth grade, where we went to Mass every day. I guess my faith has been strong all my life seeing that I attended church without my parents into my teenage years. I raised my two sons in the Catholic church through Confirmation, feeling they needed a foundation on which to base their own decisions about church and God later in life.

> I feel religious beliefs are personal—your own walk with God, however He/She appears to you. I believe all paths lead to God. I also believe organized religions are sometimes just a third dimensional club to facilitate exclusion and not at all what Jesus intended. Yes, it's a contradiction. I believe Jesus was put on this earth to show us how to love one another, and our fear prevented us from receiving his message. I believe there are many other humans who have been sent here to show us the way, including Martin Luther King, Gandhi, Marianne Williamson, Jane Elizabeth Hart, and our SOFEA sisters, to name a few. I am a student of spiritual growth and have always been drawn to Eastern belief systems such as Hinduism and Buddhism. I believe in energy, Mother

Nature, and the spirit within. Truly, I am closest to God in nature. I would describe my spirituality as energy-driven. It's all about my intentional vibration—positive and loving, flowing in and through me.

Rita

My wife Rita and I met in 2014, were engaged on the day that Ireland voted to legalize same-sex marriage and married six months later. We certainly love each other very much and are wonderfully happy together.

A common question people ask us is, "How did you meet?" At that time I was in my late fifties, and I admit to being a little hesitant to say that we met on "Match," an online service. When I created my Match profile, I hoped that being 100% myself would serve as an excellent filter: I was a mother with a doctoral degree. I didn't own a TV at the time and was very busy with lots of work responsibilities. I emphasized that I was a spiritual person, a Reiki Master, and loved hosting a monthly meditation group in my home.

My profile seemed to work because Rita liked it well enough to "favorite" me, but she is a private person and had not included a picture. As we corresponded, eventually she sent an image of herself standing far away in what looked like a desert, wearing a large, wide-brimmed hat and dark sunglasses. As we began to correspond more frequently, I realized that she was a deeply spiritual person too, and on our first date, she introduced me to Richard Rohr's Daily Meditations by reading one to me while we sat at a coffee shop. It didn't take long to realize that this woman had won my heart, and this is her story:

> Born in Belfast, Northern Ireland in 1961, I'm the second eldest of nine children. My parents had always dreamed of emigrating to California, and in 1966 with four children in tow, their dream came true, and we moved to L.A.
>
> It was the sixties and L.A was a fast-moving place compared to Ireland. So, after only six months, they decided to return. Even though the stay was short, the experience always left my family with a great love for America.

But a few years after returning to Belfast, the Troubles broke out with great unrest in Northern Ireland. As a result, my family moved south to Dublin. I went to boarding school for a few years and then to a coed day school that I absolutely loved. I had always dreamed of owning a motorbike, and on my sixteenth birthday, my mother surprised me with a beautiful red Honda 90. Wow, did I love that bike and the freedom it gave me!

After graduating college as a RN, I emigrated to Florida in 1984. I was planning to go to graduate school in Miami and study psychology, but life had other plans for me. My family had opened a small branch of our facility maintenance company, and I joined the business for what I thought would be a temporary job until college started. I was so taken with this new occupation and the opportunity to grow and create a company that I made it my life career. It's been forty years now and a tremendous journey of discovery, one that I've very grateful for. I've loved the States, loved the people that I've met on this journey, and I certainly call this home today.

Sabrina

Sabrina arrived in the group through a mutual friend who thought she would be a good fit. I also heard that she had not yet met like-minded women who would be supportive of her gifts. Because I trusted my friend enough to accept her opinion, I told her to bring Sabrina whenever she could attend.

When Sabrina started coming to the group, she had a daughter and step-daughter, both of whom were teenagers, yet she always felt as if she wanted another baby. For several years, she and her husband had tried to conceive, but with no results. A few of the women in the group, though, felt as if having this baby wasn't as impossible as it seemed; they thought that for sure a baby would come, but only under the condition of surrendering her dream to the universe—rather than controlling the situation or endlessly trying to make it happen. I don't know if all of this fortune-telling showed up in any of her readings, but it certainly did in many conversations before and after the group met. Eventually, even though it took time, she stopped talking about it so much. It seemed as if she had truly released the thought. Then, about two years later, the baby arrived. This is her story:

> I am a mother of three beautiful daughters and a wife to an amazing husband. Eventually, Kim invited one of my daughters to come and join the group, too. I found it to be amazing that my little 14-15 year-old daughter was able to be part of this group, and when she went in for the first time, she too was skeptical about herself, saying, "Mom I'm not like you. I can't do that," and I was like, "No, no, I was like that in the beginning, too. Just trust your instincts, and listen to what Spirit has to tell you. You just have to get out of your head," I told her. And she went to the group, and I heard her readings, and they were so beautiful—actually better than mine—so I knew that she, too, was feeling "at home."
>
> After about a year or so, Kim invited my other daughter to attend. She was ready, so it doesn't matter what age you are or what religion you come from because it's not based on religion—it's more spirituality and oneness with God, the Earth, and Spirit. That's what makes it amazing— when you have the sisterhood, the place where it's just peace, love, and family—no drama, no chitter chatter, no negativity, and I think that makes a good roundabout psychometry group, when you have that family oneness among the women you're in the circle with. Everyone has their own personalities—not one is the same—but we become one, connected, and it's amazing—the feeling you feel when you're together in that circle and your energies come together as one. There are no words to describe that feeling. I fell in love with the group because it was just what my body and soul had been yearning for.

Suman

Suman is wise beyond her years, and that's no overstatement. Once anyone experiences her peaceful energy, hears her discerning words, and witnesses her joyful, non-judgmental approach to life, it's very clear that her inner guidance comes from deeply abiding spiritual commitment. We are all very happy to call her a friend.

Suman has been attending almost as long as Pat, for over a decade now, and has given and received many readings through the years. I mention one of them in a previous chapter, "A Typical Evening Hosting the Group." In fact, both Suman and Pat gave me readings predicting that we would be building a new house.

I asked Suman to write down some information about herself and her experience with the group, and this is what she said:

> I was born in Bangalore, India into a Hindu Brahmin family that was very conscious of its roots and of its place in society. According to tradition, Brahmins are the uppermost caste and the keepers of the moral and religious rites, rituals, and practices of Hinduism. My maternal great-grandparents were extremely prosperous landowners, and all of their offspring were well placed in the prevailing society. The family was revered and respected throughout Bangalore for their charitable acts and for performing various "yagnas" or prayer ceremonies.
>
> On my father's side, the men were pioneers in their field of engineering and the women were all just as educated as the men. My paternal grandmother was actively involved in the struggle for independence. She organized several rallies and salt-marches, and both sets of grandparents were very involved in Mahatma Gandhi's resistance movements.
>
> After independence, my paternal grandparents settled in the seaside town of Vizag, and this is where I spent all of my summer vacations. Every evening after dinner,

my grandmother would gather all of us grandkids together and tell us stories from her youth, from the various scriptures and talk to us about the importance of education. In complete contrast to my mother's side of the family, my paternal grandmother saw no glory in being born Brahmin. As far as she was concerned, righteous thoughts, actions and living made you Brahmin no matter your lineage! She also taught us that at their core, all religions taught the same truth even if the followers believed otherwise! She insisted that love and kindness had to be the way—always.

While I consider myself Hindu, I am not particularly religious. I believe that for those seeking there are many paths to God. I also believe that I encounter God every day in every person that I meet, and I feel blessed by every encounter. For me, love and kindness will always be the way, and when negativity sets in, as it might from time to time, it doesn't last for long!

I love chanting my Sanskrit prayers—I think their effectiveness lies in the way they sound and in the energy that surrounds them rather than in the words and their meaning. My spiritual goal, if I may call it that, is to remain as much as possible in a prayerful place and imbue everything that I do with that powerful and healing energy.

Tammy

Tammy came to join us through a mutual friend, Lynda, who is a long-time member of the group. "Lynda and Amy too, encouraged me to be around the other beautiful souls there," Tammy said. She must be a brave soul because she told me, "I honestly didn't know much about it" but came anyway.

Although she might be the most peaceful and soft-spoken of the group, Tammy exudes love, and—like her hugs—her inclusive smile encompasses everyone as it spreads across the room. Since she joined the group, she started expanding her already-in-motion "Ten 2 Zen Den" workshops and then began another community service, called HEART (Honoring Emotional Alignment Reclaiming Truths) which focuses on weekend and one-day intensives for personal growth. She is the most recent member of the group, and this is her story:

> I was born and raised in Florida. (Actually, my 91-year-old dad still lives in the house I was born in.) My parents were married 52 years when my mom passed in 2004. I was blessed with very loving and devoted parents even though and especially given that my mother dealt with mental illness most of my life. I am one of four surviving children, and I have a high functioning, mentally-challenged older sister that still lives with my dad. They do a good job of taking care of each other. I feel very fortunate to still be able to go home anytime I want.
>
> My life continued to be blessed when I found a version of my dad in my husband, Glenn, 39 years ago. He is loyal, committed, hardworking, and loving. Glenn realized his childhood dream when he/we designed and built our home in the woods 33 years ago. We have been enjoying it ever since—especially now that we are officially retiring. Technically I retired in 2013 after over three decades of working at the local newspaper. Being laid off was a blessing in disguise as it (and my husband) allowed me the opportunity to start my HEART workshops in Asheville. We love it there and plan to return (at least part time) one day. Until then, I/we are working to build a community of healing and personal growth where we live now. It feeds my soul.

Final Words

A Gentle Nudge to Get Out There

I've tried to compile the best advice I can for you based on what I've learned through leading my own psychometry/meditation group. However, what I'm listing here is limited by that. There may be many other ways of leading a group that I haven't explored.

I hope this book has served as a gentle nudge for you to get out there, meet like-minded people, become part of a tribe, or create your own. Of course, growing spiritually requires alone time for meditation and self-reflection, but rather than replacing that part of your sacred practice, participating in a group like this can only add to it. Sharing your progress, your insights, joys, and even your sorrows within a close, spiritual community is where the real magic happens.

But even if you haven't yet found your tribe, trusting that it will find you sets the stage for further inner transformation and outward manifestation. So if you are even a little bit excited about it, that positive energy will expand to support whatever you need. And if you get stuck in the details, that's ok. It means you care and want the best. That's the time to remember that the Universe can help; the power of love and grace will help. Even the energy of your yet unformed, potential group can help—once your intention is clear. Trust in that, and all will be well.

Bibliography

Andrews, Ted. *How to Develop and Use Psychometry*. St. Paul: Llewellyn Publications, 1994.

Braboszcz, Claire, B. Rael Cahn, Jonathan Levy, Manuel Fernandez, and Arnaud Delorme. "Increased Gamma Brainwave Amplitude Compared to Control in Three Different Meditation Traditions." *Public Library of Science*. 12, no. 1 (January 24, 2017). https://link.gale.com/apps/doc/A478747194/STOM?u=29577_wppl&sid=bookmark-STOM&xid=4a909b1f.

Buchanan, Joseph Rodes, M.D. *Manual of Psychometry*. Boston: Frank H. Hodges, 1893.

Buchanan, Joseph Rodes, M.D. Preface to *Primitive Christianity*. Vol 1. San Jose: E. S. Buchanan, Garden City Printing House, 1897-8.

Butterworth, Eric. *The Universe is Calling*. New York: HarperSanFrancisco, 1993.

Cayce, Edgar. "Reading #239-1." Association for Research and Enlightenment. Transcript. Member Database. November 23, 1933. https://www.edgarcayce.org.

Cayce, Edgar. "Reading #255-12." Association for Research and Enlightenment. Transcript. Member Database. November 23, 1933. https://www.edgarcayce.org.

Center for Action and Contemplation. "Fruit of Our Labor," December 10, 2020, https://cac.org/daily-meditations/fruit-of-our-labor-2020-12-10/.

Choquette, Sonia. *Trust Your Vibes at Work*. Carlsbad, CA: Hay House, 2005.

Church, Dawson. "Sculpting Your Creative Brain." Episode 104. October 2023, in *Art2Life*, published by Nicholas Wilton. Podcast, audio, running time, 54:47. https://www.art2life.com/2023/10/18/sculpting-your-creative-brain-dawson-church-ep-104.

Day, Laura. *The Circle: How the Power of a Single Wish Can Change Your Life*. New York: Jeremy P. Tarcher, 2001.

Day, Laura. *Practical Intuition*. New York: Villard-Random House, 1996.

Denton, William and Elizabeth M. Foote Denton. *The Soul of Things*. Boston: Walker, Wise and Company, 1863. Internet Archive. https://archive.org/details/soulthingsorpsy00dentgoog.

Douglas-Klotz, Neil. *Prayers of the Cosmos: Reflections on the Original Meaning of Jesus's Words*. New York: Harper One, Harper Collins, 1990.

Dyer, Wayne and Esther Hicks. *Co-Creating at Its Best*. Carlsbad, CA: Hay House, 2014.

"The 'Dynamics' of the Ego." *A Course in Miracles*. Combined Volume, 2nd ed. Glen Ellen, CA: Foundation for Inner Peace, 1975.

Gordon, Jon. *The Energy Bus*. Hoboken, NJ: John Wiley and Sons, 2007.

Hasselbalch, Hagen. *Earth Prayers: 365 Prayers, Poems, and Invocations from Around the World*. Edited by Elizabeth Roberts and Elias Amidon. New York: Harper One, Harper Collins, 1991.

Heyward, Carter. *Wise Women: Over Two Thousand Years of Spiritual Writing by Women*. Edited by Susan Cahill. New York: W.W. Norton, 1996.

Holmes, Barbara. "Prophets Belong in Community." Richard Rohr's Daily Meditation, Center for Action and Contemplation. January 4, 2023. https://cac.org/daily-meditations/prophets-belong-in-community-2023-01-04.

Huffington, Ariana. *Thrive: The Third Metric to Redefining Success and Creating a Life of Well-being, Success, and Wonder.* New York: Harmony Books, 2014.

Jibrin, Janis. "How Ultra-processed Food Harms the Body and Brain." *National Geographic*, February 29, 2024. https://www.nationalgeographic.com/premium/article/ultra-processed-foods-damage-brain-depression-anxiety-cognitive-decline.

Keller, Helen. "Script for Helen Keller and Anne Sullivan's Vaudeville Appearances." American Foundation for the Blind, Helen Keller Archive. Arlington, VA. https://afb.org/about-afb/history/helen-keller/helen-keller-quotes/helen-keller-quotes-progress.

Kenton, Rebekah. "A Kabbalistic View of the Chakras." Welcome to the Kabbalah Society, November 26, 2022. www.kabbalahsociety.org/wp/articles/a-kabbalistic-view-of-the-chakras.

Mendius, Richard and Rick Hanson. *Seven Guided Practices to "Rebuild" Your Brain for Lasting Joy and Fulfillment.* Recorded 2009. Sounds True/AW01357W. Digital Audio.

Myss, Caroline. *Anatomy of the Spirit.* New York: Three Rivers Press, 1996.

Naparstek, Belleruth. *Your Sixth Sense: Activating Your Psychic Potential.* New York: HarperCollins, 1997.

New American Standard Bible. Lockman Foundation, 2020. https://www.biblegateway.com/.

Oakland, Mandy. "The Science of Bouncing Back." *Time*, May 21, 2015. https://time.com/3892044/the-science-of-bouncing-back.

Parker, Priya. *The Art of Gathering*. New York, New York: Riverhead Books, an imprint of Penguin Random House, 2018.

Peirce, Penney. *The Intuitive Way: A Guide to Living From Inner Wisdom*. Hillsboro OR: Beyond Words Publishing, 1997.

Pizzuto, Vincent. *Contemplating Christ: The Gospels and the Interior Life*. Collegeville, Minnesota: Liturgical Press, 2018.

Roman, Sanaya, and Duane Packer. *Opening to Channel: How to Connect With Your Guide*. Tiburon, CA: H.J. Kramer, 1987.

Rohr, Richard. Daily Meditations. "Third Eye Seeing," Center for Action and Contemplation, June 3, 2022, https://cac.org/daily-meditations/third-eye-seeing-2022-06-03.

Rohr, Richard. Daily Meditations. "Inner Authority." Center for Action and Contemplation, November 22, 2021. https://cac.org/daily-meditations/inner-authority-2021-11-21.

Rohr, Richard. "Faithful Resilience: Weekly Summary." Daily Meditations. Center for Action and Contemplation, January 27, 2024. https://cac.org/daily-meditations/faithful-resilience-weekly-summary.

Rosen, Rebecca. *Awaken the Spirit Within: Ten Steps to Ignite Your Life and Fulfill Your Divine Purpose*. New York: Harmony Books, 2013.

"Science of the Heart: Exploring the Role of the Heart in Human Performance. An Overview of Research Conducted by the HeartMath Institute." Heartmath Institute. Accessed February 12, 2024. https://www.heartmath.org/research/science-of-the-heart/energetic-communication.

Selig, Paul. *I Am the Word*. New York: Jeremy P. Tarcher, Penguin Group, 2010.

Selig, Paul. *The Book of Love and Creation*. New York: Jeremy P. Tarcher, Penguin Group, 2012.

Steinbrecher, Edwin C. *The Inner Guide Meditation: A Spiritual Technology for the 21ˢᵗ Century.* New York: Samuel Weiser, Inc., 1988.

Taylor, Terry Lynn and Mary Beth Crain. *Angel Journey Cards.* HarperSanFrancisco, New York: HarperCollins, 1996.

Weller, Chris. "A neuroscientist who studies decision-making reveals the most important choice you can make." *Business Insider*, Science, July 28, 2017. http://www.businessinsider.com/neuroscientist-most-important-choice-in-life-2017-7.

Wong, Laura and Kaitlyn Graña. "Psychometry." *Third Eye Bind*. Spotify podcast audio. Episode 33, May 2023, 1:17. https://open.spotify.com/episode/1WbGnNkXMdpJfI2Plt9ri0?si=46eb22bab4f54edf.

About the Author

Kim McCauley has spent most of her life learning about spirituality, intuition, and energy healing. As a Reiki Master and craniosacral therapist, she sees clients and teaches Energetics at the Central Florida School of Massage Therapy.

Before Kim started practicing energy therapy, she enjoyed teaching college writing and earned a doctorate in composition and rhetoric. Now retired from university teaching and administration, she enjoys painting and spending time with her wife, daughter, friends, and rescued dog, Pearl.

Printed in the United States
by Baker & Taylor Publisher Services